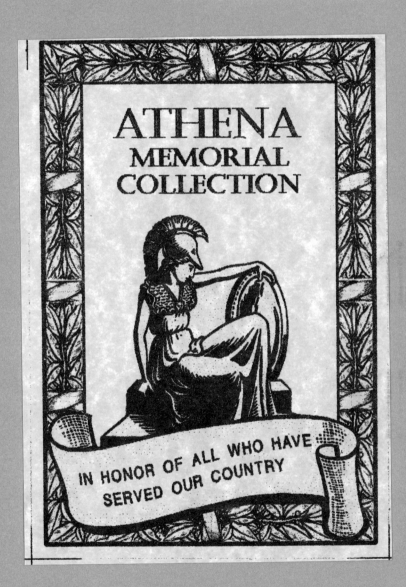

ATHENA
MEMORIAL
COLLECTION

IN HONOR OF ALL WHO HAVE
SERVED OUR COUNTRY

ICONS OF VINTAGE FASHION

PÉNÉLOPE BLANCKAERT
ANGÈLE RINCHEVAL HERNU

ICONS OF VINTAGE FASHION

DEFINITIVE DESIGNER CLASSICS AT AUCTION 1900–2000

Under the Direction of
CAROLINE LEVESQUE

Translated from the French by
DENISE JACOBS AND LENORA AMMON

ABRAMS | NEW YORK

Contents

Introduction

ICONS OF VINTAGE FASHION

Paris was the cradle of couture's greatest icons—Poiret, Lanvin, Chanel, Schiaparelli, Grès, Vionnet, Balenciaga, Dior, Saint Laurent, to name just a few. It was in Paris that couturiers practiced their craft, influencing worldwide fashion to this day. And it is from Paris still that these creations will often have a second life.

While a few British and American auction houses have entered the couture auction market, France holds an indisputably dominant position: The great auction houses such as Artcurial, Piasa, and Cornette de Saint Cyr now include fashion sales in their schedules, validating fashion's legitimacy as a true commodity.

The Hôtel Drouot, a Parisian institution like no other, has opened its prestigious auction rooms to fashion, placing it alongside modern and contemporary art, design, jewelry, and many styles of furniture and decorative objects. Today, the successful fashion auctions held at Drouot are often thematically based and unique in the world, featuring names such as Schiaparelli, Poiret, Chanel, Hermès, and Gaultier.

Fashion auctions are very much in fashion! Vintage and collection pieces are often presented side by side at the auctions. Vintage (the term is borrowed from the world of wine and has become controversial because it is often overused or used incorrectly) refers to clothing and accessories that may or may not have a brand name, but are representative of a specific time period. Just as in modern art, there is no strict temporal definition of vintage: It could start around the beginning of the twentieth century and end in the 1990s, but for some, the period is limited to the few decades between the 1940s and the 1970s. Unlike collection pieces, vintage clothes are "living garments," often acquired by someone who intends to wear them. Collection pieces on the other hand are usually acquired for conservation by museums, private collectors, and sometimes by the fashion houses themselves, who seek to buy back their lost heritage to complete their archives. This distinction does not prevent an overlap: Some museum-quality pieces might end up in a lucky woman's closet after all.

Can auctions determine the value of a vintage piece? Is it possible to accurately evaluate the price of an item based on its label, its condition, and its vintage?

While the value of a garment can be estimated with the help of an expert who can evaluate its aesthetic, technical, and historical features, one cannot really set a price and one single auction result does not set a precedent. The realized price is the result of interaction between bidders, in the room or across the world, whose infatuation, competition, and passing fancy might upend a reasonable estimate.

Potentially unique in nature, the object of desire might never appear again and two enthusiasts can easily cause prices to skyrocket. During an auction, the bidding can be fierce at one point and very slow at another. Rules are made and broken according to the passion of one buyer and the fervor of another.

Some pieces follow a more linear path; auction results for several institutions such as Chanel or Hermès, which are synonymous with excellence, are relatively predictable. Designer handbags always find their buyers, and their final price is often known beforehand. The same applies to certain periods in the history of a fashion house; a couturier or a stylist's early pieces are usually very sought after and the creator's death can quickly turn his or her designs into collector's items. Although a precise value cannot be attributed to these items, trends become apparent, perennial, and reliable.

The passion for vintage fashion is a relatively recent phenomenon, but the growth in interest in it over the past ten years has been exponential. It crosses borders, social milieus, and generations. The growing desire to own vintage pieces can be attributed to many factors (aesthetics, economics, ethics, personal desire) and belongs to a more general movement that glorifies the past. Fashion exhibits at museums are increasingly popular and fashion houses can showcase the lasting importance of their legacy; they might reissue certain styles from their archives or seek to awaken their "sleeping beauties" (e.g. Vionnet or Schiaparelli). The vintage trend is all the rage and it seems that fashion, like a good wine, ages well.

As a result of this growing enthusiasm, the places and ways to acquire vintage have multiplied. Online auctions (specifically eBay) set no limits and offer, often without any knowledgeable discrimination or expertise, an infinite number of old or new items. Vintage fashion dealers and specialized boutiques concentrate on one-of-a-kind, exceptional pieces. Secondhand shops often cater more to contemporary fashion and online marketplaces focus on the newest items. In theory, this should allow the auction houses to refocus their attention on their main purpose: fashion that is part of history and cultural heritage, fashion that tells a story.

[Note: The descriptions that follow include all the information available at the time of the auction. When a number in bold lettering appears under the name of a designer, it refers to the style number attributed by the fashion house to that particular item. The lot number that appears in parentheses after each item refers to its order of presentation during the sale and is established by the auction house.]

1900s–1920s

The Dawn of a New Century: Liberated Fashion

The beginning of the twentieth century marked a turning point in the history of fashion.

As borders opened due to increased ease of travel, textile and sartorial trends reached across the world. Couturiers were delighted and inspired by faraway places and the effect was quickly visible in their work. During World War I, the large numbers of men called up to serve at the front forced women to replace them at work. As a consequence, hemlines went up and waistlines went down, bringing about a certain androgyny. The flapper or *garçonne* style was born, reaching its peak during the 1920s.

Initiated by Paul Poiret and his orientalism-inspired designs, the disappearance of the corset became widespread, giving styles a looser and less structured silhouette, culminating in Fortuny's classical-inspired dresses. Elsewhere, the development of leisure and outdoor sporting activities in the upper echelons of society led to the emergence of sport clothes, relaxed styles, and coats meant for automobile riding.

The end of the war brought about a desire for celebrations and *fêtes* and the most elaborate embroidery enlivened ladies' finery. Pieces from those years are very difficult to find today; they suffered from the damage of time and from the lack of necessary conservation methods. Most of the designers' labels that were originally sewn into the dresses have all but disappeared today. But the anonymity of the garments does not take anything away from their brilliant construction; many can be linked to the great fashion houses: Lanvin, Doucet, Callot Soeurs, and Paquin.

The more feminine dresses, those that clung to the curves of the body, would appear in the late 1920s and serve as a preview to the following decade.

JEANNE LANVIN

WORTH

N º 79288

COUTURE, 1900s

COUTURE, 1900s

Slate blue silk crepe tea dress; bodice and long flared skirt adorned with partially embroidered chiffon; additional embroidering along the crossover V-neckline; belt. Label.

Champagne duchess satin ball gown; low neckline; uplifted bustline draped and embellished with tulle and machine-made lace; butterfly sleeves; bodice has a built-in laced corset with boning; hook-and-eye closure in the back; paneled skirt with a long train. Ivory label, gray stitching.

Estimate: 800–1,500 pounds
Sold: 1,000 pounds
Christie's, London
December 2, 2010 (lot 172)
Specialist: Patricia Frost

Estimate: 1,000–1,500 euros
Sold: 21,270 euros
Artcurial, Paris
June 11, 2012 (lot 212)
Specialist: PB Fashion

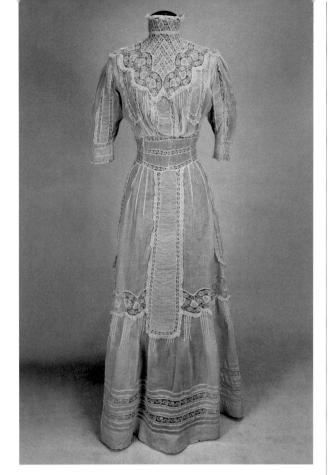

ANONYMOUS

PAQUIN

COUTURE, 1900s

COUTURE, 1900s

Ivory lawn and lace tea dress, encrusted with lace and embellished with pin-tuck panels and scalloped braiding; high-neck Bertha collar; tight-cuffed half sleeves; cinched waist; skirt is slightly pleated from the knees down; buttons in the back.

Silk and cream lace-embroidered evening coat adorned with inserts of darker silk cord lace in scroll and floral patterns; slight V-neckline; edge-to-edge facings; flared sleeves. Label "Paquin, 3 Rue de la Paix, Paris."

Estimate: 300–400 dollars
Sold: 84 dollars
Charles A. Whitaker Auction Company, Philadelphia
April 27–28, 2012 (lot 517)
Specialist: Charles A. Whitaker

Estimate: 500–700 dollars
Sold: 510 dollars
Charles A. Whitaker Auction Company, Philadelphia
October 28–29, 2011 (lot 320)
Specialist: Charles A. Whitaker

REDFERN

DRECOLL

COUTURE, 1900s

COUTURE, 1900s

Black silk velvet coat; stand-up collar with revers; loop-and-button closure repeated on the French cuffs and two flap pockets; small godets at the hemline; buckled belt. Label "The C.F. & M Co. Redfern Highest Grade."

Black wool frock coat embellished with soutache trim and fringe; edge-to-edge facings; deep cuffs. Label "Ch. Drecoll Vienna Paris."

Estimate: 500–800 dollars
Sold: 720 dollars
Charles A. Whitaker Auction Company, Philadelphia
October 28–29, 2011 (lot 312)
Specialist: Charles A. Whitaker

Estimate: 300–500 dollars
Sold: 900 dollars
Charles A. Whitaker Auction Company, Philadelphia
April 27–28, 2012 (lot 560)
Specialist: Charles A. Whitaker

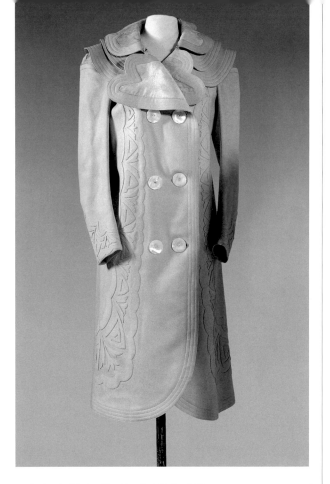

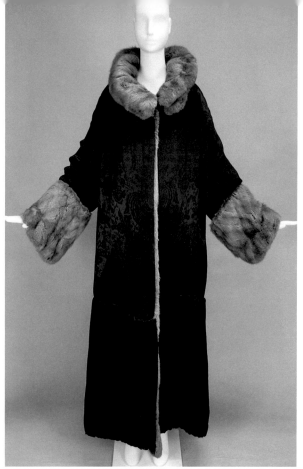

ANONYMOUS

WORTH

COUTURE, 1900s

COUTURE, 1900s

Double-breasted travel coat in ivory wool cloth adorned with topstitching; silk velvet scalloped notched collar in the shape of a small double cape; mother-of-pearl buttons; adorned with a raised leaf pattern, repeated at the wrists; wide panels on the back.

Black damask ankle-length coat with a floral pattern featuring phoenix birds and symbols; collar, wide cuffs, and lining trimmed in fur; button-and-loop closure; seam and small gathers at the hip. Label.

Estimate: 700–900 euros
Sold: 1,563 euros
Cornette de Saint Cyr, Paris
July 4, 2011 (lot 70)
Specialists: D. Chombert and F. Sternbach

Estimate: 600–800 dollars
Sold: 1,080 dollars
Charles A. Whitaker Auction Company, Philadelphia
April 27–28, 2012 (lot 562)
Specialist: Charles A. Whitaker

ANONYMOUS

PAQUIN

CALLOT SŒURS

COUTURE, 1910s

COUTURE, 1910s

COUTURE, Summer 1914

Golden brown silk satin dress lined in black taffeta; scoop neckline; bodice adorned with eight covered buttons; pleated and flounced hemline. Worn with a black tulle tunic featuring stylized leaf motifs embroidered with steel beads that create a fringe at the bottom of the half sleeves.

Printed chiffon dress with wide black and white stripes; collar, bodice, three-quarter sleeves, and godet-pleated hemline trimmed with tape lace; wide black velvet belt with a long flowing bow.

Bronze taffeta afternoon ensemble; shawl-collar jacket of asymmetric length; full back featuring a large velvet bow attached to an inner belt; bias-cut skirt. White label, gold lettering.

Estimate: 200–300 euros
Sold: 991 euros
Eve, Paris
June 18, 2012 (lot M055)
Specialist: Sylvie Daniel

Estimate: 1,500–1,800 euros
Sold: 1,611 euros
Eve, Paris
June 18, 2012 (lot M019)
Specialist: Sylvie Daniel

Estimate: 400–600 euros
Sold: 9,294 euros
Artcurial, Paris
June 27, 2011 (lot 292)
Specialist: PB Fashion

PAQUIN

N° 44971
COUTURE, Summer 1919

Black silk taffeta evening cape-jacket; shawl collar with covered single-button closure; the front of the jacket is adorned with fringe starting at the waist; the back is three-tiered; slightly bouffant sleeves and pink cotton lining. White label, black and blue lettering.

Estimate: 700–900 euros
Sold: 1,501 euros
Artcurial, Paris
November 25, 2011 (lot 419)
Specialist: PB Fashion

PAQUIN

COUTURE, 1900s

Sleeveless evening tabard of pleated black silk chiffon; small ruff; vertical panels adorned with embroidered jet beads. Label "Paquin, Rue de la Paix, Paris-London."

Estimate: 300–500 pounds
Sold: 375 pounds
Christie's, London
December 3, 2009 (lot 217)
Specialist: Patricia Frost

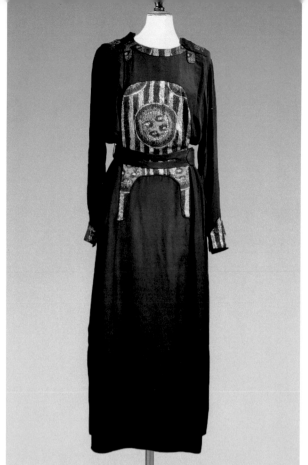

PAUL POIRET

PAUL POIRET

COUTURE, 1910s

COUTURE, 1910s

Summer dress made from a Russian woven unbleached linen tablecloth; boat neckline; part of the border of the tablecloth has been used as trim for the collar; the wide half sleeves and the bottom of the straight skirt are embroidered and hemstitched with stylized geometric motifs; seam at the waist. Worn with a wide draped belt with hook-and-eye closures under mother-of-pearl buttons. No label.

<u>PROVENANCE</u>: Denise Boulet-Poiret's wardrobe; the Colin-Poiret collection has remained in the family.

Deep blue silk dress with orientalism-inspired motifs; round neckline accentuated with shoulder tabs and cuffs; belt.

Estimate: 1,000–1,300 euros
Sold: 10,330 euros
Beaussant-Lefèvre, Paris
February 14, 2008 (lot 52)
Specialists: D. Chombert and F. Sternbach

Estimate: 6,000–8,000 euros
Sold: 14,250 euros
Eve, Paris
May 6, 2011 (lot M173)
Specialist: Sylvie Daniel

PAUL POIRET

PAUL POIRET

COUTURE, 1912
Model "Melody"

Purple damask day dress; jewel neckline with white fluting; raglan sleeves. Purple velvet tunic edged with cherry red piping; Bakelite button at the neckline; slanted patch pocket. No label.

PROVENANCE: Denise Boulet-Poiret's wardrobe; the Colin-Poiret collection has remained in the family.

BIBLIOGRAPHY: This design appears on p. 144 and p. 146 in *Poiret*, Yvonne Deslandres, éditions du Regard, 1986, and in an archive document on p. 38 in *Poiret*, Palmer White, Studio Vista London, 1973.

MUSEOGRAPHY: This design was featured as no. 151 in the *Paul Poiret* exhibit at the Musée Jacquemart-André, Paris, 1974.

Estimate: 1,200–1,500 euros
Sold: 51,043 euros
Beaussant-Lefèvre, Paris
February 14, 2008 (lot 83)
Specialists: D. Chombert and F. Sternbach

COUTURE, 1912
Model "Muscovite"

Wrap-style tunic in green duvetyn trimmed with a blue silk braid with a red and green floral motif; braided button; raglan sleeves; black and gold soutache trim runs along the front, starting at the neckline; floral bouquet–patterned silk lining on a green background inspired by a design from the atelier Martine. No label.

PROVENANCE: Denise Boulet-Poiret's wardrobe; the Colin-Poiret collection has remained in the family.

BIBLIOGRAPHY: This design, worn by Denise Boulet-Poiret, appears on p. 142 and p. 143 in *Poiret*, Yvonne Deslandres, éditions du Regard, 1986, and on p. 77 in *Poiret*, Palmer White, Studio Vista London, 1973.

Estimate: 1,200–1,500 euros
Sold: 37,674 euros
Beaussant-Lefèvre, Paris
February 14, 2008 (lot 71)
Specialists: D. Chombert and F. Sternbach

MARIANO FORTUNY

COUTURE, 1920s
Model "Delphos"

Dusty rose silk gown, hand-pleated and adorned with Murano glass beads; drawstring boat neckline. Hand-drawn label in black ink inside the dress. Worn with a coordinated silk belt stenciled in a leaf motif; belt closes in the back with two snaps and has a painted label in silver on the reverse side.

BIBLIOGRAPHY: Similar styles appear on pp. 19, 24, and 57 in *Fortuny*, Delphine Desveaux, Assouline, 1998.

Estimate: 1,000–1,500 euros
Sold: 1,487 euros

Artcurial, Paris
February 7, 2011 (lot 344)
Specialist: PB Fashion

MARIANO FORTUNY

COUTURE, 1920s
Model "Delphos"

Seafoam silk gown, hand pleated and adorned with Murano glass beads; slight V-neckline. Worn with a silk belt stenciled with gold leaf motifs. Selvedge stamped "Made in Italy Fabrique en Italie Fortuny depose."

BIBLIOGRAPHY: Similar styles appear in other colors on p. 19 and p. 57 in *Fortuny*, Delphine Desveaux, Assouline, 1998.

Estimate: 3,000–5,000 dollars
Sold: 4,500 dollars

Charles A. Whitaker Auction Company, Philadelphia
October 28–29, 2011 (lot 576)
Specialist: Charles A. Whitaker

MARIANO FORTUNY

COUTURE, 1920s
Model "Delphos"

Pumpkin-colored silk gown, hand-pleated and adorned with Murano glass beads; slight V-neckline. Worn with a silk belt stenciled in gold leaf motifs. Selvedge stamped "Made in Italy Fabrique en Italie Fortuny depose."

BIBLIOGRAPHY: Similar styles appear in other colors on p. 19 and p. 57 in *Fortuny*, Delphine Desveaux, Assouline, 1998.

Estimate: 6,000–8,000 dollars
Sold: 7,500 dollars

Charles A. Whitaker Auction Company, Philadelphia
October 28–29, 2011 (lot 575)
Specialist: Charles A. Whitaker

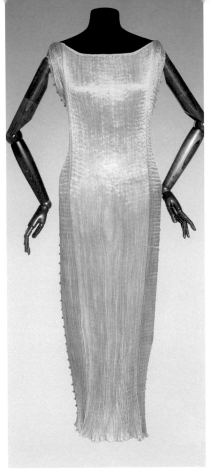

MARIANO FORTUNY

COUTURE, 1920s
Model "Delphos"

Ice blue and slate two-toned silk gown, hand-pleated and adorned with Murano glass beads; boat neckline.

Estimate: 3,000–4,000 pounds
Sold: 5,250 pounds
Christie's, London
December 3, 2009 (lot 214)
Specialist: Patricia Frost

MARIANO FORTUNY

COUTURE, 1920s
Model "Eleonora"

Medieval-style gown in jade panne velvet stenciled in a gold lace pattern; square neckline; encrusted side panels embellished with cord and blue Murano glass beads. Worn with pointed-toe heeled shoes adorned with gold metal buckles.

Estimate: 3,000–5,000 pounds
Sold: 6,250 pounds
Christie's, London
December 1, 2011 (lot 42)
Specialist: Patricia Frost

MARIANO FORTUNY

COUTURE, 1920s
Model "Eleonora"

Medieval-style gown in brown panne velvet stenciled in a gold lace pattern; square neckline; encrusted side panels embellished with cord and Murano glass beads. Label "Mariano Fortuny, Venise."

Estimate: 5,000–8,000 pounds
Sold: 6,250 pounds
Christie's, London
December 3, 2009 (lot 319)
Specialist: Patricia Frost

MARIANO FORTUNY

MARIANO FORTUNY

COUTURE, 1920s

COUTURE, 1920s

Black velvet burnoose stenciled with gold stripes and leaf motif; buttons down the front.

Honey-colored panne velvet cloak-dress partially adorned in a gold-stenciled lace motif; kimono sleeves; V-neckline. Label "Mariano Fortuny, Venise."

Estimate: 4,000–6,000 pounds
Sold: 9,375 pounds
Christie's, London
December 3, 2009 (lot 213)
Specialist: Patricia Frost

Estimate: 1,500–2,500 pounds
Sold: 1,875 pounds
Christie's, London
December 3, 2009 (lot 317)
Specialist: Patricia Frost

PAUL POIRET

PAUL POIRET

PAUL POIRET

COUTURE, 1920s
Model "Cavalier hindou"

Silk brocade gown with a fighting Hindu horseman motif on a silver-gray background; round neckline with black velvet-lined lapels; the black velvet is repeated on the cuff of the short sleeves and at the hemline; waistline emphasized by piping; gathers on each hip add fullness to the skirt. No label.

PROVENANCE: Denise Boulet-Poiret's wardrobe; the Colin-Poiret collection had remained in the family until auction.

Estimate: 1,000–1,500 euros
Sold: 9,722 euros

Beaussant-Lefèvre, Paris
February 14, 2008 (lot 70)

Specialists: D. Chombert and F. Sternbach

COUTURE, 1920s
Model "Lure"

Evening gown of embossed soft gold lamé; a sari-style belt of coral crepe and gold Lurex is attached at the hipline and drapes over one shoulder, ending as a train. No label.

PROVENANCE: Denise Boulet-Poiret's wardrobe; the Colin-Poiret collection had remained in the family until auction.

BIBLIOGRAPHY: This design, worn by Denise Boulet-Poiret, appears on p. 188 and p. 189 in *Poiret*, Yvonne Deslandres, éditions du Regard, 1986.

Estimate: 1,200–1,500 euros
Sold: 31,598 euros

Beaussant-Lefèvre, Paris
February 14, 2008 (lot 62)

Specialists: D. Chombert and F. Sternbach

COUTURE, 1920s

Russian-inspired black silk dress with alternating orange and multicolored fringe; boat neckline in the front, plunging in the back; slight draping at the hip; fluid skirt. White label, black lettering.

PROVENANCE: Mrs. Mermet, director of Paul Poiret in New York.

Estimate: 7,000–8,000 euros
Sold: 9,294 euros

Beaussant-Lefèvre, Paris
December 21, 2011 (lot 172)

Specialists: D. Chombert and F. Sternbach

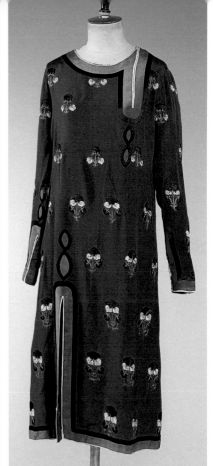

PAUL POIRET

PAUL POIRET

PAUL POIRET

COUTURE, 1920s

COUTURE, 1920s
Model "Sioux"

COUTURE, 1920s
Model "Hong Kong"

Dusty rose silk dress with scalloped boat neckline; chain-stitched embroidery in a floral pattern within a multicolored mosaic adorns the entire upper half of the dress, the kimono half sleeves, and the faced hem. No label.

PROVENANCE: Denise Boulet-Poiret's wardrobe; the Colin-Poiret collection had remained in the family until auction.

Linen dress, pocket, and cuffs adorned with a floral motif; a gold metal charm with a glass paste bead and black tassels is attached to a black linen band on the left side of the dress; black linen hem.

PROVENANCE: Denise Boulet-Poiret's wardrobe.

BIBLIOGRAPHY: This design appears on p. 172 in *Poiret*, Yvonne Deslandres, éditions du Regard, 1986.

MUSEOGRAPHY: This design was featured in the *Paul Poiret* exhibit at the Musée Jacquemart-André in Paris, 1974.

Straight dress, chain-stitch embroidered silk brocade with small repeated floral motifs in navy blue, green, and ivory; the round neckline, trimmed in green silk and navy satin, ends in a keyhole design on the left side; the trim is repeated at the wrists and on the skirt's slit hem. No label. Denise Poiret had written the name of the dress and the date in ink on a piece of silk sewn inside the hem.

PROVENANCE: Denise Boulet-Poiret's wardrobe.

Estimate: 1,000–1,200 euros
Sold: 2,430 euros

Beaussant-Lefèvre, Paris
February 14, 2008 (lot 55)

Specialists: D. Chombert and F. Sternbach

Estimate: 1,000–1,300 euros
Sold: 17,014 euros

Beaussant-Lefèvre, Paris
February 14, 2008 (lot 43)

Specialists: D. Chombert and F. Sternbach

Estimate: 800–1,000 euros
Sold: 17,014 euros

Beaussant-Lefèvre, Paris
February 14, 2008 (lot 56)

Specialists: D. Chombert and F. Sternbach

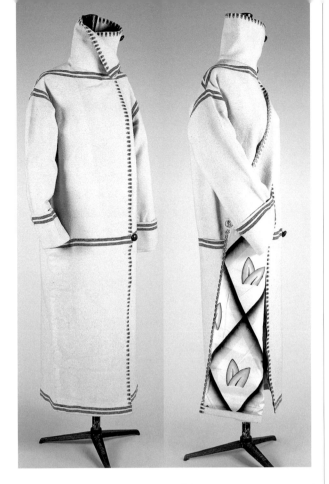

PAUL POIRET

PAUL POIRET

COUTURE, 1920s
Fabric: Rodier

North African–inspired ivory wool coat with woven brown stripes; wide stand-up collar with asymmetric closure; turnback cuffs; low waistline; silk pongee lining in a diamond-shape pattern in gray tones with peacock blue stylized leaves. White label, black lettering preceded by logo.

PROVENANCE: Denise Boulet-Poiret's wardrobe; the Colin-Poiret collection had remained in the family until auction.

BIBLIOGRAPHY: This design appears on p. 170 and p. 171 in *Poiret*, Yvonne Deslandres, éditions du Regard, 1986.

Estimate: 1,500–2,000 euros
Sold: 97,224 euros
Beaussant-Lefèvre, Paris
February 14, 2008 (lot 89)
Specialists: D. Chombert and F. Sternbach

COUTURE, 1920s

North African–inspired caftan in beige and brown linen with silver threading and geometric motifs; two blue minarets are featured on the back; square neckline; gold metallic thread embroidery on the front. The coat is made of four rectangular pieces with slits in the seams on either side. No label. The fabric was probably a purchase made by Paul Poiret during a trip to Africa.

PROVENANCE: Denise Boulet-Poiret's wardrobe; the Colin-Poiret collection had remained in the family until auction.

BIBLIOGRAPHY: This design appears on p. 164 in *Poiret*, Yvonne Deslandres, éditions du Regard, 1986.

Estimate: 1,300–1,500 euros
Sold: 9,115 euros
Beaussant-Lefèvre, Paris
February 14, 2008 (lot 88)
Specialists: D. Chombert and F. Sternbach

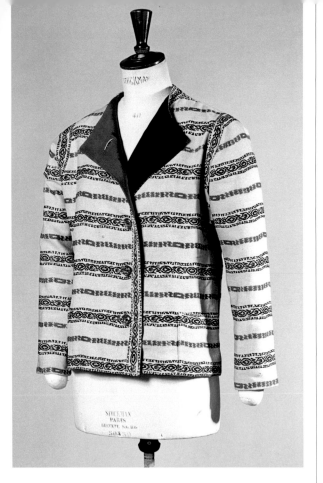

PAUL POIRET

PAUL POIRET

COUTURE, 1920s

COUTURE, 1920s

Unlined jacket of wool jacquard in a pattern of alternating red and black geometric friezes against an ivory background; black and red silk pongee trim on the facing and cuffs; asymmetric closing with five clear and black Lucite buttons; two patch pockets. No label.

PROVENANCE: Collection Paul and Denise Poiret, Collection Colin-Poiret; from the auction held February 14, 2008, in Paris at the Hôtel Drouot, Beaussant-Lefèvre, "Paul Poiret— Un visionnaire intemporel," lot 29.

Dress with a black sateen top, partially embroidered, diagonally, in honey, gold, and blue thread and adorned with metal and rhinestone sequins; V-neckline; the gathered skirt is made of red silk embroidered with silk and wool thread in a pattern of leaves and flowers. No label.

PROVENANCE: Denise Boulet-Poiret's wardrobe; the Colin Poiret collection has remained in the family.

BIBLIOGRAPHY: The same style appears on p. 187 in *Poiret*, Yvonne Deslandres, éditions du Regard, 1986.

Estimate: 800–1,200 euros
Sold: 2,627 euros
Artcurial, Paris
November 25, 2011 (lot 200)
Specialist: PB Fashion

Estimate: 1,200–1,500 euros
Sold: 13,368 euros
Beaussant-Lefèvre, Paris
February 14, 2008 (lot 53)
Specialists: D. Chombert and F. Sternbach

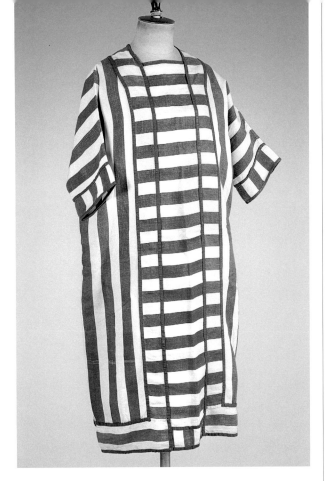

PAUL POIRET

ANONYMOUS

COUTURE, 1920s

COUTURE, 1920s

Hostess dress in white linen with tobacco-colored stripes; the dress is made of several pieces of fabric and piping that create the effect of horizontal stripes; square neckline; short kimono sleeves. No label.

PROVENANCE: Denise Boulet-Poiret's wardrobe; the Colin-Poiret collection had remained in the family until auction.

BIBLIOGRAPHY: A similar style worn by Denise Boulet-Poiret appears on p. 175, and the identical dress appears on p. 174, in *Poiret*, Yvonne Deslandres, éditions du Regard, 1986.

Beach coat in navy and ivory striped knitted fabric; wide turndown collar with two-button closure; self belt; pleats; large patch pockets on either side.

Estimate: 800–1,000 euros
Sold: 13,976 euros
Beaussant-Lefèvre, Paris
February 14, 2008 (lot 75)
Specialists: D. Chombert and F. Sternbach

Estimate: 250–350 dollars
Sold: 660 dollars
Charles A. Whitaker Auction Company, Philadelphia
April 27–28, 2012 (lot 661)
Specialist: Charles A. Whitaker

PAGE

GABRIELLE CHANEL

N °15023

COUTURE, 1920s

COUTURE, 1920s

Purple silk faille opera coat with gold lamé brocade in a floral motif; draped rolled collar; cuffs and hem in dusty rose velvet. Label "Page Paris—5 Rue Cambon."
PROVENANCE: Brooklyn Museum.

Evening cape of embossed gold silk; wide chinchilla-trimmed collar; bloused back with small gathered folds. Beige label, gold lettering.

Estimate: 500–600 dollars
Sold: 900 dollars
Augusta Auctions, New York
November 10, 2010 (lot 271)
Specialist: Karen E. Augusta

Estimate: 7,000–8,000 euros
Sold: 8,750 euros
Cornette de Saint Cyr, Paris
July 3, 2009 (lot 215)
Specialists: D. Chombert and F. Sternbach

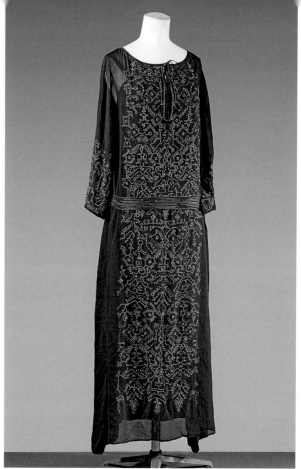

MOLYNEUX

JEANNE LANVIN

COUTURE, 1920s

N º 9606
COUTURE, Winter 1920–1921

Opera coat in dusty rose panne velvet; high rolled collar and horizontal band are embroidered with gold lamé featuring a leaf motif; bat sleeves with open cuffs; lined with gold metallic woven lamé. Beige label, black lettering.

Black chiffon gown embroidered with brown chain stitch; the front and back of the dress are adorned with coral beads in an Art Deco motif; open boat neckline ties at the front; the embroidery is repeated on the three-quarter sleeves; self belt over a skirt with two panels that begin at the waist and end at the hemline. Worn over a silk crepe slip. White label, black lettering highlighted with red.

Estimate: 1,500–2,000 euros
Sold: 4,375 euros
Cornette de Saint Cyr, Paris
July 3, 2009 (lot 189)
Specialists: D. Chombert and F. Sternbach

Estimate: 2,500–3,000 euros
Sold: 17,750 euros
Cornette de Saint Cyr, Paris
July 3, 2009 (lot 182)
Specialists: D. Chombert and F. Sternbach

GABRIELLE CHANEL

BEST & CO.

COUTURE, 1920s

COUTURE, 1920s

Black chiffon evening cape trimmed with glossy black feathers; smocking at the shoulders and the hem. Label "Chanel, Paris—31 Rue Cambon, Cannes, Biarritz."

Black and gold lamé opera coat with a chevron and arrow design; shawl collar and cuffs trimmed with white fox; button-and-loop closure.

Estimate: 2,000–4,000 pounds
Sold: 4,000 pounds
Christie's, London
December 3, 2009 (lot 303)
Specialist: Patricia Frost

Estimate: 400–600 dollars
Sold: 390 dollars
Charles A. Whitaker Auction Company, Philadelphia
April 27–28, 2012 (lot 649)
Specialist: Charles A. Whitaker

MOLYNEUX

DOEUILLET

COUTURE, 1920s

COUTURE, 1920s

Black silk chiffon faux-two-piece evening dress with a stylized floral design of gold metallic brocade; scoop neckline; draped at the sides. Label "Molyneux, 5 Rue Royale."

Black silk satin evening dress partially embroidered with stylized floral motifs in shades of orange, blue, aqua, and pink and adorned with metallic gold thread; slight drape at the bustline and waist. Label "Doeuillet Paris Londres."

Estimate: 1,000–1,500 dollars
Sold: 2,040 dollars
Charles A. Whitaker Auction Company, Philadelphia
October 28–29, 2011 (lot 561)
Specialist: Charles A. Whitaker

Estimate: 2,000–3,000 dollars
Sold: 3,120 dollars
Charles A. Whitaker Auction Company, Philadelphia
October 28–29, 2011 (lot 559)
Specialist: Charles A. Whitaker

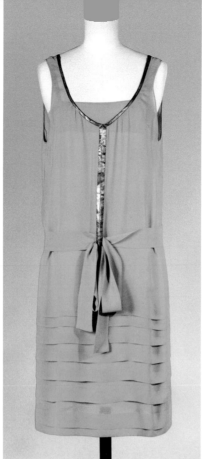

CALLOT SŒURS

COUTURE, 1920s

Ivory tulle dress with gathers and double shoulder straps; rosette trim at the low neckline, dropped waist, and hem.

Estimate: 1,000–2,000 dollars
Sold: 1,220 dollars

Leslie Hindman Auctioneers, Chicago
April 21, 2010 (lot 14)
Specialist: Abigail Rutherford

LUCIEN LELONG

N° 4144
COUTURE, 1920s

Coral crepe de chine dress with gold lamé trim; slight V-neckline with modesty panel; blind-tuck pleated skirt; self belt ties at the front. Worn with a slip and a matching cape that also ties at the front. Beige label, burgundy lettering.

Estimate: 800–1,000 euros
Sold: 2,354 euros

Artcurial, Paris
June 27, 2011 (lot 127)
Specialist: PB Fashion

GABRIELLE CHANEL

COUTURE, 1920s

Cocktail dress entirely covered with small gold bugle beads; low waist with a belt that ties at the front; fluid, asymmetric skirt. Worn over a slip. Label.

Estimate: 3,000–5,000 pounds
Sold: 5,250 pounds

Christie's, London
December 2, 2010 (lot 183)
Specialist: Patricia Frost

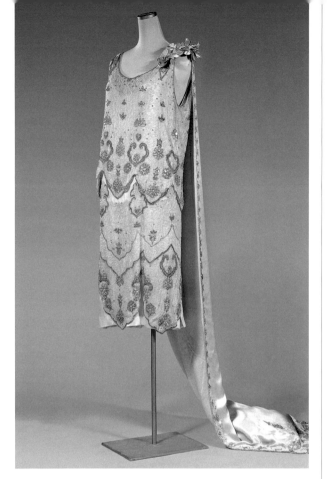

MOLYNEUX

LUCIEN LELONG

COUTURE, 1920s

COUTURE, 1920s

Formal dress in tulle-covered ivory satin entirely embroidered in glass beads and sequins; left shoulder adorned with a camellia; V-cut back with a long pearl-trimmed satin train. Label "Molyneux, 5 Rue Royale."

PROVENANCE: Mrs. Frances Jermyn Berlin wore this dress to a British Royal reception.

Cream silk cocktail dress; the top is embroidered with faceted blown-glass silver beads in an Art Deco motif; the drop waist is emphasized with a lamé belt; skirt is also in lamé and has been partially embroidered with beads that form two horizontal stripes near the hem. Label.

Estimate: 1,500–2,000 euros
Sold: 4,089 euros
Thierry de Maigret, Paris
November 22, 2011 (lot 266)
Specialist: Séverine Experton-Dard

Estimate: 1,500–2,000 pounds
Sold: 1,000 pounds
Christie's, London
December 2, 2010 (lot 164)
Specialist: Patricia Frost

ANONYMOUS

ANONYMOUS

COUTURE, 1920s

Black tulle dress embroidered with pink sequins and beads in the shape of rosettes with gold leaves in a lattice design; V-neckline; layered flounced skirt embellished with godet pleating below at the hips.

COUTURE, 1920s

Black silk satin evening dress embroidered with crystal and paste beads in a design of spread-wing pheasants on the bodice; deep neckline at the back; low waist with a tied belt; godet pleating at the hips.

ICONOGRAPHY: The bird-inspired embroidery is featured on the base of Armand-Albert Rateau's furniture.

Estimate: 800–1,000 euros
Sold: 1,000 euros
Cornette de Saint Cyr, Paris
July 4, 2011 (lot 94)
Specialists: D. Chombert and F. Sternbach

Estimate: 1,000–1,500 euros
Sold: 2,716 euros
Thierry de Maigret, Paris
November 22, 2011 (lot 265)
Specialist: Séverine Experton-Dard

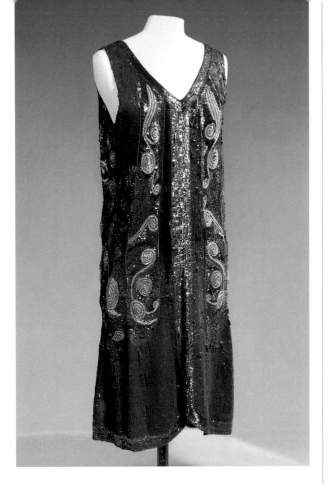

ANONYMOUS

CALLOT SŒURS

COUTURE, 1920s

COUTURE, 1920s

Dark gray and silver sequined dress embellished by stripes of small soft gold glass beads and multicolored Art Nouveau patterns; V-neckline trimmed with bias tape; slightly rounded hemline at the front.

Hunter green silk velvet dress embroidered with small beads and gold metallic thread over nude tulle that forms a decorative collar that reaches down the back; the embroidery is repeated on the low-waist fluid skirt cut on the bias with inserts. White label, black lettering.

Estimate: 1,200–1,300 euros
Sold: 1,500 euros
Cornette de Saint Cyr, Paris
July 4, 2011 (lot 205)
Specialists: D. Chombert and F. Sternbach

Estimate: 2,000–2,500 euros
Sold: 2,478 euros
Cornette de Saint Cyr, Paris
June 27, 2008 (lot 116)
Specialists: D. Chombert and F. Sternbach

  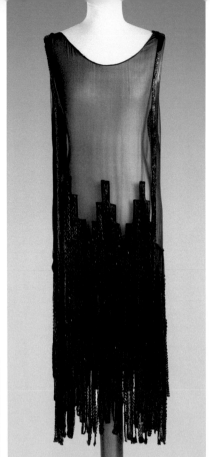

ANONYMOUS

COUTURE, 1920s

Black chiffon dress with appliqué roses; round-neck collar; dropped shoulders create a small cape at the back; fluid skirt with Chantilly lace hem.

Estimate: 800–1,000 euros
Sold: 1,000 euros
Cornette de Saint Cyr, Paris
July 4, 2011 (lot 50)
Specialists: D. Chombert and F. Sternbach

ANONYMOUS

COUTURE, 1920s

Black chiffon dress embellished with rhinestones; palm leaf design embroidered in silver metal tubular beads and tassels; V-neckline; skirt has slit on one side; two-tiered asymmetric hem.

Estimate: 150–200 euros
Sold: 250 euros
Cornette de Saint Cyr, Paris
June 30, 2012 (lot 156)
Specialists: D. Chombert and F. Sternbach

GABRIELLE CHANEL

COUTURE, 1920s

Black silk chiffon cocktail dress adorned with vertical panels embroidered in geometric shapes with beads that cascade from the hips to the hem. Label "Gabrielle Chanel, Paris."

Estimate: 1,000–2,000 pounds
Sold: 2,750 pounds
Christie's, London
December 3, 2009 (lot 293)
Specialist: Patricia Frost

GABRIELLE CHANEL | ANONYMOUS

N° 17217
COUTURE, 1920s

Black crepe de chine gown partially embroidered with tubular jet beads in geometric patterns; square halter-neck top; belt embellished with beaded tassels; two soft wing panels enhance the straight skirt. Black label, gold lettering.

Estimate: 12,000–15,000 euros
Sold: 15,000 euros
Cornette de Saint Cyr, Paris
July 2, 2010 (lot 175)
Specialists: D. Chombert and F. Sternbach

COUTURE, 1920s

Black chiffon dress; parts of the dress have scattered sequins while the rest is entirely covered with black sequins; plunging front cowl décolleté; long sleeves; bias-cut skirt starting at the hipline; sheer hem.

Estimate: 800–1,000 euros
Sold: 8,125 euros
Cornette de Saint Cyr, Paris
July 3, 2009 (lot 313)
Specialists: D. Chombert and F. Sternbach

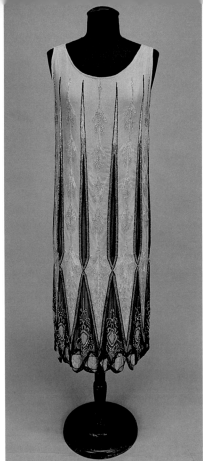

ANONYMOUS

COUTURE, 1920s

Beige chiffon gown embroidered with small beads, sequins, and silver and gold rhinestones; drop-waist is accentuated by a belt embellished with two floating panels at the front.

PROVENANCE: According to the Poiret family, this dress was made by the House of Paul Poiret.

Estimate: 300–400 euros
Sold: 744 euros
Artcurial, Paris
June 27, 2011 (lot 55)
Specialist: PB Fashion

ANONYMOUS

COUTURE, 1920s

Nude silk chiffon evening dress covered in black and white tulle embroidered with beads and rhinestones in a floral design interspersed with arrows; round neckline with bias trim; scalloped hem.

Estimate: 300–500 dollars
Sold: 1,680 dollars
Charles A. Whitaker Auction Company, Philadelphia
April 27–28, 2012 (lot 700)
Specialist: Charles A. Whitaker

MADELEINE VIONNET

N° 15823872U
COUTURE, 1920s

Black crepe dress; square neckline; shoulder straps are embroidered with gold and bronze glass beads in a Greek fresco pattern that is repeated on either side of the bodice and at the waist; asymmetric skirt. White label with embroidered pink lettering followed by the logo.

Estimate: 6,000–7,000 euros
Sold: 58,750 euros
Cornette de Saint Cyr, Paris
July 4, 2011 (lot 150)
Specialists: D. Chombert and F. Sternbach

GABRIELLE CHANEL

N º 15167
COUTURE, 1920s

Black silk cocktail dress with uneven horizontal bands of jet bead embroidery; tiered skirt. Label in ink "Gabrielle Chanel Paris."

Estimate: 10,000–15,000 dollars
Sold: 16,800 dollars
Charles A. Whitaker Auction Company, Philadelphia
April 27–28, 2012 (lot 657)
Specialist: Charles A. Whitaker

LOUISE BOULANGER

COUTURE, 1929

Ivory silk satin wedding dress; draped bodice; pleated long sleeves with buttons; the large bow on the belt covers the hips; sheath godet skirt ends in a long train.
BIBLIOGRAPHY: A similar style appears on p. 910 in *L'Art et la Mode*, no. 27, July 6, 1929.

Estimate: 600–700 euros
Sold: 805 euros
Thierry de Maigret, Paris
November 22, 2011 (lot 270)
Specialist: Séverine Experton-Dard

PAUL POIRET

ICONS OF VINTAGE FASHION
Spotlight

After an apprenticeship with an umbrella-maker, Paul Poiret changed the course of his life when he became an apprentice for the renowned couturier Jacques Doucet in 1899 and later moved to the House of Worth.

Poiret entered the world of fashion and revolutionized the field under his own name when he opened his maison de couture in 1903 at 5 Rue Auber.

POIRET REVOLUTIONIZES THE SILHOUETTE

Paul Poiret is best known for having introduced a brand-new silhouette. As of 1906, Poiret replaced the corseted and structured S-shape that had been in vogue since the beginning of the century with a column-shape silhouette. He disliked corsets and sought to liberate women from their constriction by creating Directoire-inspired high-waisted dresses that were an immediate success. This new style would define the look of the period. As the focal point shifted away from the waist and hips, the eye was drawn to the bosom, now emphasized by the empire style, and to the shoulders that supported the dress. The silhouette was narrow, linear, and meant to highlight and reveal the shape and movement of the legs. Some criticized Poiret for having hampered the way women walked and claimed that his so-called liberation was only a relative one that simply focused on the upper part of the body. However, Poiret nonetheless created a modern look with his designs that reflected simplicity, ease, and exoticism at the same time.

POIRET REVOLUTIONIZES THE PROFESSION

If Worth was known as the inventor of haute couture, Paul Poiret was undeniably the man who defined the profession of *couturier* in the modern sense of the word. Designing clothes was not enough: Poiret was the first designer to sense the far-reaching potential of a brand name. He would widen the spectrum of his activities, turning to decorative arts, designing fashion magazines, opening subsidiaries throughout the world, decorating boats, creating perfumes, and signing license agreements.

With his modern style, his oriental inspirations, his lavish fabrics, and his regal prints, Poiret was the first in his profession to be called a genius, and thus begin the ongoing debate about the couturier's role as an artist and, in a wider context, about the place of fashion within the arts. Paul Poiret was also famous for the lavish *fêtes* he hosted, where he mingled with *le Tout Paris*. He continued to hold these parties throughout his career, even after his star power began to wane, hoping to revive his fashion house and reclaim a clientele that had moved on to the next new thing after World War I.

POIRET'S LEGACY AFTER THE REVOLUTION

The 1920s saw Paul Poiret's popularity decline. The war had taken its toll and the women who had once been attracted to the decorative excess and splendor of his designs were now attracted to the idea of simplicity and comfort, the very features that were being offered by the divisive Gabrielle Chanel. Poiret fought to stay relevant, multiplying his initiatives and his innovations, but he was unable to recover his earlier popularity in the world of fashion. He died in 1944, having slipped into obscurity.

But history has not forgotten Paul Poiret; his designs are universally recognized as revolutionary and he is credited with bringing modernity to fashion. He has been the subject of multiple exhibits, in particular those presented at the Musée Galliera (1986) and at the Metropolitan Museum of Art (2007). The enormous success of the white glove auction held in 2005 at Piasa, "L'Univers de Denise et Paul Poiret," underscored the major role Poiret occupies in the history of fashion. Collectors and museums alike were in attendance and world records were set: A coat from 1914 sold for 131,648 euros and a pair of shoes belonging to Denise Poiret were scooped up for 40,912 euros, sums that had never been achieved at auction for an item of clothing or a pair of shoes. Poiret's legacy was confirmed during a second successful auction of Denise Poiret's wardrobe, this one held by Beaussant-Lefèvre in 2008.

— Auction held February 14, 2008, at Beaussant-Lefèvre: "Vêtements et accessoires provenant de la Garde-Robe de Denise Boulet-Poiret" (Clothing and accessories from the wardrobe of Denise Boulet-Poiret).
- *Left*: Silk pongee summer dress, circa 1911 (sold: 12,000 euros).
- *Center*: Day dress, bodice of wool serge and crepe skirt with small gathers, circa 1922 (sold: 5,000 euros).
- *Right*: Dinner dress, bodice in Marescot lace over crepe, circa 1920 (sold: 13,000 euros).

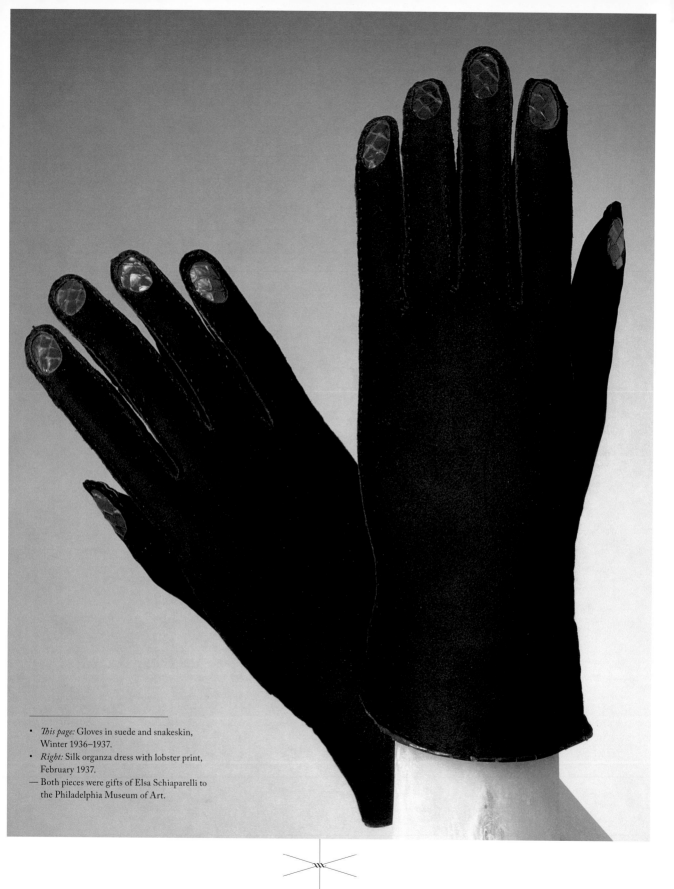

- *This page:* Gloves in suede and snakeskin, Winter 1936–1937.
- *Right:* Silk organza dress with lobster print, February 1937.
- — Both pieces were gifts of Elsa Schiaparelli to the Philadelphia Museum of Art.

ICONS OF VINTAGE FASHION
Spotlight

shade that Schiaparelli juxtaposed with black to bring out its flamboyance, the shade of pink that would become her brand, her *motto*.

Her success grew rapidly and Schiaparelli soon moved to a very symbolic place: Vendôme. The new store, designed by Jean-Paul Franck, welcomed clients that included Greta Garbo and the Duchess of Windsor.

Schiaparelli was very close to Dada and other surrealist artists. Described by Chanel as "an artist who designs dresses," Schiaparelli was one of the first designers to incorporate elements of art into fashion. Her collaborations permeated her designs: Dalí, Man Ray, and Cocteau designed jewelry, buttons, perfume bottles, and embroidery patterns for her that would become collector's items. At the "Elsa Schiaparelli: Garde-robe de 1935–1950, Haute Couture et Vintage 1900–2000" auction, held by Cornette de Saint Cyr in July 2009, a gray linen jacket designed by Jean Cocteau with embroidery by the House of Lesage fetched 174,995 euros and a metal powder compact designed by Salvador Dalí sold for 32,499 euros. Her designs were a spectacle in themselves and simply donning the clothes was considered a small artistic performance: The buttons on her dresses were often nods to surrealist art, black gloves featured red lacquered fingernails, plastic or porcelain from Sèvres could easily make its way from the pantry to the closet, upside-down shoes became hats, a telephone was transformed into a handbag, Dalí's lobsters became brooches or adorned the front of evening gowns, Cocteau's design of two faces that embellished the back of an evening coat morphed

ELSA SCHIAPARELLI

After growing up in Rome and living in New York as a young adult, Elsa Schiaparelli moved to Paris with her daughter during the 1920s. As of 1927, she gained recognition for the sweaters she made in her atelier on the Rue de Paix that had trompe-l'œil ties and sailor collars. A major fashion figure during the 1930s, Schiaparelli closed the doors of her *maison de couture* in 1954. Her short career coupled with her unbridled creativity quickly turned her creations into collector's items and vintage icons.

Schiaparelli quickly added day and evening wear to her innovative sweater lines. She also created a large range of perfumes: Schiap in 1934 and Shocking in 1938. The latter, presented in a bottle shaped like a dress mannequin, marked an important moment in the history of perfumery. Shocking was more than a perfume; it was also a specific shade of pink, the pink color that adorns the bottle and its packaging, the pink

into a vase filled with roses, and her "Le Cirque" collection of 1938 included many pieces embroidered by the House of Lesage. A standout piece was the "skeleton" dress: Its quilted padding created an optical illusion of a three-dimensional skeleton.

As testimonial to the history of fashion, Schiaparelli's creations are as likely to be found in a collector's closet as in a museum. Schiaparelli's work has been featured in many important exhibitions: The Musée des Arts Décoratifs held a large monographic retrospective of her work in 2004 and the Costume Institute of the Met presented a show in 2012 in conjunction with a pillar of Italian fashion, Miuccia Prada.

Diego Della Valle, the president and CEO of Tod's, has just taken over Schiaparelli and chosen Farida Khelfa, a former model and timeless muse, to spearhead the brand. Their first collection will be presented in 2013.

- *Left*: Madeleine Vionnet and her employees wearing hats on Saint Catherine's Day, photographed by Apic in 1923.
- *Above and Opposite*: Different views of a black silk crepe dress cut entirely on the bias. Anonymous (in the style of Madeleine Vionnet), circa 1932. Featured in the November 25, 2011, "Jolie Madame" auction held at Artcurial (sold: 5,005 euros).
- *Right*: Madeleine Vionnet, circa 1921–1923. Black crepe dress. Featured in the July 4, 2011, "Haute Couture: 50 ans de Mode Italiennes" auction held at Cornette de Saint Cyr (sold: 58,750 euros).

Although considered "a designer's designer" by her peers of both yesterday and today, and recognized as a genius by fashion professionals, Madeleine Vionnet, unlike her contemporary Coco Chanel, remains relatively unknown by the general public.

THE WOMAN

Madeleine Vionnet's unique story sheds some light on her unusual personality. Born in 1876, she was a good and serious student. Nevertheless, at the age of twelve, she was placed as an apprentice laundress with her neighbor, the wife of the village police officer. By the time she was twenty, she had lost a daughter and was divorced—an uncommon situation for the time. Her real apprenticeship in couture began in London, when she worked for Kate Reily for two years. She went on

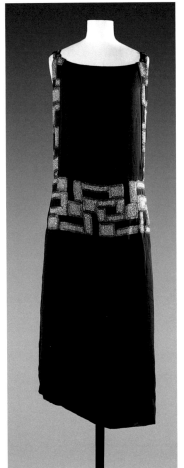

MADELEINE VIONNET

to become *première* in the ateliers of Callot Soeurs, then joined Jacques Doucet where her primary responsibility was to bring new life to the aging *maison de couture*. Wanting more creative independence, she decided to open her own house on Rue de Rivoli in 1912. Success came quickly and within ten years Vionnet moved to larger quarters on Avenue Montaigne. Her 1,200 workers occupied five ateliers and benefited from Vionnet's pioneering labor practices: a dining hall, health care, and paid holidays.

While she successfully resumed her activities after World War I, the same did not hold true in the years following World War II and the house was forced to shut down. A large part of her collections had to be sold at auction. Vionnet was one of the first designers to appreciate the importance of a fashion house's history—her own in particular—and she held on to archives that were meticulously catalogued. In 1952, she donated 122 dresses, 750 canvas patterns, and 75 albums filled with photographs to the Union Française des Arts du Costume.

VIONNET'S STYLE AND TECHNIQUE

When she began working at Doucet, Madeleine Vionnet had proposed dresses that were as lightweight as lingerie and no longer included corsets. Fascinated by ancient Greece, she favored pure shapes, created garments that used the bias cut for the entire dress. The bias became her specialty, the technique she had supremely mastered. To perfect her designs, she used small mannequins made of wood on which she could drape the fabric and work in three dimensions.

She was a purist and focused only on what was essential; she sought to reduce the number of seams and applied mathematical reasoning as she concentrated on primary forms such as the square, the rectangle, and the circle. She revolutionized the construction of a garment. Even when a dress felt and looked ethereal, its structure was nevertheless extremely complex and its technique imperceptible. Vionnet was a genius of couture, a master of savoir faire who distinguished herself by her approach to the cut and the mystery of the inner construction of her creations.

Because of the perfection of their designs and the skill of their technique, Madeleine Vionnet's pieces have become the cornerstone of fashion auctions. Relatively rare but always in demand, they fetch the highest prices. On July 4, 2011, the Cornette de Saint Cyr auction house listed a black patterned crepe dress. The estimate was between 6,000 and 7,000 euros but the dress sold for more than 58,000 euros. On November 25, 2011, at Artcurial, a black silk crepe dress, described as "in the style of Madeleine Vionnet," was estimated at between 400 and 600 euros. It sold for 5,000 euros. Regardless of its exact provenance, collectors and connoisseurs alike are prepared to pay any price to own an example of such geometric and aesthetic achievement.

- *Left*: John Galliano, Katisha-San evening gown, 2007, Museum of Fine Arts, Boston.
- *Above*: Azzedine Alaïa, ensemble with jacket, sweater, and skirt, 2008, Museum of Fine Arts, Boston.

How would you define vintage?

Vintage fashion implies that something is not "current" and has been taken out of one's closet to be sold.

Where does vintage begin and where does it end?

I think an item is considered vintage when it is twenty years old. That's usually when donors delve into their closets to give us their pieces.

What are, in your view, the consequences of vintage's current appeal?

For the special pieces, prices have soared. It's in part because of the competition between the houses themselves and also because the owners of vintage pieces are increasingly likely to try to sell them rather than donate them to a museum.

It's somewhat ironic because in the past most museums' fashion collections have served as resources for the study of fashion history for designers and artists; today, fashion houses are establishing their own collections.

Is there a difference between a vintage piece and a collection piece?

An important collection piece is characterized by its condition, its historical relevance, and/or the interest of its style. A vintage piece can simply be something that is wearable.

What are the museum collection's newest and oldest acquisitions?

We have pearl-embroidered tunics and pleated linen dresses from Egypt that date back to 2500–2300 BCE. We have recently acquired Tuyat embroidered shoes from Balmain's Spring 2012 collection.

Can you tell us about some of the more extraordinary pieces you have come across?

Some of the most extraordinary pieces have come from the most unexpected sources. A former superintendent from the museum had noticed an unlabeled Schiaparelli dress that was for sale at a local auction house. We were able to acquire it for a song. When we examined it more closely, we discovered the label sewn into an inner seam.

Another extraordinary experience: We went to a shop that was owned by two former couturiers from 1912 through the 1940s. When they closed their store, they simply covered all of their stock. We found it just as they had left it fifty years earlier. Their shop was filled with silk velvet, lamé, lace, sketches of couture and of prêt-à-porter styles from the 1920s and 1930s—some by Lucien Lelong, Paul Poiret, and Molyneux. It was like a dream! We worked on it for ten years, held an exhibition, and published a book.*

* *From Paris to Providence: Fashion, Art, and the Tirocchi Dressmakers' Shop, 1915–1947*, Rhode Island School of Design, 1999.

- *Left*: Pamela Parmal, Curator of Textile and Fashion Arts, Museum of Fine Arts, Boston

What about labels and anonymous pieces? Does that influence whether an item will be accepted into a museum's collection?

Yes. We try to recount the career of certain designers, especially those who have revolutionized the way we think about fashion. But you need more than a label; you have to know about a designer's technique and signature fabrics. There are many instances of forged labels and buyers need to be careful.

For some items, the label is less important. We recently acquired a colorblock mini dress from the late 1960s, without a label, but the print is amazing and reveals a great deal about the use of color in art at that time.

Do you think that many pieces made today will be collector's items in the future? Can real vintage pieces still be made?

Some of today's designers are incredibly creative: Japanese designers like Yamamoto or Rei Kawakubo, British designers like Gareth Pugh, Mary Katrantzou, and Sarah Burton, or American designers like Rodarte and Isabel Toledo are all incredibly interesting. And I would take absolutely anything by Azzedine Alaïa. But I do have the feeling that there are fewer great pieces being made today that will be tomorrow's vintage.

Are you personally a collector or a vintage enthusiast?

Collecting vintage clothes would be a conflict of interest for me, even if I have been known to buy a thing or two on eBay. They would not be considered "museum quality"—and I wear them!

What is the typical story behind a piece from your collections?

There are so many sources for museum-quality work. We try to look at everything that is donated to us because you never know what can be discovered in someone's attic. We also pay attention to auctions, high-end vintage, and what is on the Internet.

A Conversation with Pamela Parmal of the MUSEUM OF FINE ARTS, BOSTON

1930s

It's All About the Bias

The 1930s signaled the return of the feminine silhouette at its loveliest.

Following a decade that witnessed a vanishing waistline and an increasingly androgynous silhouette, the new styles emphasized the shape of the body, clinging softly to the curves of the women wearing them. Madeleine Vionnet spearheaded this movement with her brilliant approach to the bias, the decade's seminal cut. Collectors and museums fight over her earliest masterpieces that demonstrate unparalleled savoir faire. Other pieces that are very much in demand include those by Cristóbal Balenciaga, who was just starting his career in Paris; by Jean Patou, who was putting the finishing touches on his latest creations; and, of course, by Elsa Schiaparelli. Her numerous collaborations with surrealist artists were the ultimate representation of the period.

While the bias technique and cut led to less ornamentation and embroidery, certain design patterns remained important. The influence of Art Deco reached its peak in the graphic and geometric shapes featured on many creations. Orientalism-inspired motifs and touches of lamé balanced the decrease of embellishment. As the 1940s approached, the waistline continued to be emphasized, sometimes with a peplum—especially in the creations by Alix, better known as Madame Grès, as she began her illustrious career.

MADELEINE VIONNET

COUTURE

Black silk satin evening gown; cowl neck; V-cut back; sloped shoulders with short sleeves; cutout look; waist adorned with two panels of steel gray satin, crisscrossed and tied; full skirt cut on the bias. No label.

Estimate: 3,500–4,000 euros
Sold: 4,375 euros
Cornette de Saint Cyr, Paris
July 2, 2010 (lot 324)
Specialists: D. Chombert and F. Sternbach

MADELEINE VIONNET

COUTURE

Black panne velvet evening gown entirely cut on the bias; cowl neck crisscrossed at the back; cutout look. White label, raspberry red lettering.

Estimate: 700–900 euros
Sold: 3,098 euros
Artcurial, Paris
June 27, 2011 (lot 290)
Specialist: PB Fashion

MADELEINE VIONNET

N° 4750
COUTURE, 1934

Silk crepe garden-party dress printed with abstract ivory flowers on sage green background; draped half sleeves; inverted pleats at the bottom forming godets; belt with black Bakelite clasp. No label.

ICONOGRAPHY: Archives de la Seine, deposited by Madeleine Vionnet, 1934, album no. 54.

Estimate: 800–1,000 euros
Sold: 3,222 euros
Thierry de Maigret, Paris
November 22, 2011 (lot 275)
Specialist: Séverine Experton-Dard

MADELEINE VIONNET

COUTURE

Black silk satin evening gown cut on the bias; boat neckline with small lapels; yoke and shoulder strap look; flowing skirt cut in points. White label, blue lettering.

Estimate: 10,000–12,000 euros
Sold: 23,750 euros
Cornette de Saint Cyr, Paris
July 2, 2010 (lot 232)
Specialists: D. Chombert and F. Sternbach

ANONYMOUS

COUTURE

Raw muslin evening gown; cowl neck embroidered with small translucent gray and green tubular pearls; rhinestone highlights repeated at the waist and on the back; flowing skirt.

Estimate: 300–400 euros
Sold: 1,625 euros
Cornette de Saint Cyr, Paris
July 2, 2010 (lot 95)
Specialists: D. Chombert and
F. Sternbach

ANONYMOUS

COUTURE

Periwinkle blue dress; round neckline with two collarets, repeated at the shoulders and finishing at the back; high-waisted skirt cut on the bias; circular ribbed pattern starting at the hips.

Estimate: 300–400 euros
Sold: 250 euros
Cornette de Saint Cyr, Paris
June 30, 2012 (lot 76)
Specialists: D. Chombert and
F. Sternbach

NINA RICCI

COUTURE

Ivory satin fully pleated evening gown; V-neckline; open back with straps; waistband and skirt feature insets that offset the pleating; short raglan sleeves. White label, blue and black lettering.

Estimate: 1,500–2,000 euros
Sold: 22,749 euros
Cornette de Saint Cyr, Paris
July 3, 2009 (lot 319)
Specialists: D. Chombert and
F. Sternbach

CALLOT SŒURS

N°47028
COUTURE

Straw yellow mousseline de soie dress; V-neckline showing a satin tone-on-tone background; draping and sunburst darts are accentuated by a revers that forms a panel held by a belt fastened at the back; pagoda sleeves; box pleats on the hips, repeated at the back. White label, white lettering.

Estimate: 800–900 euros
Sold: 938 euros
Cornette de Saint Cyr, Paris
June 30, 2012 (lot 144)
Specialists: D. Chombert and F. Sternbach

MAGGY ROUFF

COUTURE

Dark red crepe evening gown partially trimmed with gold threads; V-neckline; cutout openings; skirt cut on the bias.

Estimate: 1,800–2,000 euros
Sold: 1,983 euros
Eve, Paris
June 18, 2012 (lot M042)
Specialist: Sylvie Daniel

JEAN PATOU

N°5540
COUTURE

Raw crepe evening dress; American armholes with V-neckline; front with fluted pleats embroidered with rhinestones; skirt with three sunburst-pleated bellows, repeated on the back adorned with a tied half belt. White label, pink lettering.

<u>PROVENANCE</u>: From the personal wardrobe of Mademoiselle Jack, model working for Patou in the 1930s.

Estimate: 1,200–1,300 euros
Sold: 3,500 euros
Cornette de Saint Cyr, Paris
July 4, 2011 (lot 131)
Specialists: D. Chombert and F. Sternbach

MARCELLE ALIX

COUTURE

Black silk jersey evening gown; low-cut heart-shaped neckline; three-quarter sleeves; bolero look continued on the back to the hips with smocking on a wide panel providing fullness and fluidity. White label, black lettering.

Estimate: 1,300–1,500 euros
Sold: 1,625 euros
Cornette de Saint Cyr, Paris
July 2, 2010 (lot 225)
Specialists: D. Chombert and F. Sternbach

ANONYMOUS

COUTURE

Royal blue shantung evening gown; squared neckline; small sleeves puckered by smocking and trimmed with white sequins forming a wave pattern; high-waisted look with flowing skirt. Cape with double button and a pocket; ivory Bakelite clasp with floral motif adorned with cabochons mimicking sapphires and rhinestones.

Estimate: 400–600 euros
Sold: 625 euros
Cornette de Saint Cyr, Paris
July 2, 2010 (lot 111)
Specialists: D. Chombert and F. Sternbach

JEANNE LANVIN

COUTURE, Winter 1938–1939

Black panne velvet evening gown cut on the bias; V-neckline; low armholes with half sleeves; godet skirt.

Estimate: 1,200–1,500 euros
Sold: 1,859 euros
Eve, Paris
March 16, 2012 (lot M092)
Specialist: Sylvie Daniel

ANONYMOUS

COUTURE

Lace and black muslin dress with a false two-piece look; V-neckline adorned with a scalloped neck tie trimmed with white and taupe pearls; funnel cuffs lined with ivory muslin.

Estimate: 300–400 euros
Sold: 475 euros
Cornette de Saint Cyr, Paris
June 30, 2012 (lot 345)
Specialists: D. Chombert and F. Sternbach

JENNY

COUTURE

Apricot satin evening gown cut on the bias and enhanced with cutout openings; V-neckline; pelerine look.

Estimate: 1,500–1,800 euros
Sold: 1,983 euros
Eve, Paris
October 25, 2011 (lot M027)
Specialist: Sylvie Daniel

LOUISE BOULANGER

N° 14689
COUTURE

Black satin evening gown; shoulder straps; open back; belt adorned with red Bakelite and rhinestones; trompe-l'œil knot on the front; flowing skirt cut on the bias. White label, navy lettering and logo.

Estimate: 1,800–2,200 euros
Sold: 2,750 euros
Cornette de Saint Cyr, Paris
July 2, 2010 (lot 187)
Specialists: D. Chombert and F. Sternbach

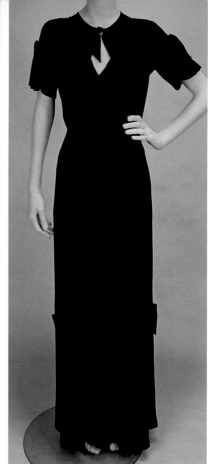

MOLYNEUX

COUTURE

Black velvet slip-on evening gown cut on the bias. Label "Modèle Molyneux."

Estimate: 500–1,000 pounds
Sold: 213 pounds
Christie's, London
December 1, 2011 (lot 69)
Specialist: Patricia Frost

GABRIELLE CHANEL

COUTURE

Black silk evening gown cut on the bias; open back with shoulder straps adorned with a large bow on the skirt forming godets. Label.

Estimate: 3,000–4,000 pounds
Sold: 4,375 pounds
Christie's, London
December 2, 2010 (lot 133)
Specialist: Patricia Frost

JEAN PATOU

N º 81070(...)
COUTURE

Black silk crepe evening gown; rounded collar with a knot over a triangular opening, repeated on the short sleeves and at the bottom of the skirt that has five box pleats and a pinched waist. Label "Jean Patou Paris."

Estimate: 1,500–1,800 dollars
Sold: 2,520 dollars
Charles A. Whitaker Auction Company, Philadelphia
April 27–28, 2012 (lot 721)
Specialist: Charles A. Whitaker

JEAN PATOU

N º 28856
COUTURE

Green-gray shimmering satin evening gown; bib bodice with open back; two long satin panels tied at the waist; slit skirt. Ivory label, pink lettering.

Estimate: 800–1,000 euros
Sold: 3,378 euros
Artcurial, Paris
June 11, 2012 (lot 477)
Specialist: PB Fashion

JEANNE LANVIN

N º 4675
COUTURE

Pleated fuchsia satin evening cape with soutache trim; crew neckline; arm openings; asymmetric length. Black label, yellow lettering.

ICONOGRAPHY: There is a similar model in the Lanvin archives.

Estimate: 1,500–2,000 euros
Sold: 1,875 euros
Cornette de Saint Cyr, Paris
June 30, 2012 (lot 167)
Specialists: D. Chombert and F. Sternbach

ELIZABETH HAWES

COUTURE

Full blue silk jersey dress with shoulder straps; draping from the V-neckline; belt draped in satin with a gold lamé triangular buckle; pink silk slip. Silk jersey cape fastened with a twisted gold lamé chain buttoned to each shoulder adorned with an identical yoke. Label "Elizabeth Hawes Inc."

<u>PROVENANCE</u>: Brooklyn Museum.

Estimate: 600–800 dollars
Sold: 1,289 dollars
Augusta Auctions, New York
March 30, 2011 (lot 283)
Specialist: Karen E. Augusta

JEAN PATOU

COUTURE

Blue, pink, and purple silk crepe evening gown with boat neckline; slightly draped shoulders and open back; pattern at the waist transforms into two small panels, repeated on the flowing skirt. Worn with a purple and blue bodice jacket with long sleeves and bouffant shoulders. No label.

<u>PROVENANCE</u>: From the personal wardrobe of Mademoiselle Jack, model at Patou in the 1930s.

Estimate: 1,000–1,200 euros
Sold: 9,500 euros
Cornette de Saint Cyr, Paris
July 4, 2011 (lot 111)
Specialists: D. Chombert and
F. Sternbach

JEAN PATOU

COUTURE

Black and yellow crepe evening gown; square neckline with wide straps; open back; two floating panels tied at the hips over a flowing skirt. No label.

<u>PROVENANCE</u>: From the personal wardrobe of Mademoiselle Jack, model at Patou in the 1930s.

Estimate: 700–900 euros
Sold: 8,750 euros
Cornette de Saint Cyr, Paris
July 4, 2011 (lot 228)
Specialists: D. Chombert and
F. Sternbach

JEAN PATOU

COUTURE

Long black lace dress decorated with velvet ribbons with a scalloped look and full skirt; hem stiffened with horsehair. No label.

<u>PROVENANCE</u>: From the personal wardrobe of Mademoiselle Jack, model at Patou in the 1930s.

Estimate: 1,500–1,700 euros
Sold: 4,500 euros
Cornette de Saint Cyr, Paris
July 4, 2011 (lot 53)
Specialists: D. Chombert and F. Sternbach

AUGUSTA BERNARD

N° 36229
COUTURE

Pearl and mouse gray dress; boat neckline; slightly draped shoulders; flowing skirt adorned with a double edging at the back; belt. White label, gray lettering.

Estimate: 1,200–1,300 euros
Sold: 2,625 euros
Cornette de Saint Cyr, Paris
July 4, 2011 (lot 60)
Specialists: D. Chombert and F. Sternbach

LUCIEN LELONG

COUTURE

Black silk satin evening gown; straps with square neckline; bavolets forming a collaret at the back; flounced hips and flowing skirt partially cut on the bias with a train. Beige label, brown lettering.

Estimate: 1,400–1,600 euros
Sold: 1,625 euros
Cornette de Saint Cyr, Paris
July 4, 2011 (lot 212)
Specialists: D. Chombert and F. Sternbach

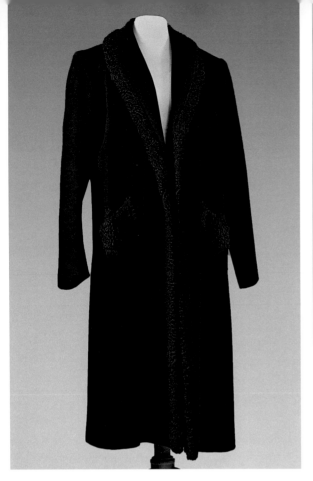

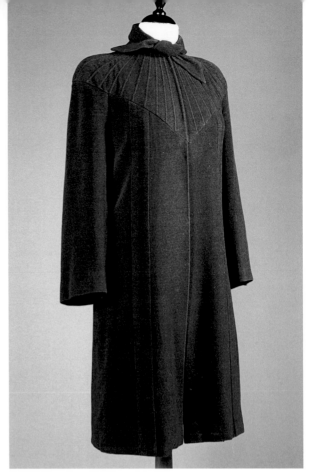

JEAN PATOU

COUTURE

Black wool drape coat; shawl collar, lapels, and pockets cut on the bias decorated with embroidery highlighted with a *Boukara astrakan* band. White label, pink lettering.

Estimate: 400–500 euros
Sold: 1,500 euros
Cornette de Saint Cyr, Paris
July 4, 2011 (lot 106)
Specialists: D. Chombert and F. Sternbach

AGNÈS DRECOLL

COUTURE

Ink blue wool coat; high neck tied at the front; pointed Bertha look; decorated with radiating ribbing; hidden hook-and-eye fasteners.

Estimate: 300–400 euros
Sold: 5,630 euros
Artcurial, Paris
June 11, 2012 (lot 475)
Specialist: PB Fashion

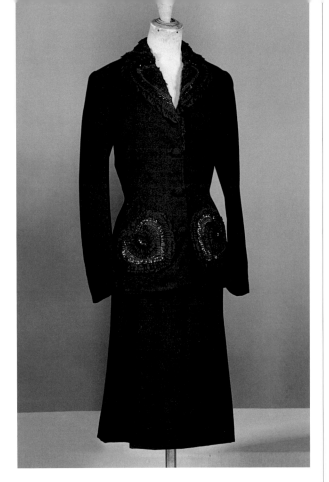

ROBERT PIGUET

JEANNE LANVIN

COUTURE

Black wool suit; tailored coat with notched collar trimmed in lace, silk, and sequins, repeated on the heart-shaped pockets; single-breasted closure with covered buttons; flared skirt. Black label, white lettering.

Estimate: 900–1,100 euros
Sold: 2,500 euros
Cornette de Saint Cyr, Paris
July 2, 2010 (lot 146)
Specialists: D. Chombert and F. Sternbach

COUTURE

Flared black velvet evening cape-coat; large cowl neck fastened with a button; kimono sleeves. Label "Jeanne Lanvin, 22 Faubg St Honoré, Paris."

Estimate: 600–1,200 pounds
Sold: 750 pounds
Christie's, London
December 3, 2009 (lot 304)
Specialist: Patricia Frost

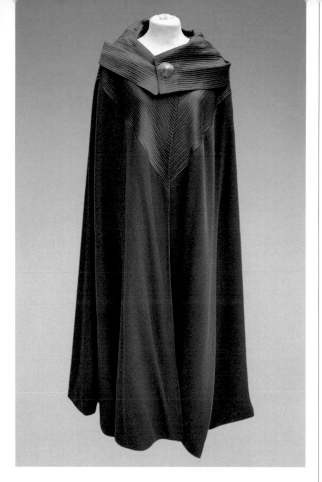

JEANNE LANVIN

BALENCIAGA

N º 100966

COUTURE, Winter 1935–1936

COUTURE, Winter 1938

Red wool crepe and satin duchesse hooded cape adorned with topstitching; wide collar over the shoulders fastened with a gadrooned metallic button.

Chocolate silk satin evening coat; double shawl collar; single-breasted closure with buttons; long sleeves with bouffant look; flared skirt forming godets at the back. White label, black lettering.

Estimate: 1,000–1,500 euros
Sold: 6,816 euros
Eve, Paris
March 16, 2012 (lot M096)
Specialist: Sylvie Daniel

Estimate: 600–700 euros
Sold: 750 euros
Cornette de Saint Cyr, Paris
June 30, 2012 (lot 235)
Specialists: D. Chombert and F. Sternbach

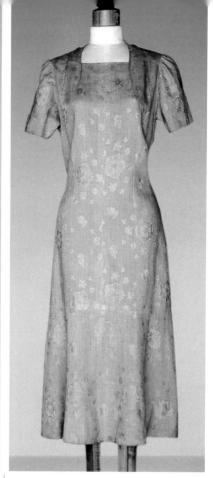

ANONYMOUS

COUTURE

Mousseline de soie dress with a red, coral, and lavender floral print on a beige background; neckline enhanced with ruffle trim set off with a flower; butterfly sleeves; hips adorned with a pleated panel over a flowing skirt forming small godets; belt.

Estimate: 100–200 dollars
Sold: 540 dollars
Charles A. Whitaker Auction Company, Philadelphia
April 27–28, 2012 (lot 717)
Specialist: Charles A. Whitaker

ANONYMOUS

COUTURE

Powder pink day dress cut on the bias; neckline with small gatherings; balloon sleeves; waist set off with a half belt attached at the back of a gored skirt.

Estimate: 60–80 euros
Sold: 62 euros
Artcurial, Paris
June 27, 2011 (lot 241)
Specialist: PB Fashion

ELSA SCHIAPARELLI

N °(...)78.F2
COUTURE, Summer 1937

Blue-green damask linen day dress with a floral motif; squared neckline with tucks on the sides; short gathered sleeves; flesh-colored plastic zippers on the neck and left side. Label "Schiaparelli Summer 1937—21 Place Vendôme Paris."

PROVENANCE: Brooklyn Museum.

Estimate: 200–300 dollars
Sold: 2,400 dollars
Augusta Auctions, New York
November 10, 2010 (lot 354)
Specialist: Karen E. Augusta

HERMÈS

ANONYMOUS

BABANI

PRÊT-À-PORTER, Spring/Summer 1938

COUTURE

COUTURE

Bathing suit printed with the signs of the zodiac on an ivory background; elasticized top over modesty shorts; back zipper. Label "Hermès Sport."

Wraparound blended wool day dress, partially embroidered like a cashmere shawl; V-neckline with lapels; short sleeves; waist fastened with two buttons; skirt adorned with a patch pocket.

Wine-colored silk crepe kimono partially embroidered with silk thread featuring landscapes and gardens; lined with steel gray silk pongee painted with a rosette pattern. Ivory label, gold lettering.

Estimate: 600–1,000 pounds
Sold: 500 pounds
Christie's, London
December 1, 2011 (lot 89)
Specialist: Patricia Frost

Estimate: 150–200 euros
Sold: 188 euros
Artcurial, Paris
November 25, 2011 (lot 410)
Specialist: PB Fashion

Estimate: 600–800 euros
Sold: 750 euros
Cornette de Saint Cyr, Paris
July 2, 2010 (lot 330)
Specialists: D. Chombert and F. Sternbach

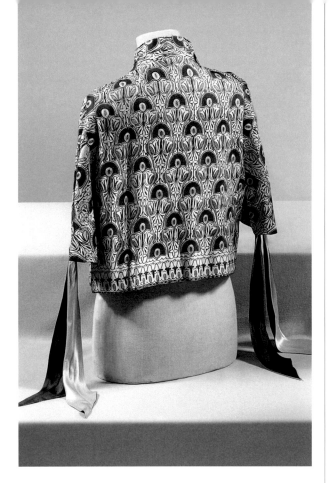

JEANNE LANVIN

N ° 5705
COUTURE, Summer 1931

Raw satin silk topcoat trimmed with Point de Beauvais needlework with an Art Deco plant motif; crew neckline; front facing without buttons; three-quarter sleeves decorated with two-sided claret red and natural-colored ribbons that can be tied. White label, black and red lettering, logo.

Estimate: 1,200–1,500 euros
Sold: 15,000 euros
Cornette de Saint Cyr, Paris
July 4, 2011 (lot 81)
Specialists: D. Chombert and F. Sternbach

ELSA SCHIAPARELLI

COUTURE

Olive green velvet jacket entirely trimmed with pearls; floral decoration in vermilion, pink, almond, and ochre tones; V-neckline enhanced with lapels; hook-and-eye fasteners. Label "Schiaparelli Paris."

Estimate: 3,000–4,000 dollars
Sold: 2,160 dollars
Charles A. Whitaker Auction Company, Philadelphia
October 28–29, 2011 (lot 577)
Specialist: Charles A. Whitaker

ELSA SCHIAPARELLI

N° 58214
COUTURE
(Buttons: Jean Clément)

Black wool crepe tailored jacket; small shawl collar; draped look in the front; single-breasted closure with black lacquer pinecone buttons. No label, atelier tag.

BIBLIOGRAPHY: The jacket is reproduced in *Elsa Schiaparelli: Empress of Paris Fashion*, Palmer White, Aurum Press, 1995.

Estimate: 4,000–5,000 euros
Sold: 11,250 euros
Cornette de Saint Cyr, Paris
July 3, 2009 (lot 72)
Specialists: D. Chombert and F. Sternbach

ELSA SCHIAPARELLI

N° 56371
COUTURE, Winter 1937/1938
(Buttons: Jean Clément)

Black, claret red, yellow, and green plaid wool jacket; shawl collar with cut panels; two front pockets with three descending accolade frills; identical hip pockets; hidden hook-and-eye fasteners adorned with three large braided leather buttons. White label, black lettering.

BIBLIOGRAPHY: The identical jacket is reproduced on p. 6 of *Vogue*, October 1937.

MUSEOGRAPHY: Sketch of the model is found in the UFAC collections of the Musée des Arts Décoratifs, inventory UF D 73-21-1363.

Estimate: 2,000–3,000 euros
Sold: 13,125 euros
Cornette de Saint Cyr, Paris
July 3, 2009 (lot 146)
Specialists: D. Chombert and F. Sternbach

ELSA SCHIAPARELLI

N ° 65158
COUTURE
(Buttons: Jean Clément)

Black wool slightly flared coat; high collar; bronze buttons with brown patina; stitching emphasizing the back waist; gored look. Label, atelier tag.

MUSEOGRAPHY: The identical cut and buttons on evening coat, Winter 1938–1939, are found in the UFAC collection, Musée des Arts Décoratifs, inventory 66-38.6; gift from Mrs. Lopez-Willshaw.

Estimate: 3,000–4,000 euros
Sold: 3,750 euros
Cornette de Saint Cyr, Paris
July 3, 2009 (lot 180)
Specialists: D. Chombert and F. Sternbach

ELSA SCHIAPARELLI

COUTURE
(Buttons: François Hugo)

Navy silk peignoir printed with shocking pink stripes and sleeve rings; round-collar blouse adorned with knotted bias-cut tie; open darts on back and yoke at the shoulders; single-breasted closure with navy resin buttons engraved with "S"; straight cuffs; wide pants; waist ties at the side; zipper. White label, black lettering.

Estimate: 1,300–1,500 euros
Sold: 5,000 euros
Cornette de Saint Cyr, Paris
July 3, 2009 (lot 266)
Specialists: D. Chombert and F. Sternbach

ELSA SCHIAPARELLI

N ° 63856
COUTURE, Fall 1938

Black crepe evening gown; square neckline, gathered with a fuchsia ribbon drawstring on an open back; high waist enhanced with two crossing panels; small sleeves with bavolets and flaps. White label, black lettering.

Estimate: 3,000–4,000 euros
Sold: 27,624 euros
Cornette de Saint Cyr, Paris
July 3, 2009 (lot 270)
Specialists: D. Chombert and F. Sternbach

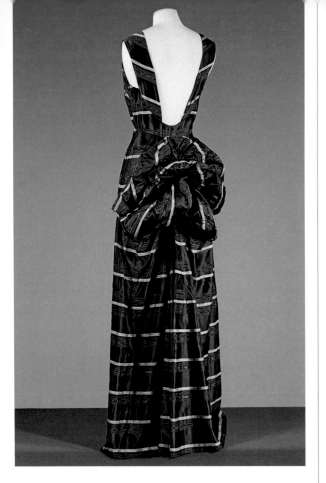

ELSA SCHIAPARELLI

N º 67695
COUTURE, Summer 1939

Pekiné and moiré silk evening ensemble; high round neckline and open back; long skirt with train made from a few hidden folds under a three-tiered bustle. White label, black lettering.

<u>MUSEOGRAPHY</u>: Sketch is found in the UFAC collections of the Musée des Arts Décoratifs, inventory UF D 73-21-2237.

<u>BIBLIOGRAPHY</u>: The model is reproduced on p. 201 in *Elsa Schiaparelli*, Dilys E. Blum, Philadelphia Museum of Art, September 28, 2003–January 4, 2004, and Musée des Arts Décoratifs, Paris, March 17–August 29, 2004; p. 150, *Hommage à Elsa Schiaparelli*, Musée de la Mode et du Costume, Palais Galliera, June 21–August 30, 1984.

<u>ICONOGRAPHY</u>: Design drawing, *Fémina*, March 1939.

Estimate: 4,000–6,000 euros
Sold: 78,748 euros

Cornette de Saint Cyr, Paris
July 3, 2009 (lot 155)

Specialists: D. Chombert and F. Sternbach

ELSA SCHIAPARELLI

COUTURE, Fall/Winter 1938

Black faille and shocking pink silk satin evening gown; wide horizontal stripes; neckline with delicate accolade cut enhanced with a small lantern sleeve on the right and strap on the left; square open back; ribbed shirring descending to the top of the hips; wide skirt cut on the bias with asymmetric length. No label.

<u>MUSEOGRAPHY</u>: Drawing of the model is in the UFAC collections of the Musée des Arts Décoratifs. Variation of the model is in the UFAC collections, inventory 66-38.3; gift from Mrs. Lopez-Willshaw.

Estimate: 4,000–5,000 euros
Sold: 43,749 euros

Cornette de Saint Cyr, Paris
July 3, 2009 (lot 256)

Specialists: D. Chombert and F. Sternbach

ELSA SCHIAPARELLI

N°65607
COUTURE, Spring 1939

Purple satin evening gown; square neckline with crossing shoulder straps on an open back. Worn under a jacket with a small straight collar with zipper; long sleeves with gathered shoulders with a multicolor satin tufted patchwork and zipped cuffs. White label, black lettering.

MUSEOGRAPHY: Sketch of the model is found in the UFAC collections of the Musée des Arts Décoratifs, inventory UF D 73-21-2139.

Estimate: 6,000–7,000 euros
Sold: 18,749 euros

Cornette de Saint Cyr, Paris
July 3, 2009 (lot 268)

Specialists: D. Chombert and
F. Sternbach

ELSA SCHIAPARELLI

N°53991
COUTURE, Fall 1937
(Embroidery: Lesage)

Crinkle crepe dress; scalloped square neckline; transparent back; skirt rounded at the back. Tailored jacket; turnback collar with look of a transparent Bertha collar; popcorn stitching.

MUSEOGRAPHY: Sketches of the model are in the UFAC collections of the Musée des Arts Décoratifs, UF D 73-21-1717.

BIBLIOGRAPHY: The identical jacket is shown on p. 113 in *Elsa Schiaparelli*, Philadelphia Museum of Art, Sept. 28, 2003–Jan. 4, 2004, on p. 39 of *Vogue*, June 1937.

Estimate: 5,000–6,000 euros
Sold: 22,499 euros

Cornette de Saint Cyr, Paris
July 3, 2009 (lot 292)

Specialists: D. Chombert and
F. Sternbach

ELSA SCHIAPARELLI

COUTURE, Winter 1934

Black crepe sheath; V-neckline with tunic-apron look made of Rhodoid sequins. No label.

BIBLIOGRAPHY: A similar model is reproduced on p. 26 of *Vogue*, July 1934, photograph by Horst.

Estimate: 7,000–8,000 euros
Sold: 11,250 euros

Cornette de Saint Cyr, Paris
July 2, 2010 (lot 237)

Specialists: D. Chombert and
F. Sternbach

ELSA SCHIAPARELLI

After a design by Jean Cocteau
COUTURE, Fall 1937
(Embroidery: Lesage)

Short gray woven linen jacket with V-neckline; long raglan sleeves; crisscrossed front facing with a hook-and-eye closure; decorated by the profile of a woman with golden hair made of interwoven tubular pearls adorned with antique gold metallic threads descending on the right sleeve. Her face is delineated with pink silk threads. Her eye, embroidered with blue silk threads, is adorned with an imitation-sapphire rhinestone; her arm is reproduced along the upper front facing in antique gold thread; her polished pink nails hold a scarf made of metallic blue thread; the signature "Jean" is embroidered with pink thread topped with a star. No label.

BIBLIOGRAPHY: The identical jacket is reproduced on p. 141 in the exhibition catalog *Elsa Schiaparelli*, Dilys E. Blum, Philadelphia Museum of Art, September 28, 2003–January 4, 2004, and Musée de la Mode et du Textile, Paris, March 17–August 29, 2004. Sketch of the jacket is reproduced on pp. 46–47 in *Elsa Schiaparelli: Empress of Paris Fashion*, Palmer White, Aurum Press, 1995. Design and details of the embroidery are reproduced on p. 65 in *Lesage, maître brodeur de la haute couture*, Palmer White, éditions du Chêne, 1988.

MUSEOGRAPHY: The identical model was presented at the exhibition *Hommage à Elsa Schiaparelli*, Musée de la Mode et du Costume, Palais Galliera, June 21–August 30, 1984.

Estimate: 12,000–15,000 euros
Sold: 174,995 euros

Cornette de Saint Cyr, Paris
July 3, 2009 (lot 200)

Specialists: D. Chombert and F. Sternbach

ICONS OF VINTAGE FASHION
1930s

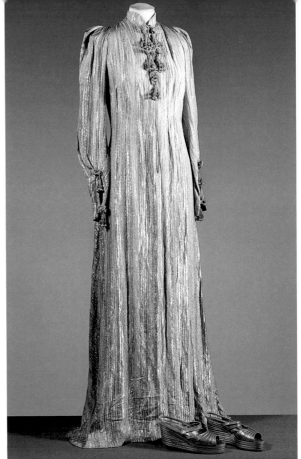

ELSA SCHIAPARELLI

ELSA SCHIAPARELLI

COUTURE

COUTURE

Electric blue velvet evening gown; squared open back; flowing skirt with inverted godet pleating. Label "Schiaparelli London."

Golden brocaded lamé evening gown with torsades in relief; high neck with zipper enhanced with pink and gold tassels, repeated on the cuffs of the long sleeves; darts at the shoulders; flowing skirt with inverted box pleats. No label.

Estimate: 3,000–5,000 pounds
Sold: 11,875 pounds
Christie's, London
December 2, 2010 (lot 173)
Specialist: Patricia Frost

Estimate: 5,000–6,000 euros
Sold: 7,500 euros
Cornette de Saint Cyr, Paris
July 3, 2009 (lot 112)
Specialists: D. Chombert and F. Sternbach

ANONYMOUS

COUTURE

Black velvet evening coat; high collar fastened with a covered button; sleeves trimmed with a floral pattern made of gold metallic thread; V-cut back.

Estimate: 100–150 euros
Sold: 125 euros

Artcurial, Paris
June 11, 2012 (lot 220)

Specialist: PB Fashion

JEANNE LANVIN

N° 21652
COUTURE

Turquoise Moroccan crepe dress; squared neckline enhanced with topstitched gold lamé that drapes over the back; belted waist with bronze buckle; flowing skirt with wide bias cut forming the hem. White label, black lettering with logo.

Estimate: 2,000–2,500 euros
Sold: 19,375 euros

Cornette de Saint Cyr, Paris
July 2, 2010 (lot 162)

Specialists: D. Chombert and F. Sternbach

ANONYMOUS

COUTURE

Black crepe evening gown decorated with gold leather applications forming a scroll pattern; thin straps; V-cut in the front with small gatherings; flowing skirt with back slit and train.

Estimate: 700–800 euros
Sold: 875 euros

Cornette de Saint Cyr, Paris
June 30, 2012 (lot 220)

Specialists: D. Chombert and F. Sternbach

CALLOT SŒURS

N° 442142
COUTURE

Sea green and silver lamé evening gown with thin straps; front adorned with a double torsade holding the small gatherings of the high-waisted slit skirt, cut on the bias; V-cut back. Worn with a separate draped cape, with double panel forming a train at the back. White label, blue lettering.

Estimate: 300–500 euros
Sold: 6,196 euros
Artcurial, Paris
June 27, 2011 (lot 171)
Specialist: PB Fashion

ANONYMOUS

COUTURE

Gold and beige metallic lace evening gown; cowl neck; low back with a tie; adorned with half belt; skirt cut on the bias forming godets. Worn with brown silk crepe slip.

Estimate: 450–650 euros
Sold: 1,376 euros
Artcurial, Paris
November 25, 2011 (lot 205)
Specialist: PB Fashion

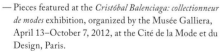

— Pieces featured at the *Cristóbal Balenciaga: collectionneur de modes* exhibition, organized by the Musée Galliera, April 13–October 7, 2012, at the Cité de la Mode et du Design, Paris.

• *Above, right*: Silk opera coat, circa 1960, Cristóbal Balenciaga, Cincinnati Art Museum, Ohio, Gift from Friends of Fashion.

BALENCIAGA

An exhibition of the personal collection of an artist whose own works are collected, the Cristóbal Balenciaga: collectionneur de modes[1] *exhibition was an opportunity for the public to discover what had inspired the couturier. It was a splendid* mise en abyme *of creation and of his collection.*

Balenciaga was a master of couture whose works have been exhibited time and time again in the museums of Paris,[2] San Francisco,[3] and New York.[4] Today, the fact that the very items that inspired the master of couture are on display in a museum seems quite fitting and offers a new perspective on his creative process.

WHAT INSPIRED THE MASTER COUTURIER?

A fashion prodigy, Cristóbal Balenciaga founded his first *maison de couture* at the age of twenty. But 1937 marked the real beginning of Balenciaga's fashion journey when he moved to 10 Avenue George-V.

His distinctive sense of elegance and perfectly cut clothes seduced the Paris fashion scene as he revolutionized the post-war silhouette. He would become the premier couturier whose work was both modern and timeless.

To reveal a fashion designer's actual sources of inspiration is akin to shattering a taboo, a daring gamble that can demystify our perception of the artist's pure sense of inspiration, one that is supposed to come from his own imagination.

Such is not the case with Balenciaga; on the contrary, the disclosure of his personal archives only reinforces his excellence and his status as a master. His allusions are intelligent and refined, and all his works reflect his own unique interpretation of these sources. When examining his sources and his designs side by side, a graceful dialogue develops between historical dresses and engravings, traditional Spanish costumes, short coats and capes dating from the nineteenth century, and the Spanish designer's haute couture creations from the mid-1950s. Guipure collars and the elaborately embroidered fabrics of the nineteenth century are subtly echoed in Balenciaga's opera capes and in the design of a dress and jacket (Haute Couture, Fall/Winter 1965); the colors and patterns of popular Spanish costumes and burnooses find their way into the history of costume in the form of a princess-shape evening gown with matching jacket and cape of embroidered tussor silk with floral motifs (Haute Couture, Spring/Summer 1960); a violet silk velvet evening coat (Haute Couture, 1958) may have drawn its monastic simplicity from the coats of the cardinals portrayed in Balenciaga's engravings.

Balenciaga will always be remembered for his preference for simple and clean lines, dramatically new shapes, and timeless classicism, and his love of volume and balance in the silhouette as well as his penchant for ornamentation, which is highlighted by his splendid and coherent collection.

THE NEW AND THE VINTAGE

Nicolas Ghesquière, universally recognized as the worthy heir to the master couturier, took over the House of Balenciaga from 1997 to 2012.

He successfully shook the house from its slumber while imposing his own name as a recognized force in fashion. He created extraordinary designs and positioned himself brilliantly at the crossroads between tradition and innovation.

He retained Balenciaga's essential codes of simplicity, architecture, volume, and radicalism. These principles were eminently adaptable to his own vision of fashion, enabling him to achieve an elegant synthesis of respect and revolution. He has openly expressed his appreciation of vintage fashion and bought many older pieces in order to take them apart and study their construction. In 2001, he gained access to the archives of the House of Balenciaga: "It was an exhilarating and breathtaking lesson in history. I am part of the ongoing Balenciaga legacy [...] I was struck by some of the similarities between my work and his. Especially the vision of a garment that is minimal, architectural, and generous in volume."[5]

If Cristóbal Balenciaga revolutionized the postwar silhouette, Nicolas Ghesquière created a radical and innovative shape, with modern lines that are in step with the times. His creations will undoubtedly be part of future vintage collections.

Some time before he announced his departure from Balenciaga at the end of 2012, Nicolas Ghesquière closed the Balenciaga Spring/Summer 2012 show with his models wearing large hats that covered their faces and reached down over their backs and shoulders, an homage to the master who had covered the head of his 1976 bride with a hat that had been inspired by the fisherman's caps of his childhood—a three-tiered level of inspiration.

1—Exhibit held by the Musée Galliera at the Docks, Cité de la Mode et du Design, April 13–October 7, 2012.
2—*Balenciaga Paris* at the Arts Décoratifs in 2006.
3—*Balenciaga and Spain* at the de Young, Fine Arts Museum of San Francisco, 2011.
4—*Balenciaga: Spanish Master* at the Queen Sofia Spanish Institute, 2010.
5—*L'Express Styles*, March 21, 2012.

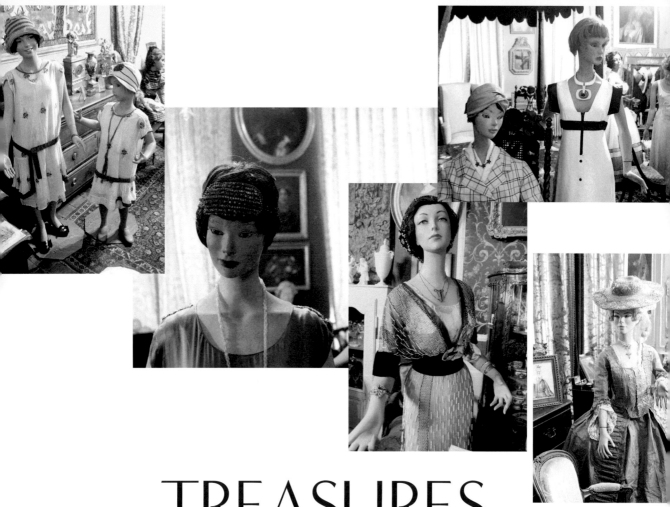

TREASURES

V intage? What is that?" asks Madame Carton, age 92, amused, as she switches on the light in the first room of the Costume Museum of Avallon.

We are in the heart of Burgundy, in a charming town of large stone houses. Among the many quaint old buildings stands one *hôtel particulier* that dates back to the seventeenth century and that once belonged to the Condé family. Madame Carton and her two daughters saved this building just as it was about to be turned into a parking facility by the town.

This happened twenty years ago. The three women arrived from Amiens, in the midst of a thunderstorm, with countless boxes filled with a treasure trove of old costumes dating from the seventeenth to the twentieth century. The storm finally passed, but the rain continued to fall inside the building. The three women were passionate about their undertaking and began the respectful renovation of the house they intended to transform into a costume museum. The building that was in ruins would become the showplace for the clothes that they had expertly collected over the years from auctions,

antique dealers, Emmaüs International, yard sales, and individuals. Their collection of more than 3,000 costumes, as well as accessories, mannequins, furniture, and archival documents, allowed them to conceive and organize yearly exhibitions, with a topic that was usually influenced by one of their latest acquisitions.

Their 2012 offering, *Telle une gravure de mode* (Like a fashion plate) presents old engravings, mostly from fashion magazines (*La Gazette du Bon Ton, Le Journal des Demoiselles, Le Petit Écho de la Mode,* and even *Vogue*) that seem to come to life through the mannequins dressed in clothing from the same period. The twelve rooms offer a panorama of fashion, ranging from the eighteenth century to the 1960s, a *tableau vivant* of the history of fashion.

In one small salon, where the walls are covered with portraits, elegant ladies from the seventeenth century converse with two men wearing suits and wigs. A little further, three women in afternoon dress are having tea. Madame Carton is quick to point out their crinolines, the revolutionary creation of

from AVALLON

Peugeot, who invented the steel crinoline that allowed women to sit without breaking the hoops that had previously been made of wood.

In a nearby boudoir with hand-embroidered curtains, a woman in her morning dress adjusts her child's baptismal outfit. The nineteenth-century chapel is filled with religious objects and is the setting for a wedding; some of the guests include men in ceremonial dress. A magnificently paneled room sets the stage for the sartorial revolution of the early twentieth century: Displayed on one side of the room is a theatrical corseted and voluminous dress of red velvet taffeta with leg-of-mutton sleeves from the late nineteenth century; on the other side, a dress that skims the body, a lighter and more linear silhouette that forecasts the fashion of the years to come. From there, we are transported to the Roaring Twenties: Two period mannequins, with short hair and suntanned skin, face each other in straight-cut dresses that show off the new flapper silhouette.

In the next room, we come across a young girl wearing a dress with a bustle who is playing with a small boy in fancy dress while two sisters pose in their hats and embroidered dresses from the 1920s.

Finally, the music room takes us to the postwar period: At the front, a geometric Courrèges dress is displayed next to a Balenciaga ensemble; alongside a harp is a tulle princess-style dress by Balmain; another dress illustrates the restrained elegance of Jean Patou; and a dress of tulle and lace exemplifies the "New Look" as interpreted by Christian Dior. In all the rooms the closets overflow with treasures. Look inside and feast your eyes on their spellbinding contents: shoes, minaudières, gloves, hats, and embroidered handkerchiefs. But there is more: a skirt that belonged to a Russian princess, a preserved bouquet, a monogrammed children's tea set, an alphabet book from the days before the letter "W" was included in the dictionary.

The Carton ladies are the museum's docents. Through their knowledge and tremendous enthusiasm, the three women have given a soul to the clothes on display and written their own very moving version of fashion history.

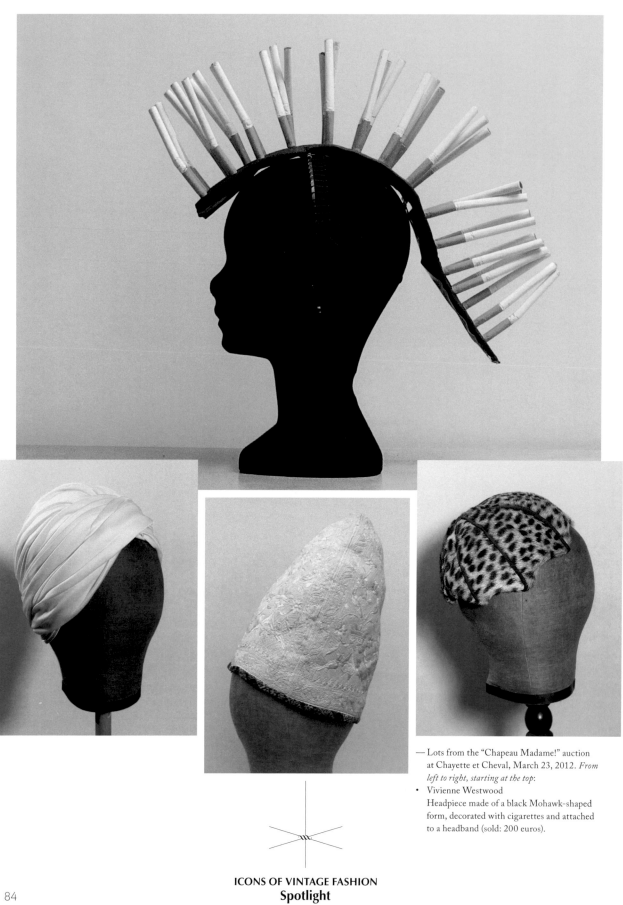

— Lots from the "Chapeau Madame!" auction
at Chayette et Cheval, March 23, 2012. *From
left to right, starting at the top*:
• Vivienne Westwood
  Headpiece made of a black Mohawk-shaped
  form, decorated with cigarettes and attached
  to a headband (sold: 200 euros).

ICONS OF VINTAGE FASHION
Spotlight

HATS OFF!

What could the names "castor, galette, hennin, capote, melon, bibi, and capuchon" have in common? They are the names of different types of hats that represent just a few of the infinite variety of shapes that this accessory—that is so much more than a simple accessory—can take. Whether it is functional or decorative, a hat is never superfluous.

HATS THROUGHOUT THE AGES

Before becoming a style accessory, hats were a necessary item of clothing. Prehistoric men fabricated hats out of wool or fur to keep their heads warm. A cone-shaped rigid hat has been traced back to 2100 BCE, in Crete. Hats, and caps in particular, did not become a mainstay of fashion until the Renaissance. With the assistance of her "fashion minister" Rose Bertin, Marie-Antoinette created an array of imaginative hats. Thereafter, the hat became the focus of all kinds of extravagance such as the coiffure "à la Belle Poule"—which involved wearing a model ship—and the famous "poufs aux sentiments"—the headdress was used as a small theater, staging subjects dear to the wearer. At the start of the nineteenth century, new shapes were created such as the wide-brimmed hat. This style of hat, originally from England, appealed at first to women living in the countryside who wanted to protect themselves from the sun, before being adopted by the more fashionable ladies.

In the twentieth century, hats were a reflection of their times. Wide-brimmed hats and *bibis* were typical of the Belle Époque while cloche and *petites têtes* (flapper hats) represented the Roaring Twenties; shaped hats with decorative details characterized the 1930s, while bowlers and small caps embodied the 1960s.

For important fashion designers, hats were a perfect canvas for creativity. Milliners (for women) and hatmakers (for men) have achieved great acclaim in the fashion industry: Philip Treacy, for example, has collaborated with many top designers (Givenchy, McQueen, Armani) and designed hats for many celebrities and royals.

- Grès, circa 1960
  Draped white silk jersey turban (sold: 600 euros).
- Anonymous, circa 1780–1820
  Persian headdress in the shape of a sugarloaf (sold: 550 euros).
- Schiaparelli, circa 1945–1950
  Leopard hat with cutouts trimmed with chocolate-colored grosgrain (sold: 750 euros).

HATS OFF TO YOU, MADAME!

Because of the constant evolution in style and the interest they arouse, hats have become an accessory that is both pleasing to wear and fun to collect. This fact was confirmed by the success of the "Chapeau Madame!" auction, featuring only hats, held by Chayette et Cheval, with the assistance of PB Fashion, in March 2012. Elsa Schiaparelli's creations, which so perfectly captured the concept of surrealism, achieved great success: a leopard *bibi* from the late 1940s, estimated at 150 euros, sold for 750 euros; a faille headdress in the shape of a hood decorated with pom-poms, pearls, and sequins, estimated at between 600 and 800 euros, fetched 3,300 euros. Hats designed by Madame Grès were also greeted with enthusiasm: A 1960 turban, estimated at between 60 and 80 euros, sold for 600 euros, and a printed silk scarf by Balenciaga, estimated at between 79 and 90 euros, sold for 900 euros.

THE SYMBOLISM OF HATS

Hats can powerfully symbolize one's association with a group, a social class, a profession, or a culture. A uniform, for instance, often includes a hat.

Hats often represent protocol. The British royal family excels at wearing hats for official events. The directive regarding hats was a crucial element of the dress code set forth by Buckingham Palace for the 2011 royal wedding: Women were required to wear a hat but asked to avoid anything too extravagant.

Beyond their symbolic and social reach, hats remain an important fashion accessory. They enhance and can even define one's personality. Celebrities use them to make a style statement: By choosing a trilby, a cloche, or a fedora, they are making a personal fashion statement, wanting to appear mysterious or self-assured. Can you even imagine the mythic Humphrey Bogart without his hat?

1940s

Haute Couture During the War Years

The hardships of war took their toll. Elegance took a back seat.

Rationing would constrict the field of possibilities for designers. Most houses would survive, but austerity had set in and fashion struggled along. The scarcity and unbridled creativity of the vintage pieces from this period justify their high prices in today's market.

While couture was scarce, most houses managed to hold on and keep working; such was the case for Germaine Krebs who would sign her creations by her other name, Grès. Today, her designs fetch the highest prices.

As the years of conflict came to an end, military style influenced fashion design. Red, white, and blue palettes were in vogue, a reflection of unequivocal patriotism, as seen in a dress with a pattern of stars and badges (Cornette de Saint Cyr, June 2012) or a jacket featuring sketches of Parisian life (Artcurial, June 2011). People often entertained at home, leading to the growing popularity of the hostess gown.

The end of the decade would signal a turning point. The silhouette took a step back in time. There was a sense of nostalgia for happier days. The "Golden Age" was about to begin and Christian Dior started it all when he presented his "New Look" collection in 1947. Other great designers—Jacques Fath, Lucien Lelong, Jacques Griffe, and Maggy Rouff—contributed to the elegant rebirth of couture. The new silhouette, with its strongly defined waist, rose from the ashes then reigned supreme.

ELSA SCHIAPARELLI

N º 72015
COUTURE, Spring 1940
(Embroidery: Lesage; buttons: Jean Clément)

Steel blue panne velvet flowing evening gown; square neckline with halter neck; worn with a jacket partially embroidered with colored silk and metallic thread in an elaborate ivy leaf pattern. White label, black lettering. Atelier tag reads "No. 512/Evelyne."

MUSEOGRAPHY: Sketch of the design is in the UFAC collection of the Musée des Arts Décoratifs, inventory UFD73-21-2539.

Estimate: 6,000–8,000 euros
Sold: 37,499 euros
Cornette de Saint Cyr, Paris
July 3, 2009 (lot 274)
Specialists: D. Chombert and F. Sternbach

ELSA SCHIAPARELLI

N º 73461
COUTURE, Summer 1940

Soft gray crepe evening gown with flounced sweetheart neckline; bodice and hips of smocked embroidery, adorned with faceted ruby-colored beads; flowing skirt cut on the bias. White label, black lettering.

Estimate: 3,000–4,000 euros
Sold: 6,875 euros
Cornette de Saint Cyr, Paris
July 3, 2009 (lot 115)
Specialists: D. Chombert and F. Sternbach

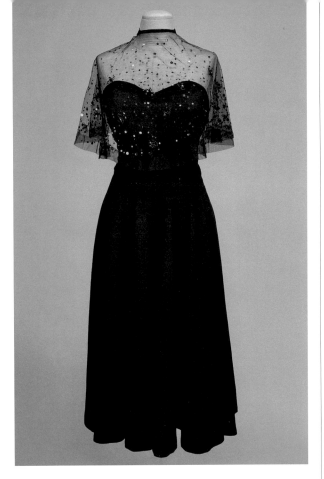 

CALLOT SŒURS

GRÈS

COUTURE

COUTURE

Black wool dress; boned bodice with velvet trim; godet skirt; worn with a sequined tulle capelet embroidered with small beaded floral motifs; jeweled neckline with hook-and-eye closure at the back of the neck. Label "Callot Soeurs 41. Avenue Montaigne Paris."

Black silk jersey evening gown; pleated in the front; V-neckline; bodice embellished with braiding at the waist; ankle-length skirt. Ivory label, black lettering.

Estimate: 1,200–1,500 dollars
Sold: 1,440 dollars
Charles A. Whitaker Auction Company, Philadelphia
April 27–28, 2012 (lot 815)
Specialist: Charles A. Whitaker

Estimate: 2,000–3,000 euros
Sold: 21,520 euros
Artcurial, Paris
June 11, 2012 (lot 376)
Specialist: PB Fashion

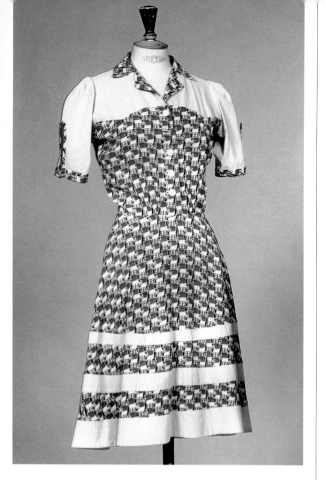

ANONYMOUS

ANONYMOUS

COUTURE

COUTURE

Dress of red, white, and blue viscose, in a print of small stars and badges; notched collar; single-breasted closure; full skirt cut on the bias with inserted bands of solid-colored shantung.

Viscose crepe jacket in a print called "*Images de Paris*" featuring annotated sketches of Parisian life; notched collar; single-breasted closure with silver mask–design buttons; jacket is flared with small gathers at the armholes.

Estimate: 150–200 euros
Sold: 188 euros

Cornette de Saint Cyr, Paris
June 30, 2012 (lot 231)

Specialists: D. Chombert and F. Sternbach

Estimate: 500–800 euros
Sold: 7,435 euros

Artcurial, Paris
June 27, 2011 (lot 170)

Specialist: PB Fashion

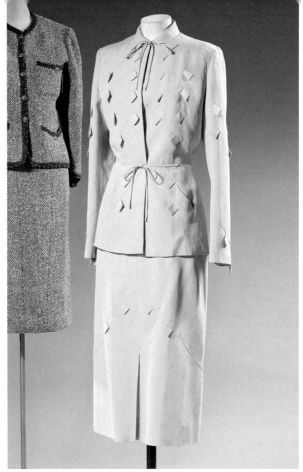

ELSA SCHIAPARELLI

ADRIAN

COUTURE

Bicycle-riding outfit of coffee and ivory striped cotton voile; bib skirt with inverted pleats starting at the hips; long bloomers.

COUTURE, Winter 1947

Fawn-colored wool suit in a checked pattern with small raised squares of fabric; fitted jacket has a small Peter Pan collar with a tie at the front, repeated at the waist; straight skirt. Label "Adrian Original."

Estimate: 800–1,000 euros
Sold: 5,625 euros
Cornette de Saint Cyr, Paris
July 3, 2009 (lot 310)
Specialists: D. Chombert and F. Sternbach

Estimate: 300–500 euros
Sold: 620 euros
Thierry de Maigret, Paris
November 22, 2011 (lot 288)
Specialist: Séverine Experton-Dard

HATTIE CARNEGIE

N º 53311-26
COUTURE

Fitted day dress of textured charcoal gray wool; small turndown collar; short kimono sleeves; slant pockets at the hips. Label.

Estimate: 600–800 pounds
Sold: 750 pounds
Christie's, London
December 3, 2009 (lot 120)
Specialist: Patricia Frost

ADRIAN

COUTURE

Black and white gingham textured wool suit with cinched waist; rounded turndown collar; single-breasted closure with gold buttons; princess seams; straight skirt. Label.

Estimate: 600–800 dollars
Sold: 240 dollars
Augusta Auctions, New York
November 10, 2010 (lot 308)
Specialist: Karen E. Augusta

I. GARNETT

COUTURE, October 1940

Fawn wool evening coat; chest and hips are adorned with cartridge-shaped objects set on gold metallic leather in a sunburst pattern; V-neckline; belt. Label.

Estimate: 500–1000 pounds
Sold: 1,875 pounds
Christie's, London
December 1, 2011 (lot 70)
Specialist: Patricia Frost

MARCEL ROCHAS

JACQUES GRIFFE

COUTURE, circa 1947–1948

COUTURE

Black rep weave suit; stand-up collar; single-breasted closure; exaggerated hipline with two slant pockets; flat pleat at the lower back; set-in sleeve; small revers at the cuffs; straight skirt, mid-calf length. Navy label, red and white lettering.

Black wool suit with slightly fitted jacket; notched collar embroidered with a floral motif of raffia and hemp; single-breasted closure with jet buttons; purple crepe lining; paneled skirt has a small slit with a button at the back left side; worn with a long-sleeve blouse made of the same purple crepe. White label, burgundy lettering.

MUSEOGRAPHY: Similar "Talisman" look appears in a sketch by Roger Rouffianges (inventory no. 1980.55.14) at the Musée Galliera.

Estimate: 500–700 euros
Sold: 610 euros
Cornette de Saint Cyr, Paris
April 25, 2008 (lot 88)
Specialists: D. Chombert and F. Sternbach

Estimate: 500–700 euros
Sold: 1,983 euros
Artcurial, Paris
February 7, 2011 (lot 285)
Specialist: PB Fashion

ANONYMOUS

COUTURE

Midnight blue panne velvet dress;
turndown collar; single-breasted closure
with covered buttons to the waist;
half sleeves are slightly draped at the
bottom; long pleated skirt; belt with
a buckle.

Estimate: 80–120 euros
Sold: 150 euros
Artcurial, Paris
June 11, 2012 (lot 380)
Specialist: PB Fashion

JEAN DESSÈS

COUTURE

Two-toned coral and ivory peignoir set;
long full sleeves; half belt that ties at
the front.

Estimate: 400–500 euros
Sold: 805 euros
Eve, Paris
March 16, 2012 (lot M107)
Specialist: Sylvie Daniel

CHRISTIAN DIOR

N º 4623
COUTURE

Red satin wraparound hostess gown;
V-neckline; tie at the waist; short raglan
sleeves are slightly draped and end in a
bow. White label, black lettering.

Estimate: 1,200–1,500 euros
Sold: 20,000 euros
Cornette de Saint Cyr, Paris
June 30, 2012 (lot 230)
Specialists: D. Chombert and
F. Sternbach

MAGGY ROUFF

MAD CARPENTIER

COUTURE

COUTURE

Midnight blue velvet peignoir; collar, lapels, and cuffs trimmed in ivory satin; matching belt. Label.

Ivory silk rep evening coat; V-neckline; wide collar with stayed revers; jeweled buttons; very full skirt of asymmetric length; fuchsia silk satin lining. White label, black lettering.

Estimate: 600–700 pounds
Sold: 500 pounds
Christie's, London
December 3, 2009 (lot 215)
Specialist: Patricia Frost

Estimate: 700–800 euros
Sold: 1,875 euros
Cornette de Saint Cyr, Paris
July 3, 2009 (lot 267)
Specialists: D. Chombert and F. Sternbach

GRÈS

COUTURE

Black crepe cocktail dress; V-neckline enhanced with bias trim; multiple small gathers on the bodice extend down the tulip sleeves; full skirt embellished with a slightly draped panel; hook-and-eye closures at the back. White label, black lettering.

Estimate: 1,500–2,000 euros
Sold: 1,875 euros
Cornette de Saint Cyr, Paris
July 2, 2010 (lot 279)
Specialists: D. Chombert and
F. Sternbach

GRÈS

COUTURE

Ivory Moroccan crepe evening gown; cowl neckline; pleated flowing skirt; silver braided double belt; trim repeated at the shoulders.

Estimate: 1,800–2,500 euros
Sold: 3,222 euros
Eve, Paris
June 18, 2012 (lot M041)
Specialist: Sylvie Daniel

GRÈS

COUTURE

Draped black silk jersey gown with velvet panels at the waist and shoulders; cape-like draping in the back.

Estimate: 1,500–2,000 euros
Sold: 2,478 euros
Eve, Paris
May 6, 2011 (lot M075)
Specialist: Sylvie Daniel

GRÈS

GRÈS

GRÈS

COUTURE, 1946

COUTURE

COUTURE

Asymmetric bottle-green and purple draped jersey silk evening dress; the diagonal drape across the bodice shows a triangle of bare skin; delicate tie belt.

<u>BIBLIOGRAPHY</u>: A sketch of the dress appears on p. 79 in *Femina*, November 1946; the identical design is featured in *Femme Chic*, Christmas 1946.

Black silk jersey evening gown, asymmetrically draped over one shoulder; very full skirt and gathered waist. White label, black lettering.

Pale yellow silk draped jersey dress; sweetheart neckline; short sleeves; asymmetric hem.

Estimate: 1,200–1,800 euros
Sold: 2,974 euros
Thierry de Maigret, Paris
November 22, 2011 (lot 292)
Specialist: Séverine Experton-Dard

Estimate: 1,200–1,500 euros
Sold: 3,125 euros
Cornette de Saint Cyr, Paris
June 30, 2012 (lot 86)
Specialists: D. Chombert and F. Sternbach

Estimate: 1,500–2,000 euros
Sold: 3,717 euros
Eve, Paris
May 6, 2011 (lot M0179)
Specialist: Sylvie Daniel

ELSA SCHIAPARELLI

N °75(...)480
COUTURE, Summer 1941
(Buttons: Jean Clément)

Brown cheviot coat; low notched collar; single-breasted closure with glazed terracotta buttons; inserts; slant pockets with flaps; slit; gathered waist and half belt at the back. White label, black lettering.

<u>PROVENANCE</u>: This coat originally belonged to Marlene Dietrich, who then gave it to Stéphane Audran.

<u>MUSEOGRAPHY</u>: A sketch of this coat is in the UFAC collections of the Musée des Arts Décoratifs, inventory UF D 73-21-2691.

Estimate: 2,000–3,000 euros
Sold: 2,500 euros
Cornette de Saint Cyr, Paris
July 3, 2009 (lot 204)
Specialists: D. Chombert and F. Sternbach

JACQUES FATH

COUTURE

Black wool cloth skirted coat; high-neck collar trimmed with glossy Hudson otter fur; single-breasted closure with self-covered buttons that are also featured on the welted pockets; godet pleats at the back. White label, black lettering.

Estimate: 1,000–1,200 euros
Sold: 1,250 euros
Cornette de Saint Cyr, Paris
July 2, 2010 (lot 125)
Specialists: D. Chombert and F. Sternbach

JACQUES FATH

COUTURE

Voluminous black wool coat with multiple godets; slim revers at the neckline; long raglan sleeves. Label.

Estimate: 800–1,000 pounds
Sold: 1,000 pounds
Christie's, London
December 3, 2009 (lot 179)
Specialist: Patricia Frost

JACQUES FATH

JACQUES FATH

COUTURE

COUTURE

Black wool crepe cocktail dress; wide shawl collar; button closure at the neckline repeated at the left hip; long sleeves with zippers. Label "Jacques Fath Paris—New York Designs for Joseph Halpert."

Black gazar cocktail dress; crossover bustier over a sheath skirt that buttons at the side and is adorned with wide ruching lined with horsehair. Worn with a shawl-collared bolero jacket. White label, black lettering and logo.

Estimate: 1,200–1,500 dollars
Sold: 1,440 dollars
Charles A. Whitaker Auction Company, Philadelphia
April 27–28, 2012 (lot 816)
Specialist: Charles A. Whitaker

Estimate: 1,500–1,800 euros
Sold: 5,000 euros
Cornette de Saint Cyr, Paris
July 2, 2010 (lot 222)
Specialists: D. Chombert and F. Sternbach

EMILIO SCHUBERTH

COUTURE

Brown and gold brocade cocktail dress; bodice with thin straps at the shoulders; square neckline; sheath skirt embellished with a tulip-shaped apron with pleats at the back and amphora-shaped pockets on each side; rounded panel runs from the waist to the back. No label.

Estimate: 1,300–1,500 euros
Sold: 2,500 euros

Cornette de Saint Cyr, Paris
July 4, 2011 (lot 200)

Specialists: D. Chombert and F. Sternbach

CHRISTIAN DIOR

N° 06402
COUTURE, Fall/Winter 1949–1950
Model "Esquisse"

Steel gray brocade day dress; crossover V-neckline bodice; short raglan sleeves; straight skirt, which was worn over a farthingale, embellished with slanted, gathered panels of asymmetric length that emphasized the hips; wide draped brown taffeta belt. White label, black lettering.

BIBLIOGRAPHY: The identical design appears in *Femina*, Winter 1949–1950, photograph by Willy Maywald, and on p. 46 of *Harper's Bazaar*, November 1949, photograph by Richard Avedon.

Estimate: 9,000–10,000 euros
Sold: 11,875 euros

Cornette de Saint Cyr, Paris
July 2, 2010 (lot 202)

Specialists: D. Chombert and F. Sternbach

BALENCIAGA

N° 55938
COUTURE

Copper silk faille dress entirely covered in black d'Alençon lace; roll collar; single-breasted closure with buttons reaching the waist; matching belt; three-quarter sleeves; full godet skirt. Label.

PROVENANCE: Brooklyn Museum.

Estimate: 700–1,000 dollars
Sold: 1,680 dollars

Augusta Auctions, New York
November 10, 2010 (lot 325)

Specialist: Karen E. Augusta

ICONS OF VINTAGE FASHION
1940s

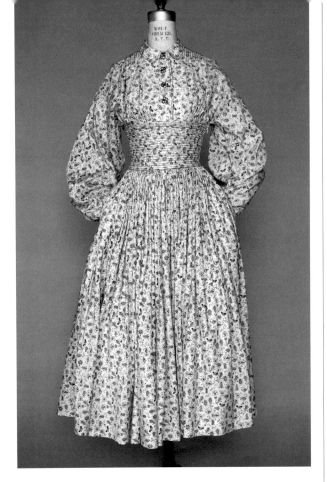 

CLAIRE McCARDELL

JACQUES GRIFFE

N° 508046
COUTURE

COUTURE, 1948

Cream cotton day dress in a pink and black floral pattern; turndown collar; "clover" buttons; wide pleated midriff yoke; long puffed dolman sleeves; full gathered skirt with two side pockets. Label "Claire McCardell clothes by Townley."
PROVENANCE: Brooklyn Museum.

Beige tulle dress with a tone-on-tone checked design to resemble faille; opening at the back; small stand-up collar; velvet bib front adorned with buttons; short raglan sleeves; full skirt over horsehair crinoline; patch pockets. White label, black lettering.

Estimate: 200–300 dollars
Sold: 360 dollars
Augusta Auctions, New York
November 2, 2011 (lot 396)
Specialist: Karen E. Augusta

Estimate: 200–250 euros
Sold: 21,250 euros
Cornette de Saint Cyr, Paris
June 30, 2012 (lot 364)
Specialists: D. Chombert and F. Sternbach

PIERRE BALMAIN

N° 4147
COUTURE

Black and brown silk evening ensemble printed with
a striped pattern; bodice has a small turndown collar
embellished with trim and guipure encrusted with sequins;
three-quarter sleeves with revers; full taffeta skirt cut on
the bias; double-faced capelet in velvet and silk; shawl collar;
kimono sleeves.

Estimate: 1,500–2,000 euros
Sold: 1,750 euros
Cornette de Saint Cyr, Paris
June 30, 2012 (lot 80)
Specialists: D. Chombert and F. Sternbach

JACQUES FATH

N° 211516
COUTURE

Ruby red satin evening gown; draped fitted bodice; halter
back with button; embellished at the hips by two bows that
gather the pleats of the full and flared skirt. White label,
black lettering with logo.

Estimate: 1,000–1,200 euros
Sold: 1,875 euros
Cornette de Saint Cyr, Paris
July 2, 2010 (lot 300)
Specialists: D. Chombert and F. Sternbach

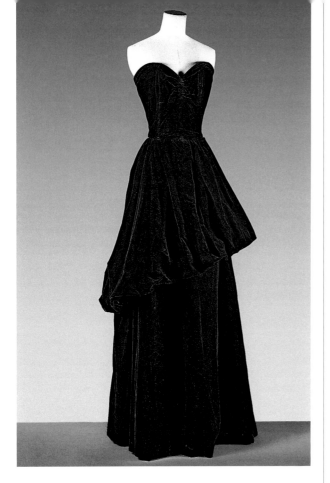

ROBERT PIGUET

N° **42869**
COUTURE

Black velvet evening gown; bustier with double scalloped design; shirred asymmetric pinafore over the full skirt. Worn with a matching short jacket embroidered with gold sequins in a floral pattern. Black label, gold lettering.

Estimate: 1,500–2,000
Sold: 10,625 euros
Cornette de Saint Cyr, Paris
July 3, 2009 (lot 221)
Specialists: D. Chombert and F. Sternbach

LUCIEN LELONG

COUTURE

Navy blue tulle gown; draped bustier embellished with smocking that extends to the waist; bottom of the skirt is flounced. White label, brown lettering.

Estimate: 1,300–1,500 euros
Sold: 2,550 euros
Piasa, Paris
November 8, 2010 (lot 147)
Specialists: D. Chombert and F. Sternbach

EISA

CHRISTIAN DIOR

N °7(...)004
COUTURE
COUTURE, Spring/Summer 1948
Model "Martinique"

Black and white polka-dot silk taffeta day dress; turndown
collar; covered buttons to the waist; white belt; bubble skirt
with bustle at the back. Label.
PROVENANCE: Anne Moen Bullitt.

Green, ivory, and indigo striped organza ball gown; square
neckline with wide straps; belted waist over a partially
draped full skirt.

Estimate: 800–1,500 pounds
Sold: 1,125 pounds
Christie's, London
December 3, 2009 (lot 125)
Specialist: Patricia Frost

Estimate: 15,000–18,000 pounds
Sold: 23,750 pounds
Christie's, London
December 1, 2011 (lot 80)
Specialist: Patricia Frost

CHRISTIAN DIOR

JACQUES FATH

N º 9333
COUTURE, Fall/Winter 1948
Model "Lahore"

N º 15176
COUTURE

Midnight blue velvet evening dress partially embroidered with silver beads and rhinestones in an Indian-inspired motif; upturned collar with a small notch at the neckline adorned with a bow, repeated on the back; wide flaring of the skirt below the knees. Label.

ICONOGRAPHY: The Duchess of Windsor wore an identical dress.

Evening dress with gold lamé bustier covered in tulle that has been embellished with ruched metallic braiding, sequins, and rhinestones; the left shoulder is adorned with a pink velvet panel that floats down the back; draped ankle-length wraparound skirt features pleats that gather at the waist. White label, navy blue lettering.

Estimate: 15,000–18,000 pounds
Sold: 63,650 pounds
Christie's, London
December 1, 2011 (lot 79)
Specialist: Patricia Frost

Estimate: 1,500–2,000 euros
Sold: 3,753 euros
Artcurial, Paris
June 11, 2012 (lot 299)
Specialist: PB Fashion

- *Left*: Madame Grès with one of her models in 1945.
- *Opposite*: Two of the gowns featured in the *Madame Grès— La Couture à l'oeuvre* exhibition at the Musée Bourdelle, March 25–July 24, 2011, organized by the Musée Galliera.

Madame Grès, born Germaine Krebs in 1903, began her career in fashion in 1934 when she opened a small atelier under the name Alix. Despite her immediate success, it would take her eight years to establish her own maison de couture, in 1942. She named it Madame Grès.

A SCULPTOR OF FABRIC

The symbolism behind the name *Grès* is revealed when one learns that the grande dame of couture had originally wanted to become a sculptor. Grès is a partial anagram of Serge, the name of her husband, who was in fact a sculptor. Grès is also the French word for sandstone, a sedimentary rock that lends itself perfectly to sculpture.

ICONS OF VINTAGE FASHION
Spotlight

MADAME GRÈS

While she chose fabric over stone, Madame Grès approached fabric with the unrelenting discipline of a sculptor. She would drape yards of fabric around mannequins until she perfected the art of drapery. Similarly, her legendary pleating, so precise that three meters of fabric would be reduced to seven centimeters, was executed on the garment as it was being constructed. The suppleness of her favorite fabric, silk jersey, offered endless creative possibilities.

Given her brilliant techniques of draping and pleating, and her scrupulous consistency, Madame Grès's creations are more than couture—they are true works of art.

MUSEUMS AND THE WORK OF MADAME GRÈS

In 2011, Madame Grès was the subject of the first Parisian retrospective organized by the Musée Galliera but held elsewhere—in this instance, at the Musée Bourdelle. Eighty-four pieces by the woman who wanted to be a sculptor were harmoniously displayed among Emile Antoine Bourdelle's statues—her creations seemed perfectly at home in the atelier of the master sculptor.

This rare juxtaposition revealed what great designers have in common: Madame Grès's work is instantly recognizable. All her designs reflect her signature style, exceptional savoir faire, and technical skill as well as her penchant for pure lines and her mastery of complexity. Yet each piece is special and affirms its individuality. Such is the achievement of an artist who can create a piece that clearly bears his or her imprint but still feels unique.

CONTEMPORARY AND TIMELESS

Unlike many others in her field, Madame Grès enjoyed a long career—over fifty years working under her own name. For nearly six decades she resisted the changing fashion trends, inventing instead her own timeless lexicon. All her designs from the 1930s to the 1980s were characterized by their extraordinary modernity.

Though she was not well known by the general public, she has been a serious reference and a source of inspiration for many contemporary designers. She was a pioneer of minimalism, the queen of austerity in search of simplified complexity; her creations had the look of monastic simplicity but their sophistication was the result of brilliant construction, extreme purity of lines, and economy of form and seams. Her work influenced many others during the 1990s, notably the *École Belge* and many Japanese designers. The Grès pleat elicited the admiration of Issey Miyake, the founder of Pleats Please. The sensuality conveyed through her sober and restrained designs still serves as a model of balance for today's designers.

Azzédine Alaïa and Dominque Sirop, both great admirers of Madame Grès, are also avid collectors of her work. Following the insolvency proceedings of the House of Grès in 1987, her remaining creations were sold. Some pieces have been acquired by museums or by knowledgeable enthusiasts for their archives while others occasionally turn up at auctions. So few items are left that it is difficult to evaluate their precise value. Dresses from the period between the 1950s and 1970s turn up occasionally and have achieved prices ranging from 1,000 to 4,000 euros; some do not sell while others fetch over 6,000 euros. At the Piasa auction in November 2010, a black taffeta dress sold for 6,630 euros.

Madame Grès, so admired for her virtuosity in couture, was destitute and unknown at the time of her death in 1993, leaving behind a bittersweet legacy.

FALBALAS *at the*

*F*albala is a French word with many meanings, a word that is full of surprises, connotations, and subtle references. Classically defined, it is a masculine word for a most feminine item: a flounce, a pleated piece of material used to hem a dress. Over time, the term has taken on pejorative connotations, meaning a trinket or something in bad taste.

In its plural form, *Falbalas* refers to a film by Jacques Becker (*Paris Thrills*, 1945) about the fashion industry, its cast of smooth characters and designers, the world of the *"petites mains"* and the wedding dress in all its biting symbolism.

Falbalas is also the name of a shop from another time, proudly situated in the Saint-Ouen Flea Market in Paris. Erwan and Françoise de Fligué are the heart and soul of this temple that honors the history of fashion.

Erwan de Fligué has rejected the term "vintage" as he feels there is no need to use an English word borrowed from wine terminology. When describing his numerous acquisitions, he prefers to define the items—many of which are much older than he is—as historical or collectible. Erwan de Fligué secures his inventory piece by piece, in the traditional way, from specialists in the field or from individuals, and, only occasionally, at auctions. Based on their nature and his own sense of style, his discoveries have three possible destinations. Some—but fewer and fewer—will end up in his personal collection. He has no idea how many pieces he owns at this point, but they "occupy an entire house and an apartment!" Others will become part of his wife's wardrobe that he manages with perfection. And finally, the bulk of them—"I am an opportunist and I can't allow myself to be too restrained"—will end up on the racks and mannequins of his shop in the Puces, waiting for new owners.

Erwan de Fligué knows his clientele so well that he will often buy a piece with them in mind: "someone knowledgeable" who is interested in a specific period or a particular style; a

PARIS FLEA MARKET

stylist who has come by without something definite in mind but just to be inspired, especially by the small details (a group of clients who have become increasingly rare as the financial crisis has restricted research and development budgets in many fashion houses); and wardrobe specialists, more so for the film industry than the theater, who are seeking clothes that suit the aesthetic and temporal coherence of their project. Private collectors are also his clients. In fact, the collection of one of their clients, Dominique Miraille, has recently been converted into a museum, the Musée de la Mode d'Albi. Designers Dominique Sirop and Azzedine Alaïa, and the dandy and journalist Hamish Bowles have also bought items for their private collections. Rarely will a piece be sold to a large institution because of the complex acquisition procedures and the small budgets, but a few items have made their way to the Musée des Arts Décoratifs or to foreign museums, such as the Kyoto Costume Institute.

Erwan and Françoise de Fligué describe their love of old clothes in a few words: a certain inventiveness, the savoir faire, the beauty of the way a garment is made and finished—all the features they believe have disappeared, or nearly, from contemporary fashion. They don't adhere to any particular rules, going as far back in time as they can. Their oldest pieces date from the eighteenth century, such as a man's suit from 1755 displayed on a mannequin. Their enthusiasm dips noticeably after 1960, although they have made exceptions for "major nontraditional couturiers such as Alaïa, Mugler, or Gaultier in his good days."

Falbalas is more museum than shop because of the unique quality of the garments and accessories, the sense of nostalgia, and the opportunity of a guided tour by the masters of the house—a journey through time.

• *Above*: The Falbalas shop and its owners, Erwan and Françoise de Fligué.

- *Left*: Dress with gold lamé bustier, Christian Dior, prêt-à-porter collection by John Galliano, Spring/Summer 2003. Photograph by Laziz Hamani.
- *Below*: Barbara Jeauffroy-Mairet by Solène Auréal.
- *Right*: Pink organdy "Grand Bal" gown adorned with Valenciennes lace. Photograph by Pottier from the Musée Marmottan, Paris, published in *L'Officiel*, no. 327–328, 1949.
- *Below, right*: Stereochrome of the Villa Les Rhumbs, now the Christian Dior Museum in Granville, France.

Barbara Jeauffroy has been the curator for the Christian Dior Museum for over sixteen years, but she never tires of hunting down treasures that could further enrich the museum's collections dedicated to the most famous French couturier.

It is often said that the past is the past and legacy is, by its very essence, frozen in time, but Barbara Jeauffroy does not accept any of these clichés. She continues to explore the *maison de couture*'s archives of infinite treasures for delightful surprises and endless originality.

The Christian Dior Museum is housed in the Villa Les Rhumbs, Dior's childhood home in Granville. The museum is home to the elaborate creations designed by the master couturier during his short time at the helm of his company, as well as to the pieces designed by his successors in the House of Dior. The museum also features many other symbolic items that reveal more about the man than the couturier. Barbara Jeauffroy remembers with great emotion the moment when the museum bought back Mr. Dior's Jaeger Le Coultre watch that the designer had given, along with other presents and drawings, to his close friend Jacques Tiffeaut. After a circuitous journey, the watch made its way back to the museum, where it is kept with, among other personal effects, Dior's datebook

and his famous good-luck star—probably an old street crossing marker found on the sidewalk—that became his talisman.

Barbara Jeauffroy has enriched the museum's collections through acquisitions from auction houses—notably the sublime gold bustier dress adorned with bows from Artcurial—or from fashion experts like Didier Ludot. But she much prefers when items are donated, which actually happens quite often. A donated item comes with a story, a life, a human perspective, all welcome in a museum that is already quite personal.

She shares one of her most memorable experiences that began with a phone call from the owners of a dry cleaning store in Coutances—a small town located near the Christian Dior Museum. One of their customers, an Englishwoman, had brought in a Dior wedding dress and veil that she was going to sell. Believing that the incomparable dress might be better suited for the museum's collection, the owners suggested

Bonnefond pointed to two trunks from which she removed two sumptuous dresses from the late 1940s, veritable *millefeuilles*, with profusions of organza petticoats. The dresses were some of the most emblematic ball gowns the House of Dior had ever made. In addition, she would learn their history and come away with three more dresses: two especially rare rose-printed cotton designs from the 1950s and a lamé dress from the Bohan years. She left in shock, her arms filled with these unexpected treasures that most definitely would not fit in her small white plastic bag.

Barbara Jeauffroy could tell these stories endlessly and admits that they are probably the most rewarding surprises of her job: the snippets of tales she gathers from generous strangers; the joy she felt at the sight of the extraordinary pair of leopard skin pants that came to the museum through a colleague who specialized in fur; or the gift "from the heavens" that appeared just as she was curating the *Christian Dior et le monde* exhibit in 2006—a scarf that had once belonged to Lady Mosley (better known as one of the Mitford sisters) that led to the following correspondence from her sister, Nancy Mitford, a writer and Dior devotee: "I have decided on a style and I will stay with it; I have chosen Dior's current collection. I think it is quite perfect." During the course of her meeting with Charlotte Mosley, Nancy Mitford's daughter-in-law, who donated the scarf, a painting on the wall caught her attention. It was a small portrait of Nancy Mitford, painted by the Danish artist Mogens Tvede, in which she is wearing a black wool day suit—the "Daisy" look from the Spring/Summer collection of 1947—that Barbara Jeauffroy had dreamed of acquiring for the museum's collection. This is a hint to any potential donors reading this…

A Conversation with Barbara Jeauffroy-Mairet of THE CHRISTIAN DIOR MUSEUM

a meeting at the dry cleaner. An incongruous rendezvous with an elegant Englishwoman ended with Barbara Jeauffroy "moved to tears" as she carried off the wedding dress that encompassed "a part of the history of the House as well as its own."

Another time, she received a telephone call from a Madame Bonnefond who simply mentioned "a dress" that she wanted to donate to the Christian Dior Museum. On her way to meet the woman, Barbara Jeauffroy brought a small plastic bag in which she could place the dress. When she arrived, Madame

1950s

The Golden Age

Optimism and exhilaration characterized the postwar years as life returned to normal.

Following years of shortages and rationing, fashion started to come back to life in the late 1940s.

At the helm of his eponymous house of couture until 1957, Christian Dior presented a large number of diverse style options: The 1947 "Corolle" line would become one of the key looks of the 1950s, closely followed by the "ZigZag" and "Tulip" lines, and the "A," "Y," and "H" (for *haricot vert* or string bean) lines. Each one of his twenty-two collections was considered revolutionary. Today, museums and collectors vie for Monsieur Dior's pieces when they turn up at auctions. Creations by Yves Matthieu Saint Laurent, the young prodigy who succeeded Dior at the couture house in 1957, have met with equal success.

The fashion terminology of the period—day suits, bias-cut skirts, afternoon dresses, cocktail dresses, and ball gowns—may seem old-fashioned today, but they accurately describe the strict sartorial conventions that allowed for a wide variety of styles and shapes. The stars of this golden age of couture—Balmain, Balenciaga, Jacques Griffe, Jean Dessès, or Grès—alternatively embraced opulent luxury or restrained simplicity. Their creations influenced fashion around the world and have become today's vintage treasures.

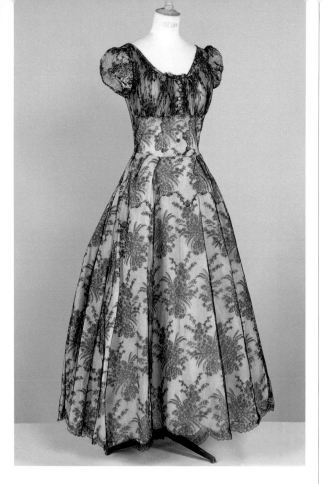

CHRISTIAN DIOR

CHRISTIAN DIOR

N° 16335 and N° 3724
COUTURE, Spring/Summer 1953

COUTURE

Black lace evening gown with floral bouquet pattern over ivory horsehair underdress; round neckline; bust set off with a multitude of small folds; covered buttons topped with a bow; balloon sleeves; very full skirt with darts. Black label, white lettering.

Silk shantung evening ensemble with white and orange floral print on golden yellow background; yellow organza bodice with draped halter top and open back; waist set off with a bias-cut print; very full skirt with sunray pleats and darts. Worn under a buttoned bolero jacket with small shawl collar; three-quarter raglan sleeves. White label, black lettering.

Estimate: 3,000–4,000 euros
Sold: 5,625 euros
Cornette de Saint Cyr, Paris
July 2, 2010 (lot 150)
Specialists: D. Chombert and F. Sternbach

Estimate: 6,000–7,000 euros
Sold: 50,000 euros
Cornette de Saint Cyr, Paris
July 4, 2011 (lot 100)
Specialists: D. Chombert and F. Sternbach

CHRISTIAN DIOR

CHRISTIAN DIOR

N°54075
COUTURE, Spring/Summer 1955

N°75394
COUTURE, Fall/Winter 1956–1957

Cocktail dress; crisscrossed bodice with accolade neckline and an ivory net covering with plant and floral motifs; high-waisted with full black silk skirt over petticoat. White label, black lettering.

Gradated gray brocade cocktail dress with peony pattern; crisscrossed, slightly draped bodice with a boat neckline higher in the back and over the shoulders; full skirt with inverted pleats adorned with a bow at the waist. No label.
BIBLIOGRAPHY: The model is reproduced on p. 72 of *L'Officiel de la Mode*, no. 401.

Estimate: 2,500–3,500 euros
Sold: 3,125 euros
Cornette de Saint Cyr, Paris
July 2, 2010 (lot 80)
Specialists: D. Chombert and F. Sternbach

Estimate: 5,000–6,000 euros
Sold: 16,250 euros
Cornette de Saint Cyr, Paris
July 2, 2010 (lot 230)
Specialists: D. Chombert and F. Sternbach

CHRISTIAN DIOR

CHRISTIAN DIOR

N º 25713
COUTURE

COUTURE, 1952

Silk shantung dress; bodice with round neckline; short kimono sleeves; waist set off with the small gatherings of the wraparound skirt, adorned with tone-on-tone fringe; left hip enhanced with two sashes with same fringed trim. Label "Christian Dior Europe."

Black silk cocktail outfit; blistered bodice with round neck; satin pencil skirt; bow at the gathered waist. No label.

Estimate: 500–800 euros
Sold: 1,859 euros
Artcurial, Paris
June 27, 2011 (lot 323)
Specialist: PB Fashion

Estimate: 4,000–5,000 pounds
Sold: 1,375 pounds
Christie's, London
December 1, 2011 (lot 81)
Specialist: Patricia Frost

CHRISTIAN DIOR

CHRISTIAN DIOR

COUTURE

COUTURE

Emerald silk satin blouse; high draped turndown neck with velvet coffee-colored tie; small hook-and-eye fasteners; peplum cut. Black label, white lettering.

Black satin faux two-piece; bodice with square neckline; single-breasted closure; draped cap sleeves; back belt at the waist; wide gathered skirt. Label "Christian Dior New York."

Estimate: 30–40 euros
Sold: 186 euros
Artcurial, Paris
June 27, 2011 (lot 430)
Specialist: PB Fashion

Estimate: 500–800 euros
Sold: 1,735 euros
Artcurial, Paris
June 27, 2011 (lot 172)
Specialist: PB Fashion

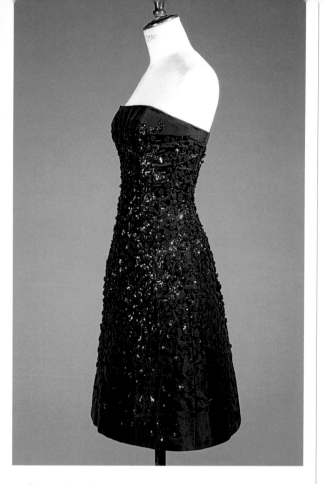

CHRISTIAN DIOR

N º 76457
COUTURE, Fall/Winter 1955

Strapless dress with a silk faille corset adorned with
sequins, beads, and small metallic springs forming gradating
roses; slightly flared skirt over slip providing fullness in the
back. White label, black lettering.

Estimate: 2,500–3,500 euros
Sold: 17,516 euros

Artcurial, Paris
June 11, 2012 (lot 370)
Specialist: PB Fashion

CHRISTIAN DIOR

N º 45069
COUTURE, Fall/Winter 1954–1955

Black silk dress; short, slightly draped sleeves; boat neckline
with square-cut in the back with self buttons reaching the
waist; attached partial belt forming two half-bows at the
front; full skirt pleated at the hipline.

Estimate: 800–1,200 euros
Sold: 1,239 euros

Artcurial, Paris
November 15, 2010 (lot 430)
Specialist: PB Fashion

CHRISTIAN DIOR

COUTURE
by Yves Saint Laurent

Pleated navy gazar cocktail dress; round neckline and short raglan sleeves adorned with overlaid lace frills, repeated on the full skirt; gazar and tulle slips. Black label, white lettering.

Estimate: 2,500–3,000 euros
Sold: 3,125 euros
Cornette de Saint Cyr, Paris
December 12, 2011 (lot 182)
Specialists: D. Chombert and F. Sternbach

CHRISTIAN DIOR

COUTURE, Spring/Summer 1958
Model "Bal masque" by Yves Saint Laurent

Black leadwork tulle dress adorned with jet sequins over brown tulle, gathered with forty-two black satin bows; round scalloped neckline embroidered with beads, repeated at the bottom of the three-quarter sleeves; reinforced bustier under sheer top; gathered bell-shaped skirt over layered petticoat with satin hem. No label.

BIBLIOGRAPHY: The identical model is on p. 342 in *Yves Saint Laurent*, Petit Palais, March 11–August 29, 2010, F. Müller and F. Chenoune, Abrams, 2010; details are shown on p. 87 in *Twentieth-Century Fashion in Detail*, C. Wilcox and V. Mendes, V&A Publishing, 2009.

MUSEOGRAPHY: The identical dress belonged to the Duchess of Windsor, Victoria & Albert Museum, London.

Estimate: 4,000–6,000 euros
Sold: 13,631 euros
Artcurial, Paris
June 27, 2011 (lot 326)
Specialist: PB Fashion

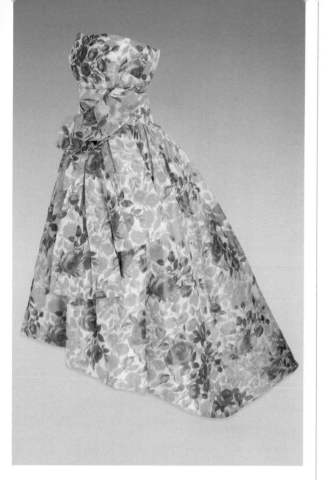

CHRISTIAN DIOR

CHRISTIAN DIOR

N º 1999203
COUTURE, 1956
Model "Rosée"

N º 089663
COUTURE, Fall/Winter 1957

Silk taffeta evening gown with a pink and green floral pattern; strapless bustier set off with a wide draped belt on a full skirt; train at the back. Label.

Faux two-piece silk ottoman dress printed with a black floral motif on a red background; bodice with square neckline and three-quarter sleeves; skirt with draped coattail look in the front. White label, black lettering.

Estimate: 3,000–5,000 pounds
Sold: 4,750 pounds
Christie's, London
December 1, 2011 (lot 92)
Specialist: Patricia Frost

Estimate: 3,000–3,500 euros
Sold: 4,375 euros
Cornette de Saint Cyr, Paris
July 3, 2009 (lot 283)
Specialists: D. Chombert and F. Sternbach

CHRISTIAN DIOR

ANONYMOUS

N º 92502
COUTURE, Spring/Summer 1958
by Yves Saint Laurent

COUTURE

Turquoise green silk faille cocktail dress; bustier decorated with a rose in the center of a bow, repeated on the hem of the full skirt with horsehair-stiffened petticoat. This dress is a variation of the "Aurore" model. Label "Christian Dior Paris."

White nylon dress with a blue and yellow floral print; V-neckline; draped skirt with vertical gatherings, white gauze, and tulle slip.

Estimate: 5,000–8,000 dollars
Sold: 19,200 dollars
Charles A. Whitaker Auction Company, Philadelphia
April 27–28, 2012 (lot 822)
Specialist: Charles A. Whitaker

Estimate: 50–80 euros
Sold: 583 euros
Bailly-Pommery & Voutier, Paris
April 23, 2012 (lot 389)
Specialist: PB Fashion

CHRISTIAN DIOR

CHRISTIAN DIOR

N º 45141
COUTURE, Fall/Winter 1954

N º 90886 and N º 908877
COUTURE, Fall/Winter 1957

Gingerbread and black embossed wool suit with herring-bone weave; tailored jacket with notch collar and single-breasted closure; hips with false flap pockets; pencil skirt. Label "Christian Dior Paris."

BIBLIOGRAPHY: The identical model is reproduced on p. 126 in *Dior in Vogue*, Brigid Keenan, Random House Value Pub., 1983.

Black wool bouclé ensemble; dress with accolade neckline; small kimono sleeves; straight skirt; crossover jacket; round neckline and scarf with fringe trim; double-breasted closure; long kimono sleeves. White labels, black lettering.

Estimate: 4,000–6,000 dollars
Sold: 8,400 dollars
Charles A. Whitaker Auction Company, Philadelphia
October 28–29, 2011 (lot 703)
Specialist: Charles A. Whitaker

Estimate: 1,000–1,200 euros
Sold: 7,507 euros
Artcurial, Paris
June 11, 2012 (lot 211)
Specialist: PB Fashion

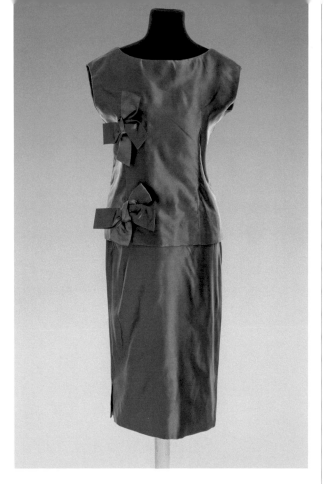

CHRISTIAN DIOR

CHRISTIAN DIOR

N° 090086
COUTURE, Fall/Winter 1957–1958

N° 00391
COUTURE, Spring/Summer 1959

Gray silk cocktail ensemble; bodice with a boat neckline adorned with two bows on the right side; low armholes; straight skirt. Label.

Black silk and woven linen outfit; sleeveless dress with boat neckline; jacket with shawl collar adorned with a bow; three-quarter sleeves.

PROVENANCE: Brooklyn Museum.

Estimate: 4,000–6,000 pounds
Sold: 3,000 pounds
Christie's, London
December 1, 2011 (lot 85)
Specialist: Patricia Frost

Estimate: 800–1,200 dollars
Sold: 2,280 dollars
Augusta Auctions, New York
March 21, 2012 (lot 295)
Specialist: Karen E. Augusta

CHRISTIAN DIOR

COUTURE, Fall/Winter 1958
by Yves Saint Laurent

Black woven wool coat; large collar folded over to form a pelerine; double-breasted closure; long raglan sleeves. White label, black lettering.

Estimate: 1,200–1,500 euros
Sold: 6,500 euros
Cornette de Saint Cyr, Paris
December 12, 2011 (lot 274)
Specialists: D. Chombert and F. Sternbach

CHRISTIAN DIOR

N º 98965
COUTURE, Fall/Winter 1958–1959
by Yves Saint Laurent

Plum wool bouclé three-quarter length coat with cape look due to the attachment of the three-quarter sleeves; large turndown, slightly asymmetric collar; double-breasted closure. White label, black lettering.

Estimate: 1,500–1,800 euros
Sold: 6,250 euros
Cornette de Saint Cyr, Paris
December 12, 2011 (lot 266)
Specialists: D. Chombert and F. Sternbach

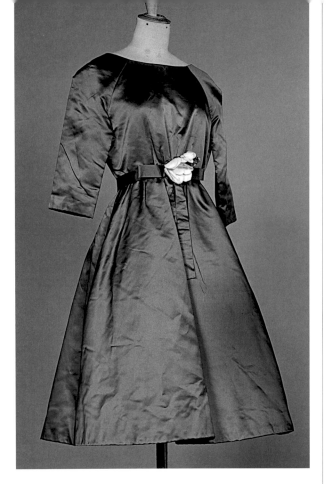

CHRISTIAN DIOR

CHRISTIAN DIOR

N ° 13010
COUTURE, Fall/Winter 1959–1960
by Yves Saint Laurent

Emerald satin cocktail dress; mid-length raglan sleeves; back buttons; full skirt with darts and small open pleats; thin belt adorned with a camellia. White label, black lettering.

BIBLIOGRAPHY: The identical model is reproduced on p. 60 in *L'Officiel 1,000 Modèles, Dior, 60 ans de création*, no. 81, January 2008, éditions Jalou.

Estimate: 2,000–2,500 euros
Sold: 3,125 euros
Cornette de Saint Cyr, Paris
December 12, 2011 (lot 272)
Specialists: D. Chombert and F. Sternbach

N ° 13037
COUTURE, Fall/Winter 1959–1960
by Yves Saint Laurent

Black taffeta cocktail dress; draped bodice with straps crisscrossed at the back and adorned with bows; gathered waist and full skirt with three ruffled tiers enhanced with lace. Black label, white lettering.

BIBLIOGRAPHY: The identical model is reproduced on p. 218 of *L'Officiel de la Mode*, no. 449–450.

Estimate: 3,000–3,500 euros
Sold: 3,750 euros
Cornette de Saint Cyr, Paris
July 2, 2010 (lot 351)
Specialists: D. Chombert and F. Sternbach

CHRISTIAN DIOR

N º 102610
COUTURE, Fall/Winter 1959
by Yves Saint Laurent

Tomato red ottoman silk coat; turndown collar; single-breasted closure with black beaded buttons, repeated at the bottom of the three-quarter sleeves.

Estimate: 1,500–2,500 dollars
Sold: 2,684 dollars
Leslie Hindman Auctioneers, Chicago
September 16, 2010 (lot 280)
Specialist: Abigail Rutherford

CHRISTIAN DIOR

COUTURE
by Yves Saint Laurent

Silk brocade cocktail dress with pink and apricot floral print; bodice with criss-crossed look; V-neckline; belt with a bow at the waist; full skirt with a few pleats.

Estimate: 400–600 dollars
Sold: 519 dollars
Leslie Hindman Auctioneers, Chicago
September 16, 2010 (lot 279)
Specialist: Abigail Rutherford

CHRISTIAN DIOR

N º 101354
COUTURE, Fall/Winter 1959
by Yves Saint Laurent

Pale pink cocktail dress; sleeveless bodice entirely embroidered with shell and silver mother-of-pearl sequins; full skirt with godets. Worn with a short open jacket with three-quarter sleeves.

Estimate: 800–1,200 dollars
Sold: 1,952 dollars
Leslie Hindman Auctioneers, Chicago
December 16, 2010 (lot 292)
Specialist: Abigail Rutherford

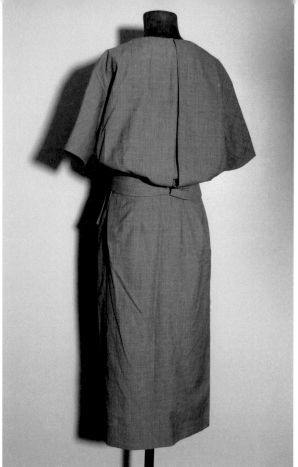

EISA

JEANNE LANVIN

COUTURE

COUTURE
by Antonio Castillo

Raw silk and wool suit with polka-dot motif; fitted single-breasted jacket with notch collar; two flap pockets at the hip; notches at jacket hemline; three-quarter sleeves; pencil skirt. Label.

<u>PROVENANCE</u>: Anne Moen Bullitt.

Gray and black mottled wool dress; round neckline with large inverted pleat; blousy look; short kimono sleeves; bow at the waist; straight skirt. Worn with a fitted fabric belt. White label, black lettering.

Estimate: 600–800 pounds
Sold: 1,125 pounds
Christie's, London
December 3, 2009 (lot 136)
Specialist: Patricia Frost

Estimate: 350–450 euros
Sold: 1,983 euros
Deburaux & Associés, Paris
October 13, 2011 (lot 391)
Specialist: PB Fashion

EISA

ANONYMOUS

COUTURE

COUTURE

Ice blue wild-silk suit; basque-cut bodice adorned with
a wide turndown collar with a sailor inspiration; single-
breasted closure with covered buttons, repeated at the
bottom of the balloon half sleeves; pleated skirt; thin belt
with matching buckle. White label, gray lettering.

<u>PROVENANCE</u>: Anne Moen Bullitt.

Nattier-blue woven wool suit; slightly mottled, fitted jacket;
small notched collar; single-breasted closure with galalith
buttons, repeated on the two bias-cut pockets; three-quarter
sleeves with slit at the bottom; peplum look at the back;
A-line skirt.

Estimate: 120–150 euros
Sold: 310 euros
Artcurial, Paris
June 27, 2011 (lot 324)
Specialist: PB Fashion

Estimate: 400–600 euros
Sold: 475 euros
Artcurial, Paris
November 25, 2011 (lot 409)
Specialist: PB Fashion

ANONYMOUS

GRÈS

COUTURE

COUTURE

Blue and white striped woven cotton suit; peplum-cut jacket; small notched collar; single-breasted closure with buttons, repeated on the two pockets; three-quarter sleeves with cuffs; straight skirt.

Two-tone melon and apricot wool jersey dress, reversible front to back; bias-cut bodice; boat neckline draped over sloping shoulders; waist with gathered small pleats on flowing skirt; buttoned half belt. Black label, white lettering.

Estimate: 30–50 euros
Sold: 87 euros
Artcurial, Paris
June 27, 2011 (lot 48)
Specialist: PB Fashion

Estimate: 1,500–2,000 euros
Sold: 11,260 euros
Artcurial, Paris
November 25, 2011 (lot 480)
Specialist: PB Fashion

JACQUES HEIM

LILLI ANN

COUTURE

COUTURE

Black wool skirted coat; collar with lapels; single-breasted closure; fitted with darts at the hips; piped pockets; godets at the back. Black label, white lettering and logo.

Gray, black, and white mottled wool skirted coat with darker diamond inlays; V-neckline with wide lapels. Label.

Estimate: 600–700 euros
Sold: 3,750 euros
Cornette de Saint Cyr, Paris
July 2, 2010 (lot 365)
Specialists: D. Chombert and F. Sternbach

Estimate: 200–400 dollars
Sold: 660 dollars
Augusta Auctions, New York
November 2, 2011 (lot 272)
Specialist: Karen E. Augusta

JACQUES FATH

SCHIAPARELLI

COUTURE

COUTURE

Black wool bouclé jacket; turndown collar; single-breasted closure; peplum cut set off with a belt buckle; three-quarter sleeves. Black label, white lettering, logo.

Carmel-colored wool herringbone coat; turndown collar; single-breasted closure; three flat pockets; sloping shoulders. Logo on lining.

<u>PROVENANCE</u>: Brooklyn Museum.

Estimate: 400–500 euros
Sold: 1,188 euros
Cornette de Saint Cyr, Paris
December 12, 2011 (lot 106)
Specialists: D. Chombert and F. Sternbach

Estimate: 200–400 dollars
Sold: 420 dollars
Augusta Auctions, New York
November 2, 2011 (lot 273)
Specialist: Karen E. Augusta

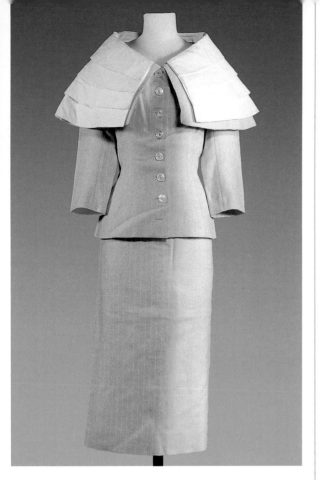

EMILIO SCHUBERTH

SCHIAPARELLI

N º 96731-2076

COUTURE

COUTURE

Yellow wool suit with white stripes; fitted jacket with wide turndown collar falling over the shoulders and a second removable white collar with four flat folds; three-quarter sleeves; straight skirt, mid-calf length with inverted pleats at the back. Label "Emilio Schuberth Roma."

Seersucker dress; Provençal quilting printed with ferns and other green and ochre plants on white background; accolade neckline; sloping shoulders; bust set off with a yoke; A-line skirt. White label, black lettering.

Estimate: 1,200–1,300 euros
Sold: 1,500 euros
Cornette de Saint Cyr, Paris
July 4, 2011 (lot 54)
Specialists: D. Chombert and F. Sternbach

Estimate: 2,500–3,000 euros
Sold: 3,750 euros
Cornette de Saint Cyr, Paris
June 30, 2012 (lot 132)
Specialists: D. Chombert and F. Sternbach

JEAN DESSÈS

N° 2352
COUTURE

Black velvet dress; V-neckline and asymmetric buttons; shoulders with a cape look; draped waist adorned with a quill of asymmetric length; full skirt. White label, black lettering.

Estimate: 1,300–1,500 euros
Sold: 1,500 euros
Cornette de Saint Cyr, Paris
July 2, 2010 (lot 164)
Specialists: D. Chombert and F. Sternbach

EMILIO SCHUBERTH

COUTURE

Black wool and silk suit; fitted jacket adorned with a large organza collar with four layers of decreasing size stiffened with horsehair; single-breasted closure; straight skirt with small inverted pleats. Label "Emilio Schuberth Roma."

Estimate: 2,000–2,500 euros
Sold: 4,375 euros
Cornette de Saint Cyr, Paris
July 4, 2011 (lot 248)
Specialists: D. Chombert and F. Sternbach

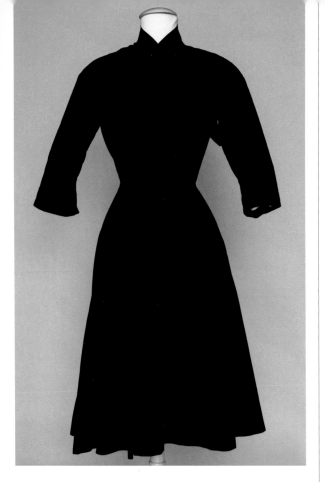

JEANNE LANVIN

JACQUES FATH

N° 16078
COUTURE
by Antonio Castillo

COUTURE

Black silk faille dress; bodice with high neck that is also a tie; three-quarter sleeves; fitted waist on full skirt with godets.
PROVENANCE: Brooklyn Museum.

Black wool crepe dress; small V-neckline on button placket; long raglan sleeves; straight skirt with full pinafore-like arch of draped moiré. White label, black lettering, logo.

Estimate: 300–600 dollars
Sold: 900 dollars
Augusta Auctions, New York
November 2, 2011 (lot 311)
Specialist: Karen E. Augusta

Estimate: 1,300–1,500 euros
Sold: 2,250 euros
Cornette de Saint Cyr, Paris
July 2, 2010 (lot 105)
Specialists: D. Chombert and F. Sternbach

JEAN DESSÈS

COUTURE

Navy wool dress with pinafore-bustier sprinkled with black studs; V-neckline; flared skirt with asymmetric length.

Estimate: 200–250 euros
Sold: 149 euros
Camard & Associés, Paris
March 18, 2012 (lot 15)

CHRISTIAN DIOR

N° 4332
COUTURE

Black wool day dress; bodice with high neck; three-quarter sleeves; fitted waist set off by full flared skirt forming godets. Label "Christian Dior London."

Estimate: 400–600 dollars
Sold: 915 dollars
Leslie Hindman Auctioneers, Chicago
September 16, 2010 (lot 276)
Specialist: Abigail Rutherford

CHANEL

N° 023318
COUTURE

Pink wool bouclé suit; silk lining with multicolor abstract print; small notched collar; front adorned with four flaps; gored skirt with two slits at the back. Worn with a matching toque. Beige labels, brown lettering.

Estimate: 600–800 euros
Sold: 1,000 euros
Cornette de Saint Cyr, Paris
February 13, 2012 (lot 93)
Specialists: D. Chombert and F. Sternbach

CHANEL

N° 18177
COUTURE

Beige and ivory tweed suit; jacket trimmed in wool jersey; small notched collar; single-breasted closure with pierced gold metal buttons carved with lion heads; four overlaid pockets, two on two; straight skirt. Worn with a wool jersey sleeveless blouse with round neckline. Beige label, brown lettering.

Estimate: 400–500 euros
Sold: 750 euros
Cornette de Saint Cyr, Paris
June 30, 2012 (lot 359)
Specialists: D. Chombert and F. Sternbach

CHARLES JAMES

COUTURE, Fall/Winter 1951–1952

Chesterfield wool skirted coat; multicolor flecks on brown background; black wool notched collar; two Lucite buttons on slightly asymmetric facings; two bias-cut hip pockets. No label.

BIBLIOGRAPHY: The model is reproduced on p. 41 of *Harper's Bazaar*, July 1951, and on p. 13 of the *New York Times*, October 2, 1955.

Estimate: 900–1,000 euros
Sold: 1,125 euros
Cornette de Saint Cyr, Paris
July 2, 2010 (lot 274)
Specialists: D. Chombert and F. Sternbach

JEAN DESSÈS

COUTURE

Aqua lace dress; slightly draped bodice; V-neckline; cap-sleeve look; full gathered skirt. Label "Jean Dessès Rd. Pt. Champs-Elysées Paris."

Estimate: 1,000–2,000 dollars
Sold: 1,342 dollars
Leslie Hindman Auctioneers, Chicago
April 21, 2010 (lot 30)
Specialist: Abigail Rutherford

CHANEL

N° 4161
COUTURE, 1958

Navy blue lace cocktail dress with round, slightly scalloped neckline; flared skirt with godets adorned with layered ruffles at the hem. Label.

Estimate: 2,000–4,000 dollars
Sold: 3,904 dollars
Leslie Hindman Auctioneers, Chicago
September 16, 2010 (lot 285A)
Specialist: Abigail Rutherford

GRÈS

COUTURE

Sleeveless red silk jersey cocktail dress; bustier draped with crisscrossing bands in the front; skirt forming small godets. Label "Grès, 1 Rue de la Paix Paris."

Estimate: 1,500–2,000 dollars
Sold: 4,560 dollars
Charles A. Whitaker Auction Company, Philadelphia
October 28–29, 2011 (lot 706)
Specialist: Charles A. Whitaker

EISA

CHARLES JAMES

COUTURE

COUTURE, 1951

Black wild-silk cocktail dress; high collar; balloon mid-length sleeves; fitted waist and full gathered skirt. Label.
PROVENANCE: Anne Moen Bullitt.

Tomato red silk faille cocktail dress; bodice with whalebone stays; short draped cape forming mid-length sleeves; corset look on pencil skirt; a few pleats at the hips. Label "Charles James."
PROVENANCE: Mrs. Cornelius Vanderbilt Whitney.

Estimate: 800–1,200 pounds
Sold: 1,000 pounds
Christie's, London
December 3, 2009 (lot 172)
Specialist: Patricia Frost

Estimate: 8,000–10,000 dollars
Sold: 18,000 dollars
Charles A. Whitaker Auction Company, Philadelphia
October 28–29, 2011 (lot 719)
Specialist: Charles A. Whitaker

JEAN DESSÈS

EISA

N° 9852
COUTURE

COUTURE, Winter 1953

Black faille cocktail dress; bodice with a wide neckline enhanced with a high draped collar; three-quarter sleeves; asymmetric wraparound skirt cut on the bias. Worn with a satin belt and a black horsehair slip. White label, black lettering.

PROVENANCE: Anne Moen Bullitt.

Black satin cocktail dress with white polka dots; draped bust set off with a horizontal cut; three-quarter kimono sleeves; buttoned back with two trailing sashes tied together; peplum look; straight black skirt. Worn with a fitted belt. Black label, white lettering.

BIBLIOGRAPHY: The model in identical material and with the same type of bodice is reproduced on p. 179 in *Balenciaga and Spain*, Hamish Bowles, Fine Arts Museums of San Francisco and Skira Rizzoli, 2011.

PROVENANCE: Anne Moen Bullitt.

Estimate: 1,000–1,200 euros
Sold: 4,337 euros
Artcurial, Paris
June 27, 2011 (lot 293)
Specialist: PB Fashion

Estimate: 1,000–1,200 euros
Sold: 4,957 euros
Artcurial, Paris
June 27, 2011 (lot 370)
Specialist: PB Fashion

HENRY À LA PENSÉE

MAGGY ROUFF

PRÊT-À-PORTER

COUTURE

Black silk bathing suit; corset look; coral and tone-on-tone print; skating skirt. Label.

Ivory silk damask dress with floral motif; asymmetric neckline with slightly draped strap; wide peplum over draped skirt. Label "Maggy Rouff 25. Avenue Matignon Paris."

Estimate: 150–250 pounds
Sold: 325 pounds
Christie's, London
December 3, 2009 (lot 202)
Specialist: Patricia Frost

Estimate: 800–1,200 dollars
Sold: 5,700 dollars
Charles A. Whitaker Auction Company, Philadelphia
October 28–29, 2011 (lot 714)
Specialist: Charles A. Whitaker

MAGGY ROUFF

EISA

COUTURE

Midnight blue woven silk dress, partially pleated; halter top and open back; wide turndown collar over small slit; fitted waist and full skirt. White label, black lettering.

COUTURE

Burnout silk velvet day dress with floral motif; round neckline; balloon sleeves; full bias-cut skirt forming godets; belted waist.

<u>PROVENANCE</u>: Anne Moen Bullitt.

Estimate: 400–600 euros
Sold: 2,502 euros
Artcurial, Paris
June 11, 2012 (lot 481)
Specialist: PB Fashion

Estimate: 600–800 pounds
Sold: 750 pounds
Christie's, London
December 3, 2009 (lot 183)
Specialist: Patricia Frost

EISA

EISA

COUNTURE

COUTURE, 1954

Black dress with fitted crepe bodice; V-neckline extended with two covered buttons; small sleeves; full faille skirt with gathered low waist forming numerous godets. Label.
 PROVENANCE: Anne Moen Bullitt.

Black ottoman silk dress; round neckline with button placket on the back; fitted look; wide bias-cut skirt with godets. White label, black lettering.
PROVENANCE: Anne Moen Bullitt.

Estimate: 600–1,000 pounds
Sold: 2,125 pounds
Christie's, London
December 3, 2009 (lot 165)
Specialist: Patricia Frost

Estimate: 200–300 euros
Sold: 867 euros
Artcurial, Paris
June 27, 2011 (lot 404)
Specialist: PB Fashion

EISA

NINA RICCI

COUTURE

PRÊT-À-PORTER

Black silk cocktail dress; boat neckline; V-cut back with winged-lapel look; single-breasted closure; sloping shoulders; full gathered skirt adorned with a fringed ruffle at the hips; waist with fitted belt. Worn with a slip. Black label, white lettering.

Black gazar cocktail dress with small permanent pleats intercut with thin braiding; turndown collar on low neckline; hook-and-eye fasteners; ruffled skirt; belt. Label "La Boutique de Nina Ricci."

Estimate: 700–800 euros
Sold: 4,000 euros
Cornette de Saint Cyr, Paris
July 2, 2010 (lot 252)
Specialists: D. Chombert and F. Sternbach

Estimate: 300–400 euros
Sold: 438 euros
Cornette de Saint Cyr, Paris
June 30, 2012 (lot 249)
Specialists: D. Chombert and F. Sternbach

JEAN DESSÈS

ANONYMOUS

COUTURE

COUTURE

Black silk chiffon cocktail dress; wide velvet straps; draped bust; V-neckline; bias-cut fluted skirt forming godets over a slip. White label, black lettering.

Evening dress; black silk velvet bodice fitted to the top of the hips; V-neckline; full tulle skirt adorned with velvet leaves enhanced with silver beads and sequins. Worn with a slip.

Estimate: 600–800 euros
Sold: 867 euros
Deburaux & Associés, Paris
October 13, 2011 (lot 392)
Specialist: PB Fashion

Estimate: 600–700 euros
Sold: 625 euros
Cornette de Saint Cyr, Paris
July 2, 2010 (lot 87)
Specialists: D. Chombert and F. Sternbach

ANONYMOUS

COUTURE

Strapless draped silk chiffon dress; wide skirt enhanced with satin and adorned with a bow; horsehair slip.

Estimate: 60–80 euros
Sold: 150 euros
Artcurial, Paris
June 11, 2012 (lot 227)
Specialist: PB Fashion

JACQUES GRIFFE

COUTURE

Black organza cocktail dress with horizontal pleats; long bustier fitted to the hips; wide skirt with godets stiffened with horsehair. No label.

Estimate: 900–1,000 euros
Sold: 1,938 euros
Cornette de Saint Cyr, Paris
July 4, 2011 (lot 261)
Specialists: D. Chombert and F. Sternbach

JEAN DESSÈS

EISA

COUTURE

COUTURE

Navy lace strapless dress; waist with a tie in the front; full skirt forming godets. Worn with a bolero that has three-quarter sleeves. Label.

Black lace cocktail dress; round collar with scalloped edge, repeated at the bottom of the three-quarter raglan sleeves and at the hem of the full skirt; gathered waist set off with a bright purple belt. Worn over a strapless dress. White and black labels, black and blue lettering.

Estimate: 800–1,200 dollars
Sold: 1,220 dollars
Leslie Hindman Auctioneers, Chicago
December 6, 2011 (lot 29)
Specialist: Abigail Rutherford

Estimate: 800–1,000 euros
Sold: 2,750 euros
Cornette de Saint Cyr, Paris
July 2, 2010 (lot 321)
Specialists: D. Chombert and F. Sternbach

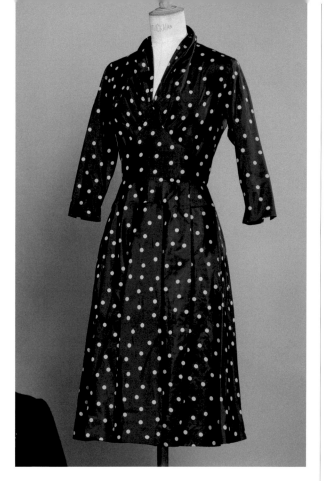

JACQUES FATH

JACQUES ESTEREL

COUTURE

COUTURE

Black taffeta day dress with white polka dots; V-neckline with turned-back shawl collar; half sleeves with slits at the bottoms; fitted under the chest with gatherings; full skirt with round pleats and basque look. Black label, white lettering, logo.

Gray and white dress, partially striped; spaghetti straps and uplifted bust adorned with a small bow; full skirt with inverted pleats and trompe-l'œil styling.

Estimate: 2,000–2,500 euros
Sold: 3,125 euros
Cornette de Saint Cyr, Paris
December 12, 2011 (lot 270)
Specialists: D. Chombert and F. Sternbach

Estimate: 150–200 euros
Sold: 3,500 euros
Cornette de Saint Cyr, Paris
April 4, 2012 (lot 440)
Specialists: D. Chombert and F. Sternbach

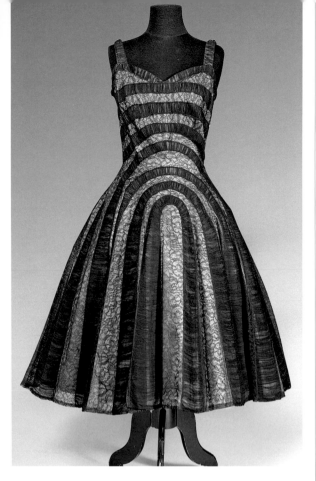

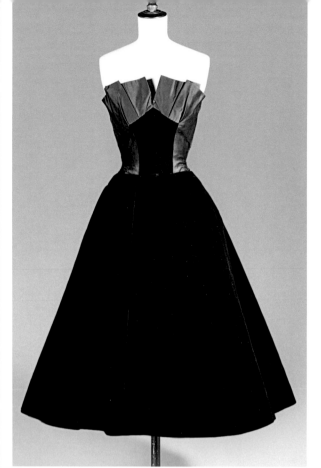

JACQUES GRIFFE

JACQUES FATH

N º 6672

COUTURE

COUTURE

Cocktail dress with alternating black tulle and lace on a background of flesh-colored silk; accolade neckline; full skirt forming godets.

Black silk velvet and satin duchesse evening dress; folding on the front of the bustier resembling a shirt dickey; full wraparound skirt. White label, black lettering.

<u>PROVENANCE</u>: Anne Moen Bullitt.

Estimate: 300–400 euros
Sold: 991 euros
Coutau-Begarie, Paris
December 10, 2011 (lot 65)

Estimate: 1,000–1,200 euros
Sold: 11,153 euros
Artcurial, Paris
June 27, 2011 (lot 173)
Specialist: PB Fashion

PIERRE BALMAIN

ANONYMOUS

N º 108011
COUTURE

COUTURE

Evening gown; bustier draped with coral and olive gazar; full ivory organza skirt printed with large flowers; waist set off with a black, velvet fitted belt. White label, black lettering.

White satin-stitched lace cocktail dress; bustier overlaid with black Chantilly, repeated at the hips; wide skirt over tulle and horsehair slips.

Estimate: 1,000–1,200 euros
Sold: 2,750 euros
Cornette de Saint Cyr, Paris
July 4, 2011 (lot 231)
Specialists: D. Chombert and F. Sternbach

Estimate: 800–1,000 euros
Sold: 1,125 euros
Cornette de Saint Cyr, Paris
July 4, 2011 (lot 154)
Specialists: D. Chombert and F. Sternbach

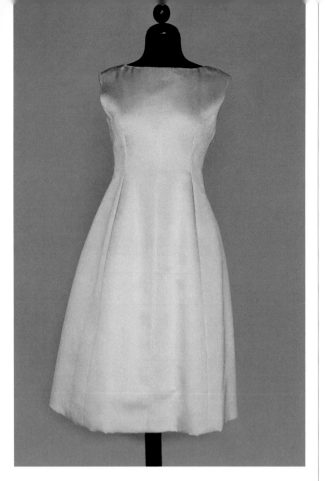

GIVENCHY

CHANEL

COUTURE, 1955

COUTURE, 1956

Pale yellow silk cocktail dress; boat neckline; flared panel skirt. Label.

 PROVENANCE: Brooklyn Museum.

Cocktail dress; bustier with ivory and burgundy stripes adorned with a bow; satin-stitched ivory tulle full skirt; stripes repeated at the hem; worn over a synthetic gauze slip trimmed with lace. Label.

PROVENANCE: Brooklyn Museum.

Estimate: 400–600 dollars
Sold: 451 dollars
Augusta Auctions, New York
March 30, 2011 (lot 202)
Specialist: Karen E. Augusta

Estimate: 300–600 dollars
Sold: 1,920 dollars
Augusta Auctions, New York
November 2, 2011 (lot 376)
Specialist: Karen E. Augusta

PAULINE TRIGERE

JEANNE LANVIN

COUTURE

COUTURE
by Antonio Castillo

Chocolate brown wool crepe cocktail dress; "pierced" with a silk faille tone-on-tone half bow. Label.

Oat-colored wool dress; short sleeves; flared skirt with godets. Worn with a short jacket with turndown collar; crossed rounded facings fastened with snaps; three-quarter sleeves. Label.

Estimate: 300–600 dollars
Sold: 1,080 dollars
Augusta Auctions, New York
November 2, 2011 (lot 321)
Specialist: Karen E. Augusta

Estimate: 150–200 euros
Sold: 223 euros
Camard & Associés, Paris
March 8, 2012 (lot 57)

GRÈS

COUTURE

Ivory silk evening gown, entirely pleated; asymmetric neckline with one shoulder strap; open back with two cross straps; long flowing skirt. White label, black lettering.

Estimate: 700–900 euros
Sold: 3,503 euros
Artcurial, Paris
June 11, 2012 (lot 213)
Specialist: PB Fashion

PIERRE BALMAIN

N° 95632
COUTURE, Fall/Winter 1956

Black silk jersey draped sheath; asymmetric neckline; bust set off with two velvet ribbons. Black label, white lettering.

BIBLIOGRAPHY: The "Calcédoine" model, a variation of the model displayed, is reproduced on p. 210 in the exhibition catalog *Pierre Balmain, 40 années de créations*, Musée de la Mode et du Costume, Palais Galliera, December 20, 1985–April 6, 1986.

Estimate: 600–700 euros
Sold: 4,375 euros
Cornette de Saint Cyr, Paris
June 30, 2012 (lot 280)
Specialists: D. Chombert and F. Sternbach

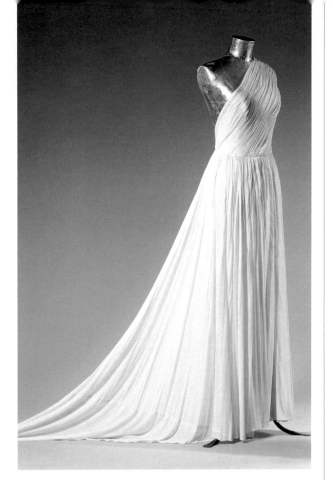

GRÈS

EISA

COUTURE

Ivory silk jersey draped dress; asymmetric neckline with one
draped shoulder; skirt with side train. Label "Grès, 1 Rue de
la Paix Paris."

COUTURE

Ball gown; champagne satin duchesse bustier with tailored
points on each side, repeated on the small basque; absinthe-
colored silk tulle skirt. White label, gray lettering.
<u>PROVENANCE</u>: Anne Moen Bullitt.

Estimate: 1,000–1,500 euros
Sold: 1,487 euros
Thierry de Maigret, Paris
November 22, 2011 (lot 294)
Specialist: Séverine Experton-Dard

Estimate: 1,800–2,200 euros
Sold: 2,478 euros
Artcurial, Paris
June 27, 2011 (lot 294)
Specialist: PB Fashion

JEAN DESSÈS

COUTURE

Lemon yellow silk chiffon evening gown; bodice with crisscross look reinforced with whalebone stays; slightly draped halter neckline; open back; skirt with numerous small godets.

Estimate: 1,500–2,000 pounds
Sold: 2,750 pounds
Christie's, London
December 1, 2011 (lot 68)
Specialist: Patricia Frost

PIERRE BALMAIN

N º 59749
COUTURE

Sheath completely covered with black metallic sequins; bustier reinforced with whalebone stays. Label "Pierre Balmain Paris."

Estimate: 4,000–6,000 dollars
Sold: 15,600 dollars
Charles A. Whitaker Auction Company, Philadelphia
April 27–28, 2012 (lot 827)
Specialist: Charles A. Whitaker

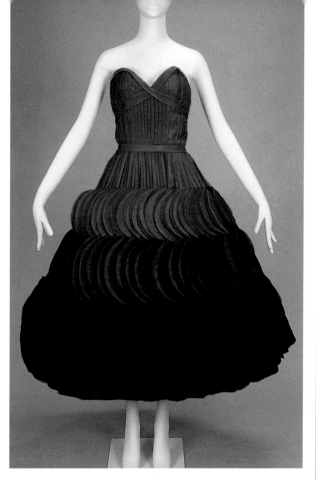 

JEAN DESSÈS

COUTURE

Bright purple organza dress; pleated bustier set off with crossing bands, repeated at the belted waist; wide skirt decorated with overlaid geometric petals. Label "Jean Dessès 17. Avenue Matignon. Paris."

Estimate: 3,000–4,000 dollars
Sold: 15,000 dollars
Charles A. Whitaker Auction Company, Philadelphia
October 28–29, 2011 (lot 718)
Specialist: Charles A. Whitaker

BALENCIAGA

N° 51773
COUTURE, Winter 1951

Black taffeta evening gown draped with tulle adorned with flowerets; bum-roll look and bow at the back; full skirt with a ruffled hem. Label "Balenciaga 10, Avenue George V. Paris."

Estimate: 4,000–6,000 dollars
Sold: 14,400 dollars
Charles A. Whitaker Auction Company, Philadelphia
April 27–28, 2012 (lot 825)
Specialist: Charles A. Whitaker

Chanel Boutique
Wool tweed jacket with a silk crepe peplum.
"Haute Couture, Accessoires, Bijoux Fantaisie"
auction held at Artcurial, June 11, 2012
(sold: 400 euros).

ICONS OF VINTAGE FASHION
Spotlight

The CHANEL JACKET

"The Chanel jacket has become the symbol of a certain elegance that is feminine, nonchalant, always in style and enduring—in other words, timeless."
—Karl Lagerfeld

THE HISTORY

The Chanel jacket was born in 1954 when Gabrielle Chanel, following a fifteen-year absence from the fashion world, returned with a collection of tweed suits inspired by the jackets of grand Austrian hotel elevator operators.

And what a spectacular return it was! Chanel positioned herself at the other extreme of Christian Dior's "New Look" that was the style of the moment; instead of the reactionary opulence of the postwar silhouette, Mademoiselle Chanel proposed a simple and practical tweed jacket—so practical that it has been part of the Chanel collections ever since, reinterpreted each season. As such, it has become one of the most sought-after pieces at vintage auctions.

AN ICON

Since 1983, Karl Lagerfeld has been the creative force of the Rue Cambon couture house: He has orchestrated infinite variations of the jacket's shape, fabric, texture, and color and has succeeded in turning the famous jacket into an essential foundation of any wardrobe.

It was his idea to exhibit the jacket at the Grand Palais, in the same manner that great works of art are presented under the museum's glass roof. It was the subject of a giant sculpture that served as the centerpiece for the Spring/Summer 2008 Haute Couture show.

In 2012, it was the exclusive subject of a book published by Steidl, *The Little Black Jacket: Chanel's Classic Revisited* by Karl Lagerfeld and Carine Roitfeld. The book features 108 photographs of celebrities from the world of film, fashion, and music: both men (Romain Duris, Kanye West) and women (Vanessa Paradis, Sofia Coppola), ranging in age from the very young (Hudson Kroening, age four) to the slightly less young (Yoko Ono). The book demonstrates that the jacket, while hard to capture in a photograph because of its color, is always different. Even when worn by an impressive cast of characters, the jacket remains the true star.

THE SYMBOL

The little tweed jacket is a style icon. As a symbol of the Chanel brand, the jacket represents the house, along with the quilted bag, the camellia, and the universal double C. Often reproduced, copied, even parodied, it will always be part of Chanel mythology: The tweed jacket *is* Chanel.

As a cardigan that has been turned into a jacket, it retains a suppleness that makes it comfortable to wear while still keeping its shape. There are no darts or shoulder pads, just a straight cut, a simple and straightforward neckline, and impeccable drape. Ever since it was first created, small chain weights have been placed inside the lining to make sure that the jacket hangs perfectly. Such attention to detail has made the jacket the ideal uniform of independent and liberated women who want chic but functional clothes that do not hinder their movements.

In addition, like so many of Mademoiselle Chanel's designs, it found its inspiration in the world of men's clothing, which in turn led to a transference of values normally associated with men. The women who wore tweed were modern, feminine, and elegant but also liberated and powerful; they were, like the designer herself, women of character who sought to project their unique personalities. It comes as no surprise then to learn that the jacket was the sartorial choice of women in powerful positions: Simone Veil, who fought for the legalization of abortion in France in 1974, or International Monetary Fund Managing Director Christine Lagarde, photographed in 2011 in front of the Élysée Palace in a pink and black jacket.

THE MYTH

Almost half a century earlier, the Chanel jacket entered the world of myth. The First Lady of the United States, Jackie Kennedy, known for her elegance, had chosen the Chanel suit as her favorite outfit. She was wearing a pink Chanel suit on November 22, 1963, the day of her husband's assassination. On that day, with its heartbreaking red bloodstain, the jacket achieved legendary status.

DIDIER LUDOT AND VINTAGE

Vintage is experiencing unprecedented popularity. Didier Ludot believes the phenomenon started when Yves Saint Laurent presented his 1940s-themed collection in the early 1970s ("Homage aux années 40") and "gave women the idea of rummaging through their grandmothers' attics in search of wedge-heeled shoes. At the time, it was called 'retro' not 'vintage.'" It does not really matter since, as he says, "the term vintage is bandied about and often used incorrectly."

He prefers the term *grand cru*, which allows him to disregard the temporal limitations of vintage. He can then include more recent pieces, even current pieces, whose condition, rarity, and significance as representation of a specific fashion trend or designer give their presence complete legitimacy. Among the *grand crus* that do not need to age to reach the status of *noblesse* are John Galliano's creations for Dior, Gaultier's draped designs (an homage to Madame Grès), Viktor and Rolf's pillow dresses, Montana's sensual sculptural shapes, as well as the timeless pieces of Yohji Yamamoto. Ludot recognizes that fewer clothes made today will be collector's pieces, that there is an increase in "deplorable faux-couture happening right now" and that prêt-à-porter, while capable of great things, can never achieve the sense of exclusivity that belongs to haute couture. Didier Ludot avoids the pitfalls of mass production and still finds charm within the world of prêt-à-porter by going to sample sales where he can buy one-of-a-kind pieces, unusual items that are not on the market.

A Conversation with
DIDIER LUDOT

Didier Ludot was always interested in fashion and clothes. He grew up in a small town but vividly remembers that his mother had copies of Parisian haute couture dresses made by a local seamstress and that his cousins would model their wedding dresses on Lanvin's designs. He may have been far from Paris but he would discover and learn the art of couture, the savoir faire, the first muslin fittings, the beauty of handwork and refined finishing from his mother's dressmaker.

Today, Didier Ludot lives in the very heart of Paris. He is one of the most celebrated vintage couture dealers and the ultimate specialist in the field. Since 1975, he has owned several shops tucked into the arcades of the Palais-Royal.

Didier Ludot loves the history behind his clothes. That is the point of vintage, after all: a piece with a past that is given a second chance. His clothes are his treasures and he is sensitive to the emotional pull of vintage items, becoming attached to them, finding it hard to let them go.

He particularly adores clothes that can still be worn and does not mind loaning his pieces for exhibitions, "because you have to take them out from time to time." He likes selling to fashion houses, allowing his treasures to "return home."

Ludot believes that vintage fashions play a role in the preservation of a cultural heritage and in the memory and transmission of Parisian savoir faire and quality.

- *Above:* Didier Ludot, in October 2012, in front of his window display dedicated to the work of Claude Montana during Fashion Week in Paris.

- *Left:* A dress by Pierre Balmain Haute Couture with embroidery by François Lesage, 1953.
- *Above:* Didier Ludot's boutique in the arcade of the Palais-Royal.
- *Below:* A dress by Yves Saint Laurent Haute Couture, 1974.

A KNOWLEDGEABLE CLIENTELE

Ludot is always interested in anecdotes related to his treasures. He enjoys buying from individuals as it often gives him the opportunity to talk about the past with "older ladies in slippers" whose closets reveal the glamour and beauty of their earlier days. He dreams about the clothes that once belonged to celebrities whose elegance he admires and considers Catherine Deneuve's collection of Yves Saint Laurent clothes to be his most precious acquisition.

He is as passionate about the clothes as his most faithful clients who travel from across the world intent on wearing what they buy. These daring women, who "know, understand, and appreciate fashion," have succumbed to the cachet of real couture and know that by wearing vintage clothes, "they will attract all the attention and envy of others." He speaks fondly of his devoted clients such as Stephanie Seymour, who can, better than anyone, gracefully slip into one of his haute couture dresses, and his customers from China and India, who are knowledgeable about fashion and have the panache to wear a gala dress in the middle of the day. Unafraid to speak his mind, he adds mischievously "unlike French women, who no longer know how to dress."

WHY NOT PRODUCTIONS PRÉSENTE

SÉLECTION OFFICIELLE
FESTIVAL DE CANNES

CHIARA **MASTROIANNI** • Catherine **DENEUVE** • Ludivine **SAGNIER**

Les Bien-Aimés

Un film de **CHRISTOPHE HONORÉ**

LOUIS **GARREL**   MILOS **FORMAN**   PAUL **SCHNEIDER**   Avec la participation de MICHEL **DELPECH**

Avec RASHA **BUKVIC**   Musique originale ALEX **BEAUPAIN**

Image RÉMY CHEVRIN (a.f.c.) – Décors SAMUEL DESHORS – Costumes PASCALINE CHAVANNE – Son GUILLAUME LE BRAZ – Montage CHANTAL HYMANS – Une coproduction WHY NOT PRODUCTIONS, FRANCE 2 CINÉMA, SIXTEEN FILMS, NEGATIV – Avec la participation de CANAL +, FRANCE TÉLÉVISIONS, ORANGE CINÉMA SÉRIES – Avec le soutien de la RÉGION ÎLE-DE-FRANCE et du FONDS D'ACTION SACEM – En association avec la SOFICA SOFICINÉMA 7 – Ventes internationales CELLULOID DREAMS – Distribution France LE PACTE

ICONS OF VINTAGE FASHION
Spotlight

FASHION *and* FILM

Fashion loves the movies and the feeling is mutual. The two art forms have developed strong connections, an ambiguous but nonetheless passionate relationship, and a mutual dependency.

Far from playing a supporting role, costume design has become one of film's stars; clothes can help create unforgettable characters and scenes.

THE ACTRESS AND THE DESIGNER

If a film achieves cult status, the main character's wardrobe will follow suit. The clothes become a symbol of the period and, in time, vintage icons.

Such is the case for the outfits born from the collaboration between an actress and a designer. Who can forget the close relationship that developed between Audrey Hepburn and Hubert de Givenchy? It all started with a misunderstanding: When they first met, Givenchy was expecting Katharine Hepburn but immediately fell under the charm of the beautiful petite brunette. As a result of this first meeting, Givenchy would design the clothes for Billy Wilder's film *Sabrina* (1954) as well as those worn by Holly Golightly in Blake Edwards's *Breakfast at Tiffany's* (1961), the film that turned the little black dress into a fashion icon. Givenchy also designed the dreamy white ball gown for the film *Ariane* (1957). The gown sold at auction at Kerry Taylor in London for 6,500 pounds on December 8, 2009.

Another strong actress-designer relationship existed between Catherine Deneuve and Yves Saint Laurent. Their lasting friendship began when Saint Laurent designed the elegant outfits Catherine Deneuve wore in Buñuel's *Belle de Jour* (1967). The deceivingly demure dress of black and ivory satin *grain de poudre*, the dress Michel Piccoli described as that of a "precocious schoolgirl," has become emblematic of the late 1960s even though the skirt was longer in length than most styles of the time. Today, the dress is part of the Saint Laurent archives and was featured next to nine other outfits belonging to Catherine Deneuve at the major Yves Saint Laurent retrospective held at the Petit Palais in 2010.

Catherine Deneuve also wore Roger Vivier's pilgrim-buckle pumps in *Belle de Jour*. Today they are considered vintage icons and have been reissued by the company with resounding success.

NEW FILMS AND VINTAGE CLOTHES

While the above-mentioned films reflected the time period of their storyline, others go back in time or use flashbacks whose credibility depends in great part on the accuracy of the costume design. Sometimes the main function of an actor in period costume is to establish the mood and look of the time. Costume designer Theoni V. Aldredge won an Oscar for costume design for Jack Clayton's 1974 film, *The Great Gatsby*. The magnificent flapper dresses and other sequined and beaded creations worn by Mia Farrow and the rest of the cast immediately transported the viewers to the 1920s.

That same decade was also celebrated in *Midnight in Paris* (2011). Woody Allen captured a picture-perfect Paris shot through a romantic lens, with Marion Cotillard, as Adriana, wearing authentic vintage dresses. Costumes are the main temporal reference in the film's many flashbacks. At one point, when the storyline shifts from the 1920s to the Belle Époque, one of the characters remarks on the avant-garde style of Adriana's dress.

For *The Artist* (2011), Oscar-winning costume designer Mark Bridges created clothes that accurately reflected the time period of the 1930s. He created the main character's outfits from scratch but turned to the vintage shops of Los Angeles to dress all the supporting actors.

Christophe Honoré's two-hour film *Les Bien-Aimés* (2011) spans four decades. Costume designer Pascaline Chavanne concentrated on timeless designs, following the lead of the director for whom "today is always filled with references to yesterday." Featured are Roger Vivier's famous "Chiquette" shoes that have come to symbolize the 1960s. The film's main character will resort to sexual encounters so that she can buy those shoes.

Finally, one must mention Sofia Coppola's *Marie Antoinette* (2005) in which she humorously accessorizes a perfectly re-created eighteenth-century wardrobe with delightfully anachronistic Converse sneakers.

— Poster for the film *Les Bien-Aimés* by Christophe Honoré (2011), starring style icon Catherine Deneuve.

The CARRÉ
HERMÈS

ICONS OF VINTAGE FASHION
Spotlight

As the ultimate icon, the Hermès silk square is both a symbol of the house that created it and the supreme example of a scarf. It has sailed through the years without so much as a wrinkle and has the ability to renew itself again and again without ever losing any of its authenticity.

THE HISTORY OF THE SILK "CARRÉ"

The *carré* was first introduced in 1937 when Robert Dumas, the director of Hermès, was inspired by the company's creative enthusiasm to produce the first 90 cm by 90 cm silk scarf; he named the design "Jeu des Omnibus et des Dames Blanches." It was a success and illustrators were soon called upon to create new patterns to offer clients more choices when purchasing the new accessory that would come to represent the Hermès myth. Hugo Grygkar designed the best-selling "Brides de Gala" in 1957 and Cathy Latham created "Les Clés" in 1965, which quickly became a classic. As of today, more than 2,000 designs have been created, each one weaving its own story.

EXCEPTIONAL SAVOIR FAIRE

From the illustrator's initial design to the printed scarf draped around the neck, the multi-step process of making a scarf begins in the company's textile division near Lyon. For more than fifty years, Perrin & Fils has been the silk supplier for Hermès. They weave the Brazilian raw silk into rolls of twill; the next step involves the "décreusage," the removal of the gum. The silk is then ready for printing. A 90 cm by 90 cm scarf requires 450,000 meters of thread. The scarf's pattern is reproduced in its actual size on a template that goes to the engraving workshops where multiple screens are created, one for each color (each scarf has about thirty colors). The colorists step in at this point. Choosing from a palette of 75,000 shades, they will select the different colors in which a specific design will be produced. Once the silk is printed, the finishing process can begin. The colors are fixed, washed, and dried, followed by the famous "roulottage," the hand-rolled hemming with silk thread that takes forty-five minutes. The scarf is ready.

CONTEMPORARY AND TIMELESS

The silk square has become a classic, a timeless piece that never goes out of style and is passed down from generation to generation. New styles and shapes have been developed: In 1980, a pleated, fan-like silk was introduced, followed by chiffon, crepe, and even plain cotton. Newer shapes included a triangular scarf known as "pointu," and a silk ribbon called "twilly." To celebrate its seventieth anniversary, Hermès introduced a 70 cm square version of its *carré*.

The various designs have made the *carré* a favorite of collectors. The scarves are a mainstay at auctions, put up for sale by those who want something new and acquired by connoisseurs who want to give the scarves a second life. While some designs do not fetch more than 100 euros, most sell for between 100 and 200 euros, even with holes and stains; some even reach 300 euros (more than the retail price of the scarf). A scarf featuring the Egyptian jewelry pattern sold at Piasa for 318 euros in 2012. The price realized depends on the popularity of the design, the condition of the piece, and also on the possible presence of the small indelible mark Hermès stamps on its sale items.

Emblematic of elegance, Hermès scarves have been worn by Jackie Kennedy and Grace Kelly. They appeal equally to elegant women who wear them traditionally and to younger trendsetters who use them as hair accessories, belts, bustiers, or even jewelry.

— Silk Square Scarf with an Egyptian Jewelry Design, Hermès, Paris.
Featured at the "Mode, Haute Couture" auction at Piasa, April 25, 2012 (sold: 318 euros).

1960s

The Swinging Sixties

The years of austerity were a distant memory.

The Swinging Sixties were under way, making a clean sweep of the past. Everything felt new, contemporary, and up-to-date. Modern and easy to wear, sixties fashions continue to be a favorite of vintage enthusiasts.

In 1966, the launch of Yves Saint Laurent's "Saint Laurent Rive Gauche" signaled the beginning of prêt-à-porter and a certain democratization of fashion. In time, all the other houses would follow suit.

The clothing revolution gave birth to a host of new super-star designers who embraced prêt-à-porter, including Karl Lagerfeld, Sonia Rykiel, Christiane Bailly, Michèle Rosier, and Emmanuelle Khanh.

The appeal of Chanel's narrow-shouldered suit, the symbol of the decade, has never wavered. It continues to be one of the most popular auction items.

The mod dress, offered in a rainbow of shapes, colors, and fabrics, is another perennial favorite. Dramatically and unapologetically short, it mirrored the generation's second revolution: the mini.

Cardin and Courrèges both claimed to have invented the mini dress, but even the more traditional houses such as Patou, Lanvin, and Marc Bohan at Dior took the bold step of raising hemlines.

The influence of graphic and futuristic designs can be seen in the geometric shapes adopted by Givenchy and Balenciaga and in the materials used by Paco Rabanne, such as plastic and metal.

Evening wear also had a fresh new look as simpler and straighter lines replaced the crinolines and full skirts of earlier years.

CHANEL

N° 29324
COUTURE

Navy blue bouclé wool suit; round neckline and cuffs enhanced with white piqué cotton; four gold metal buttons; two vertical pockets; straight wraparound skirt. Black label, white lettering.

Estimate: 800–900 euros
Sold: 2,500 euros
Cornette de Saint Cyr, Paris
April 4, 2012 (lot 338)
Specialists: D. Chombert and F. Sternbach

CHANEL

N° 40972
COUTURE

Ivory bouclé wool suit with navy blue jersey trim; edge-to-edge jacket embellished with eight mock pockets, each adorned with a button, with a similar design repeated at the cuffs; flared paneled skirt. White label, black lettering.

Estimate: 600–700 euros
Sold: 2,375 euros
Cornette de Saint Cyr, Paris
April 4, 2012 (lot 368)
Specialists: D. Chombert and F. Sternbach

CHANEL

CHANEL

N º 29914
COUTURE

N º 45792
COUTURE

Pink tweed suit with matching print silk lining; jacket trimmed with black wool cord; round neckline; frog closures; four patch pockets; black silk cuffs; tie collar and flared skirt with small inverted pleats. Beige label, brown lettering.

Beige multicolor fantasy tweed bouclé suit; edge-to-edge jacket with matching trim enhanced with pink silk shirring; pockets and cuffs adorned with gold metal buttons; flared paneled skirt. Worn over a sleeveless pink blouse in rippled silk with tie collar. Beige label, brown lettering.

Estimate: 800–900 euros
Sold: 2,000 euros
Cornette de Saint Cyr, Paris
April 4, 2012 (lot 375)
Specialists: D. Chombert and F. Sternbach

Estimate: 700–800 euros
Sold: 3,750 euros
Cornette de Saint Cyr, Paris
April 4, 2012 (lot 376)
Specialists: D. Chombert and F. Sternbach

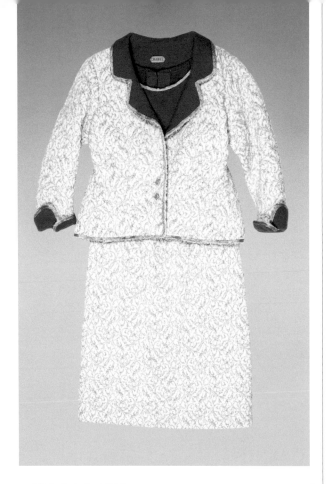

CHANEL

N º 05799
COUTURE

Evening suit of ivory silk embroidered in a gold foliage pattern; jacket has trim and notched collar; fuchsia wool jersey lining appears on revers of collar and cuffs; two gold metal buttons; straight skirt. Worn over a matching wool jersey blouse. Beige label, brown lettering.

Estimate: 1,000–2,000 dollars
Sold: 1,708 dollars
Leslie Hindman Auctioneers, Chicago
April 17, 2012 (lot 208)
Specialist: Abigail Rutherford

CHANEL

COUTURE

Black and beige tweed suit trimmed with navy double braid and fuchsia grosgrain; round neckline; single-breasted closure with gold metal buttons featuring a lion's head, repeated on the four pockets and cuffs. Worn over a fuchsia silk pongee blouse with tie collar; long sleeves with French cuffs. No label.

BIBLIOGRAPHY: Similar styles appear in *Vogue,* March 1961, and in *Femme Chic,* no. 486, Summer 1961. A similar style appears on pp. 154–155 in the exhibition catalog *Chanel,* Harold Koda and Andrew Bolton, Metropolitan Museum of Art of New York, May 5–August 7, 2005, Yale University Press.

Estimate: 2,000–2,500 euros
Sold: 2,750 euros
Cornette de Saint Cyr, Paris
February 25, 2010 (lot 160)
Specialists: D. Chombert and F. Sternbach

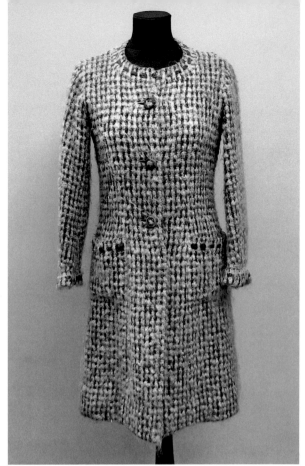

CHANEL

N ° **42603**
COUTURE

Brown and white tweed suit; jacket trim in white bouclé wool; round neckline; single-breasted closure; three pockets, one of which has a silk pocket square; flared skirt. Worn with matching brown silk blouse and scarf. White label, black lettering.

Estimate: 700–800 euros
Sold: 1,750 euros
Cornette de Saint Cyr, Paris
April 4, 2012 (lot 396)
Specialists: D. Chombert and F. Sternbach

CHANEL

COUTURE, Spring/Summer 1963

Ink blue, red, and gray coat in wool and mohair tweed; size 9/10; round neckline and patch pockets with drawstring ribbon of fuchsia and blue printed silk; matching buttons and lining. Beige label, brown lettering.

Estimate: 600–700 euros
Sold: 1,220 euros
Chayette & Cheval, Paris
February 5, 2012 (lot 343)
Specialist: PB Fashion

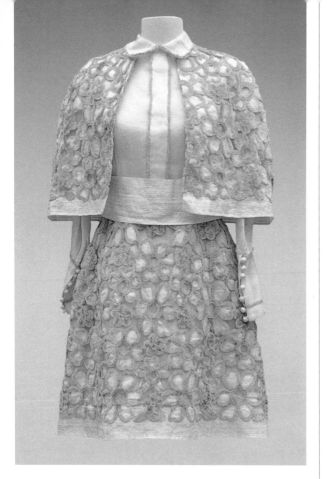

TED LAPIDUS

COUTURE

White organdy ensemble with bubble-gum pink chenille appliqués; turndown collar over a flat pleat that reaches the waist; buttons on the cuffs; flared skirt; short edge-to-edge cape; belt.

Estimate: 100–150 euros
Sold: 446 euros
Eve, Paris
June 18, 2012 (lot M109)
Specialist: Sylvie Daniel

CHRISTIAN DIOR

COUTURE, Spring/Summer 1960
by Yves Saint Laurent

Woven silk evening gown in a pink floral motif on ivory background; draped panel attached to the back of the bustier runs along the full skirt; scalloped hem adorned with large bows. No label.

Estimate: 2,000–4,000 pounds
Sold: 3,000 pounds
Christie's, London
December 1, 2011 (lot 90)
Specialist: Patricia Frost

CHANEL

BALENCIAGA

COUTURE

N° 104430
COUTURE, Summer 1968

Fuchsia rippled silk cocktail dress with gazar ruffles; V-neckline; wraparound bodice and skirt; matching belt. Beige label, brown lettering.

Gazar cocktail dress in a fuchsia floral pattern on white background; jewel neckline; raglan sleeves, ending with a flounce that is reprised on the skirt starting at the hipline. White label, black lettering.

BIBLIOGRAPHY: A similar style appears on pp. 244–247 in *Balenciaga*, Cristóbal Balenciaga Museoa, éditions du Regard, 2011.

Estimate: 400–500 euros
Sold: 2,875 euros
Cornette de Saint Cyr, Paris
February 13, 2012 (lot 272)
Specialists: D. Chombert and F. Sternbach

Estimate: 1,500–1,700 euros
Sold: 1,875 euros
Cornette de Saint Cyr, Paris
June 30, 2012 (lot 73)
Specialists: D. Chombert and F. Sternbach

JEANNE LANVIN

JEANNE LANVIN

COUTURE

COUTURE

Nut-brown jersey cashmere dress; round neckline with piping; short sleeves adorned with glossy marabou feathers in the same shade. Label "Lanvin Paris."

Flared coatdress in burgundy tweed with yellow and cherry red mottling; two patch pockets. Worn under a short jacket with turndown collar and scarf with fringe; single-breasted closure with covered buttons.

Estimate: 300–400 dollars
Sold: 480 dollars

Charles A. Whitaker Auction Company, Philadelphia
October 28–29, 2011 (lot 726)
Specialist: Charles A. Whitaker

Estimate: 80–100 euros
Sold: 104 euros

Camard & Associés, Paris
March 18, 2012 (lot 44)

ANONYMOUS

COUTURE

Tan and ivory double-faced wool and cashmere ensemble; double-breasted short jacket with turndown collar; long cuffed sleeves; wraparound skirt; sleeveless top with square neckline.

Estimate: 40–60 euros
Sold: 149 euros
Artcurial, Paris
November 15, 2010 (lot 316)
Specialist: PB Fashion

VALENTINO

COUTURE

Ivory double-faced wool suit with topstitching design; double-breasted jacket with round neckline; long raglan sleeves; paneled skirt. Label "Valentino Roma."

Estimate: 400–500 euros
Sold: 813 euros
Cornette de Saint Cyr, Paris
June 30, 2012 (lot 209)
Specialists: D. Chombert and F. Sternbach

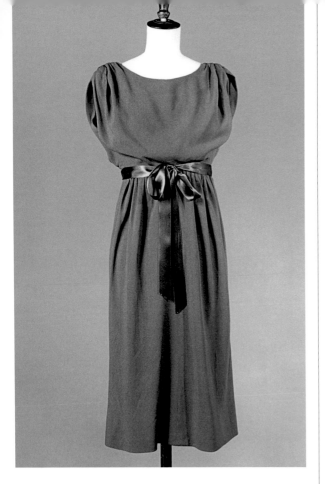 

ANONYMOUS

EISA

COUTURE

COUTURE

Light brown crepe cocktail dress; bodice with round neckline and gathered shoulders; high waist enhanced with a satin ribbon tied in a bow over flowing straight skirt.

Black crepe wraparound dress; slightly draped neckline; dropped shoulders; tie belt. Black label, white lettering.

Estimate: 200–300 euros
Sold: 248 euros
Artcurial, Paris
June 27, 2011 (lot 126)
Specialist: PB Fashion

Estimate: 200–300 euros
Sold: 626 euros
Artcurial, Paris
June 11, 2012 (lot 378)
Specialist: PB Fashion

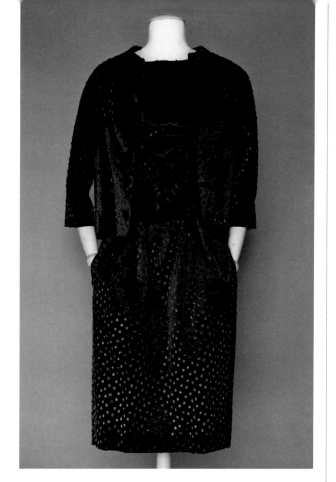

CHRISTIAN DIOR

GEOFFREY BEENE

N º 106419
COUTURE, Fall/Winter 1960–1961
by Marc Bohan

COUTURE

Black silk satin dinner ensemble with rust-colored velvet polka dots; sleeveless blouse with boat neckline; belt with a bow; straight skirt is slightly gathered at the waist and has two pockets; the single-breasted jacket has a round neckline and covered buttons; three-quarter kimono sleeves.

<u>PROVENANCE</u>: Brooklyn Museum.

Day dress in black and ivory cane-work patterned wool; small turndown collar with a silk bow; slightly flared paneled skirt. Label.

<u>PROVENANCE</u>: Brooklyn Museum.

Estimate: 600–800 dollars
Sold: 8,400 dollars
Augusta Auctions, New York
March 21, 2012 (lot 352)
Specialist: Karen E. Augusta

Estimate: 200–400 dollars
Sold: 60 dollars
Augusta Auctions, New York
November 2, 2011 (lot 58)
Specialist: Karen E. Augusta

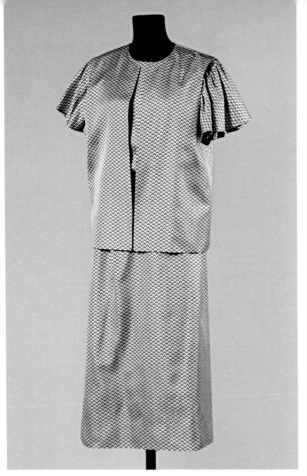

GRÈS

COUTURE

Silk twill ensemble with small geometric black-on-white pattern; blouse has round neckline and butterfly sleeves; sleeveless edge-to-edge cardigan; straight skirt. White label, black lettering.

Estimate: 120–150 euros
Sold: 310 euros
Artcurial, Paris
June 27, 2011 (lot 325)
Specialist: PB Fashion

YVES SAINT LAURENT

PRÊT-À-PORTER

Navy and white geometric print tussore ensemble; tunic has round neckline with bias trim and buttons, design repeated on the cuffs; straight skirt. Label "Yves Saint Laurent Boutique."

Estimate: 200–300 euros
Sold: 250 euros
Cornette de Saint Cyr, Paris
April 4, 2012 (lot 537)
Specialists: D. Chombert and F. Sternbach

GRÈS

GIVENCHY

COUTURE

PRÊT-À-PORTER

White and navy wool suit with a diagonal pattern; two-button jacket with round neckline and three-quarter sleeves; flared wraparound skirt.

Cotton piqué ensemble with light blue and white houndstooth pattern; single-breasted jacket with turndown collar; three-quarter raglan sleeves with cuffs; two vertical pockets; skirt has pleats starting at the hipline. Label "Givenchy Nouvelle Boutique."

Estimate: 100–150 euros
Sold: 248 euros
Eve, Paris
June 18, 2012 (lot M049)
Specialist: Sylvie Daniel

Estimate: 70–90 euros
Sold: 87 euros
Artcurial, Paris
June 27, 2011 (lot 103)
Specialist: PB Fashion

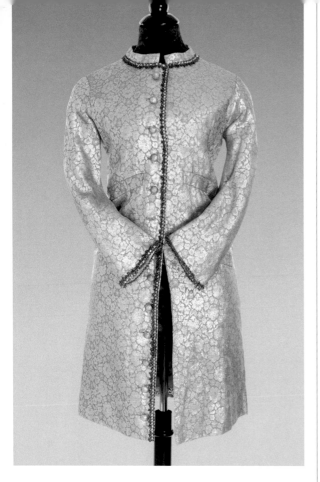

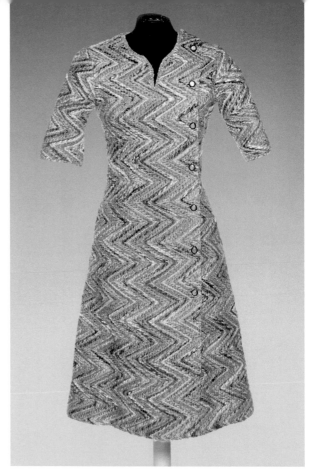

YVES SAINT LAURENT

N° 2844
COUTURE, 1962

Green silk tunic with gold lamé floral brocade, trimmed with metallic-colored braid; short stand-up collar; single-breasted closure with covered buttons; two mock pockets. Label.

ICONOGRAPHY: This look was featured at the first Yves Saint Laurent fashion show in Paris, in 1962.

Estimate: 2,500–3,500 pounds
Sold: 2,000 pounds
Christie's, London
December 1, 2011 (lot 96)
Specialist: Patricia Frost

CHANEL

N° 37800
COUTURE

Multicolored tweed coatdress in a stylized horizontal chevron pattern; round neckline with small opening; asymmetric closing; three-quarter sleeves; flared skirt. Label.

PROVENANCE: From Mademoiselle Chanel's personal wardrobe, sold at Christie's in December 1978.

Estimate: 1,500–2,000 pounds
Sold: 4,375 pounds
Christie's, London
December 3, 2009 (lot 230)
Specialist: Patricia Frost

YVES SAINT LAURENT

COUTURE, Fall/Winter 1966

Trapeze dress of multicolored woven silk enhanced with gold sequins; round neckline; short sleeves. No label.

ICONOGRAPHY: A similar style appears in *L'Officiel 1,000 Modèles, Yves Saint Laurent 1962–2002*, special edition no. 14, éditions Jalou.

Estimate: 400–500 euros
Sold: 875 euros
Cornette de Saint Cyr, Paris
June 30, 2012 (lot 331)
Specialists: D. Chombert and F. Sternbach

JEANNE LANVIN

COUTURE

Multicolored cotton dress adorned with gold and silver lamé and trimmed with braiding; round neckline; loop closure with pearl buttons along opening; short sleeves; draped mock belt at hipline.

Estimate: 120–150 euros
Sold: 186 euros
Eve, Paris
October 25, 2011 (lot M053)
Specialist: Sylvie Daniel

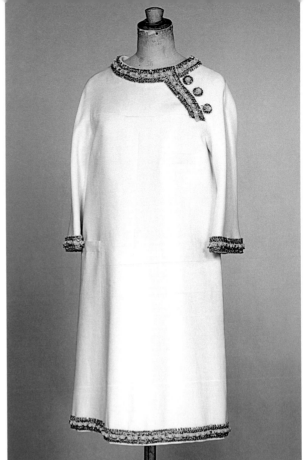

ANONYMOUS

VALENTINO

COUTURE

COUTURE, Summer 1967

Black silk gazar cocktail dress; round neckline; sheer sleeves and slightly flared skirt trimmed with ivory frayed silk. Worn with a satin belt adorned with a bow and a petal boa.

Ivory linen dress enhanced with gold and silver metallic thread embroidery and white and turquoise beads; scoop neckline; diagonal button-and-loop closure; two horizontal mock pockets; three-quarter raglan sleeves. Label "Valentino Roma."

Estimate: 250–350 euros
Sold: 438 euros
Artcurial, Paris
June 11, 2012 (lot 374)
Specialist: PB Fashion

Estimate: 800–1,000 euros
Sold: 1,625 euros
Cornette de Saint Cyr, Paris
June 30, 2012 (lot 188)
Specialists: D. Chombert and F. Sternbach

CHANEL

JEANNE LANVIN

COUTURE

N° 55242
COUTURE
by Antonio Castillo

Black cocktail dress with chiffon bustier; flared skirt with sunray pleated ruffles. Black label, white lettering.

Black velvet cocktail dress embroidered with beads and rhinestones in an arabesque design; boat neckline; straight skirt. White label, black lettering.

Estimate: 1,000–1,200 euros
Sold: 2,125 euros
Cornette de Saint Cyr, Paris
February 13, 2012 (lot 214)
Specialists: D. Chombert and F. Sternbach

Estimate: 200–300 euros
Sold: 563 euros
Cornette de Saint Cyr, Paris
July 2, 2010 (lot 119)
Specialists: D. Chombert and F. Sternbach

CHRISTIAN DIOR

N °106420

COUTURE, Fall/Winter 1960–1961
by Yves Saint Laurent

Chocolate brown lace cocktail dress; square neckline; short scalloped full sleeves, similar hem design on gathered, low-waist full skirt.

<u>PROVENANCE</u>: Brooklyn Museum.

Estimate: 600–800 dollars
Sold: 2,040 dollars
Augusta Auctions, New York
March 21, 2012 (lot 294)
Specialist: Karen E. Augusta

CHRISTIAN DIOR

COUTURE

Bottle-green mock two-piece dress in guipure with scalloped edging; square neckline; three-quarter sleeves; wide ribbon with a bow at the waist. Label "Christian Dior New York."

Estimate: 300–500 dollars
Sold: 519 dollars
Leslie Hindman Auctioneers, Chicago
September 16, 2010 (lot 278)
Specialist: Abigail Rutherford

NORMAN NORELL

JAMES GALANOS

COUTURE

COUTURE

Black silk satin cocktail dress; round neckline; bustier adorned with bow; drop waist; gathered skirt. No label.

Black silk taffeta cocktail dress; V-neckline with ruffle; large bow at the waist; gathered skirt.

Estimate: 400–600 dollars
Sold: 580 dollars
Leslie Hindman Auctioneers, Chicago
April 17, 2012 (lot 20)
Specialist: Abigail Rutherford

Estimate: 300–500 dollars
Sold: 732 dollars
Leslie Hindman Auctioneers, Chicago
April 17, 2012 (lot 34)
Specialist: Abigail Rutherford

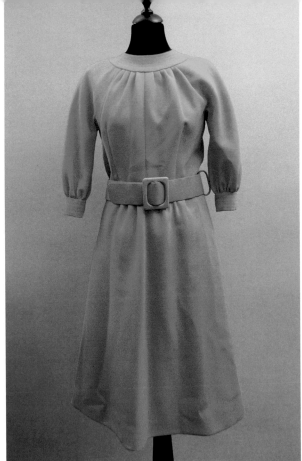

BALENCIAGA

NINA RICCI

N º 102018
COUTURE, Summer 1967

PRÊT-À-PORTER

Chartreuse and pink shantung silk shirtdress; turndown collar; single-breasted closure; cuffs; tie belt. White label, black lettering.

Cotton-candy pink wool crepe dress; round neckline; bottom of half sleeves enhanced with topstitching; bodice and flared skirt are slightly gathered; wide belt with buckle. Label "Nina Ricci Boutique."

Estimate: 1,500–1,800 euros
Sold: 1,875 euros
Cornette de Saint Cyr, Paris
June 30, 2012 (lot 326)
Specialists: D. Chombert and F. Sternbach

Estimate: 80–120 euros
Sold: 114 euros
Bailly-Pommery & Voutier, Paris
April 23, 2012 (lot 348)
Specialist: PB Fashion

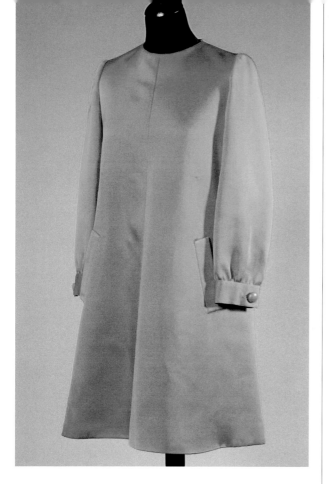
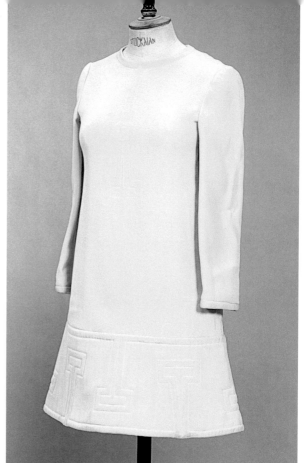

CHRISTIAN DIOR

PIERRE CARDIN

N° 50489
COUTURE, Fall/Winter 1966
by Marc Bohan

PRÊT-À-PORTER

Raspberry pink silk gabardine trapeze dress; round neckline; buttons down the back and on the cuffs; two slant pockets. White label, black lettering.

Light salmon–colored silk crepe A-line dress with geometric topstitching design; round neckline; quilting at the hemline; rolled hem at the sleeves. Label "Pierre Cardin Boutique."

Estimate: 100–150 euros
Sold: 500 euros
Artcurial, Paris
June 11, 2012 (lot 469)
Specialist: PB Fashion

Estimate: 300–400 euros
Sold: 813 euros
Cornette de Saint Cyr, Paris
June 30, 2012 (lot 381)
Specialists: D. Chombert and F. Sternbach

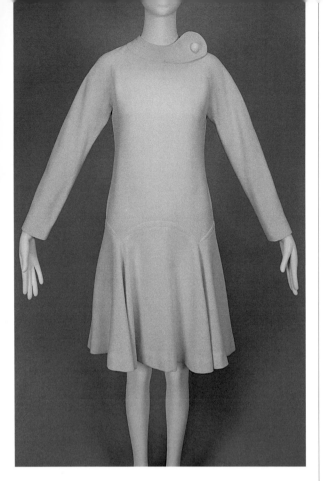
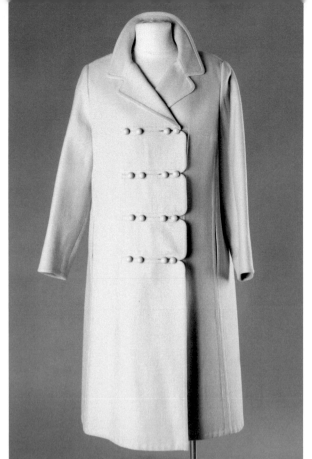

PIERRE CARDIN

PIERRE BALMAIN

N º 162623

COUTURE

COUTURE

Ivory wool dress; round neckline with topstitching; tab
neckline with a button; long raglan sleeves; scallop design
at the hipline above godet skirt. Label "Pierre Cardin Paris
New York."

Winter white wool coat; size 9/10; notched collar; double-
breasted closure with notched facings, similar design
repeated on the half belt; side-seam pockets. White label,
black lettering.

Estimate: 200–400 dollars
Sold: 720 dollars

Charles A. Whitaker Auction Company, Philadelphia
October 28-29, 2011 (lot 727)
Specialist: Charles A. Whitaker

Estimate: 100–150 euros
Sold: 140 euros

Artcurial, Paris
November 15, 2010 (lot 465)
Specialist: PB Fashion

EMANUEL UNGARO

N° 1746-10-69
COUTURE, Fall/Winter 1969

Yellow wool A-line coat; turndown neckline; single-breasted closure; cutouts and topstitching design; two breast pockets with flaps, two curved pockets at the hipline; cuffs. White label, black lettering.

Estimate: 600–700 euros
Sold: 1,187 euros
Cornette de Saint Cyr, Paris
July 3, 2009 (lot 265)
Specialists: D. Chombert and F. Sternbach

YVES SAINT LAURENT

N° 013757
COUTURE

Red wool coat; turndown round collar; double-breasted closure; two flap pockets; long sleeves with adjustable tabs at the wrists; half belt.

Estimate: 80–100 euros
Sold: 620 euros
Camard & Associés, Paris
March 18, 2012 (lot 124)

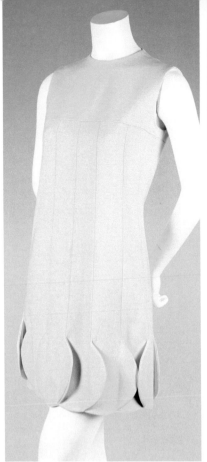
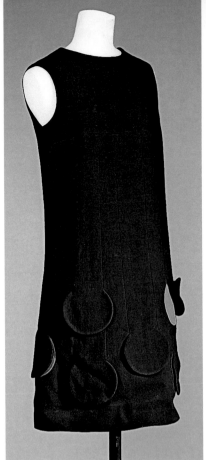

PIERRE CARDIN

COUTURE

Ivory wool crepe mini dress; vertical sections end in small round panels along the hemline.

PIERRE CARDIN

COUTURE

Black wool crepe dinner dress; jewel neckline; bottom of dress is adorned with round floating petals over a red crepe background. White label, black lettering.

PIERRE CARDIN

COUTURE

Pumpkin-colored wool crepe straight dress; round neckline enhanced with large scalloping, reprised on the long-sleeve seams; tie belt. Worn under a cape that attaches to the left shoulder with a snap; hem trimmed in crystal fox. White label, black lettering.

Estimate: 300–500 dollars
Sold: 1,952 dollars
Leslie Hindman Auctioneers, Chicago
April 21, 2010 (lot 60)
Specialist: Abigail Rutherford

Estimate: 500–600 euros
Sold: 1,375 euros
Cornette de Saint Cyr, Paris
July 3, 2009 (lot 314)
Specialists: D. Chombert and
F. Sternbach

Estimate: 1,500–1,700 euros
Sold: 6,250 euros
Cornette de Saint Cyr, Paris
July 3, 2009 (lot 269)
Specialists: D. Chombert and
F. Sternbach

BALENCIAGA

JACQUES HEIM

N° 102783
COUTURE
(Button: Roger Jean-Pierre)

PRÊT-À-PORTER

Black wool suit; jacket with asymmetric collar, notched on one side; jewel button enhanced by rounded yoke, design repeated as a mock pocket; flared skirt. White label, black lettering.

Black wool crepe dinner dress; round neckline with geometric cutout opening; cutouts repeated at the bottom of slightly flared skirt. Label "Heim Actualité."

Estimate: 800–900 euros
Sold: 12,500 euros
Cornette de Saint Cyr, Paris
June 30, 2012 (lot 187)
Specialists: D. Chombert and F. Sternbach

Estimate: 100–150 euros
Sold: 150 euros
Artcurial, Paris
November 25, 2011 (lot 128)
Specialist: PB Fashion

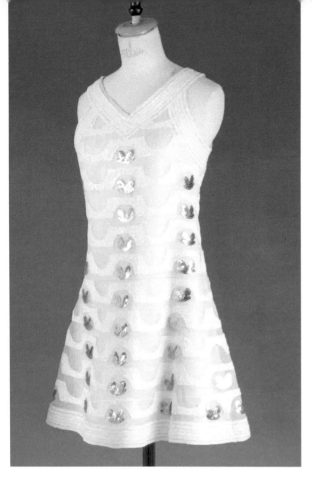

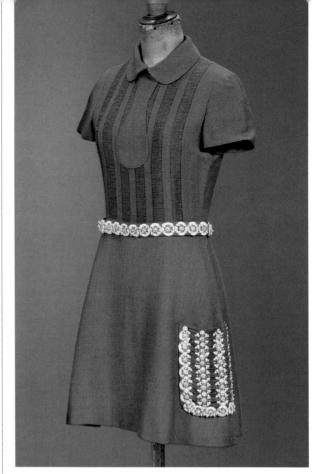

COURRÈGES

JACQUES ESTEREL

COUTURE

COUTURE

White organdy A-line cocktail dress, embroidered with purple and tone-on-tone sequins in a geometric garland adorned with butterflies; V-neckline; halter top armhole. White label, black lettering.

Fuchsia silk and linen mini dress; openwork striped design on bodice; rounded turndown collar; tear-shaped inset; bias-cut skirt; pockets and belt are adorned with Rhodoid, rhinestones, and sequins. White label, black lettering.

<u>BIBLIOGRAPHY</u>: The identical dress appears on p. 137 in *Courrèges*, Erik Orsenna, éditions Xavier Barral, 2008.

Estimate: 1,300–1,400 euros
Sold: 2,875 euros
Gros & Delettrez, Paris
December 19, 2011 (lot 158)
Specialists: D. Chombert and F. Sternbach

Estimate: 200–300 euros
Sold: 625 euros
Cornette de Saint Cyr, Paris
June 30, 2012 (lot 403)
Specialists: D. Chombert and F. Sternbach

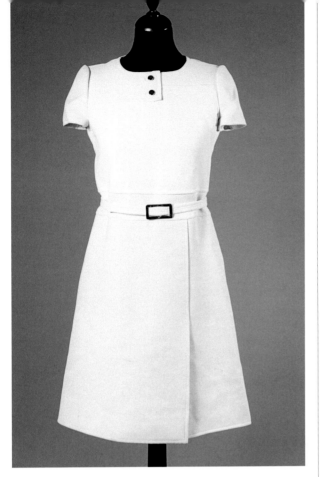

COURRÈGES

N º 036203
COUTURE

Ivory wool crepe dress; round neckline with two gold metal buttons; wraparound flared skirt; belt with a gold metal buckle. Label "Courrèges Couture Future."

Estimate: 60–80 euros
Sold: 250 euros
Artcurial, Paris
June 11, 2012 (lot 309)
Specialist: PB Fashion

COURRÈGES

COUTURE

Pink wool crepe day ensemble; sleeveless dress with buttons; empire waist and flared skirt; short-sleeve jacket; turndown collar; single-breasted closure with two patch pockets.
<u>PROVENANCE</u>: Constance St. Clair Estate.

Estimate: 100–200 dollars
Sold: 1,080 dollars
Augusta Auctions, New York
March 21, 2012 (lot 97)
Specialist: Karen E. Augusta

COURRÈGES

COURRÈGES

COURRÈGES

COUTURE

COUTURE

COUTURE, 1967

Navy blue wool crepe day ensemble; sleeveless single-breasted jacket; turndown collar; oval inlays; flared skirt (belt is missing).

PROVENANCE: Barbara A. Walter, Santa Rosa, California.

Ivory wool crepe dress; geometric neckline and asymmetric closing with buttons; slightly flared skirt. Label "Courrèges exclusively for Bonwit Teller."

Black wool crepe coat; notch collar; double-breasted closure with gold-toned buttons, repeated at the cuffs, on the two patch pockets, and the half belt.

Estimate: 400–600 dollars
Sold: 915 dollars

Leslie Hindman Auctioneers, Chicago
December 6, 2011 (lot 43)

Specialist: Abigail Rutherford

Estimate: 500–700 dollars
Sold: 915 dollars

Leslie Hindman Auctioneers, Chicago
December 16, 2010 (lot 269)

Specialist: Abigail Rutherford

Estimate: 600–800 dollars
Sold: 1,342 dollars

Leslie Hindman Auctioneers, Chicago
April 11–12, 2011 (lot 65)

Specialist: Abigail Rutherford

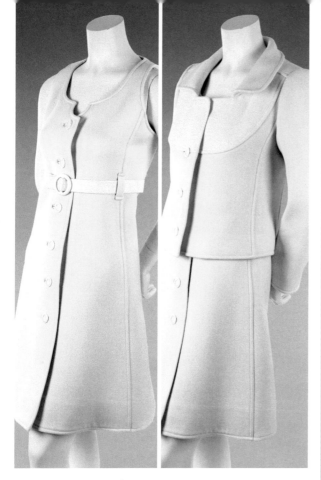

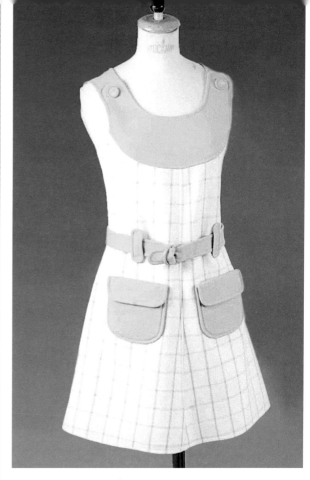

COURRÈGES

COURRÈGES

N° 38445
COUTURE

COUTURE

Lime green and ivory wool crepe ensemble; sleeveless mod dress has a rounded notched collar and buttons down the front; empire waist with a white leather belt; cropped jacket; turndown collar; single-breasted closure with a yoke.

White and green check A-line dress in wool; round collar with buttoned straps; two slightly rounded patch pockets; belt. White label, black lettering.

Estimate: 1,000–2,000 dollars
Sold: 1,464 dollars
Leslie Hindman Auctioneers, Chicago
April 21, 2010 (lot 65)
Specialist: Abigail Rutherford

Estimate: 500–550 euros
Sold: 813 euros
Gros & Delettrez, Paris
December 19, 2011 (lot 183)
Specialists: D. Chombert and F. Sternbach

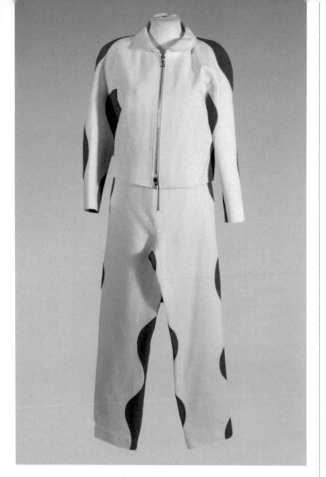

COURRÈGES

COURRÈGES

PRÊT-À-PORTER

PRÊT-À-PORTER

Red and white crepe ski suit; jacket has turndown collar; one-piece jumpsuit and the jacket have zippers. No label.

BIBLIOGRAPHY: A similar style appears on p. 91 in *Courrèges*, Erik Orsenna, éditions Xavier Barral, 2008.

Orange vinyl cropped jacket; adjustable stand-up collar; snap button closure repeated on wrists. White logo on the front.

Estimate: 400–500 euros
Sold: 620 euros
Ève, Paris
October 25, 2011 (lot M012)
Specialist: Sylvie Daniel

Estimate: 400–600 dollars
Sold: 475 dollars
Leslie Hindman Auctioneers, Chicago
April 21, 2010 (lot 66)
Specialist: Abigail Rutherford

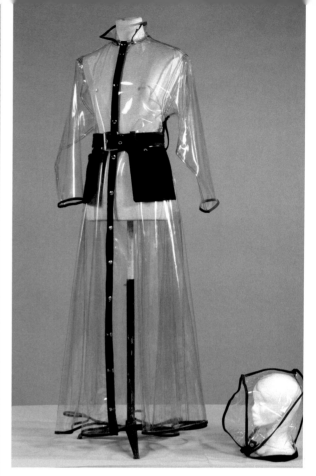

COURRÈGES

COURRÈGES

N º 102570
COUTURE

PRÊT-À-PORTER

Cropped jacket with white mink strips over cream silk, trimmed with orange vinyl; turndown collar; snap closure; flap pockets. Worn with a maxi skirt with snaps. White label, black lettering.

Maxi-length sheer vinyl raincoat with khaki trim; small collar with removable hood; snap closure on black cotton facing, repeated on pockets; belt. No label.
ICONOGRAPHY: Twiggy wore this raincoat in 1967 in New York.

Estimate: 3,000–3,500 euros
Sold: 6,250 euros
Cornette de Saint Cyr, Paris
July 3, 2009 (lot 275)
Specialists: D. Chombert and F. Sternbach

Estimate: 1,000–1,200 euros
Sold: 1,500 euros
Cornette de Saint Cyr, Paris
June 30, 2012 (lot 48)
Specialists: D. Chombert and F. Sternbach

ANONYMOUS

COUTURE

Silkscreen tissue paper dress with "Campbell's Soup" design.

Estimate: 1,000–1,500 pounds
Sold: 2,000 pounds
Christie's, London
December 3, 2009 (lot 283)
Specialist: Patricia Frost

ROBERTA DI CAMERINO

PRÊT-À-PORTER

Trompe-l'œil printed jersey dress with Scottish vest in red, burgundy, and brown plaid; turndown collar; button closure with logo; brown and black pleated skirt. No label.

Estimate: 60–80 euros
Sold: 87 euros
Bailly-Pommery & Voutier, Paris
September 26, 2011 (lot 460)
Specialist: PB Fashion

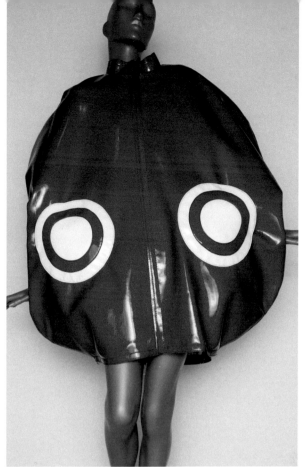

PIERRE CARDIN

PIERRE CARDIN

COUTURE

PRÊT-À-PORTER

Bright red leather dress has geometric yoke that ties around the neck; A-line mini skirt; belt with buckle.

Bright red vinyl "Satellite" cape; stand-up collar; front zipper; arm slits; white bull's-eye patch pockets. Label "Création Pierre Cardin."

BIBLIOGRAPHY: The same design appears on p. 49 in *Pierre Cardin: 60 Years of Innovation*, Jean-Pascal Hesse, Assouline, 2010; Patrick Bertrand's photograph appears in *L'Officiel*, March 1969.

Estimate: 1,000–2,000 dollars
Sold: 3,172 dollars
Leslie Hindman Auctioneers, Chicago
April 11–12, 2011 (lot 67)
Specialist: Abigail Rutherford

Estimate: 2.000–3,000 dollars
Sold: 20,400 dollars
Augusta Auctions, New York
March 21, 2012 (lot 300)
Specialist: Karen E. Augusta

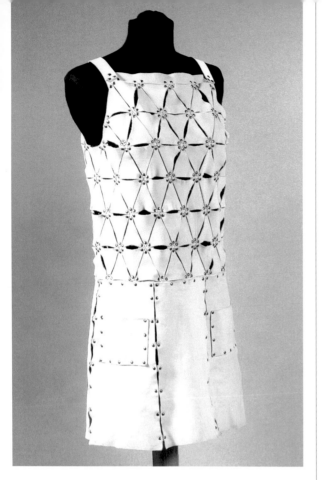 

PACO RABANNE

PACO RABANNE

COUTURE

COUTURE

Low-waisted mini dress made of white leather triangular patches held together with small rivets; square neckline; two patch pockets on the skirt. No label.

Mini dress made of navy, white, and clear Rhodoid discs arranged in a geometric chevron pattern; boat neckline; pagoda sleeves.

Estimate: 1,200–1,500 euros
Sold: 3,875 euros
Cornette de Saint Cyr, Paris
June 30, 2012 (lot 162)
Specialists: D. Chombert and F. Sternbach

Estimate: 3,000–5,000 pounds
Sold: 6,000 pounds
Christie's, London
December 1, 2011 (lot 78)
Specialist: Patricia Frost

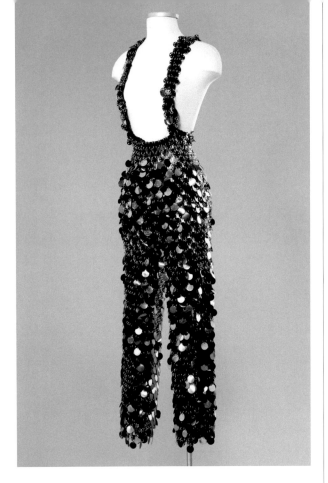

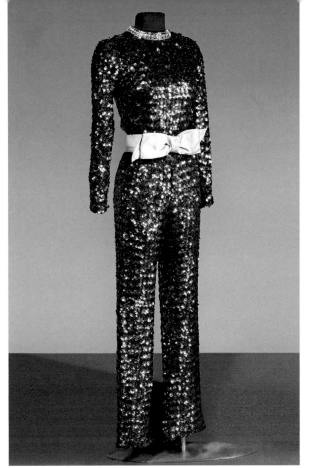

PACO RABANNE

PIERRE CARDIN

COUTURE

COUTURE

Evening overalls made of black and silver Rhodoid discs linked by small metallic rings. No label.

Black sequined jumpsuit; round neckline embroidered with rhinestones and beads in a floral design; chartreuse satin belt with a bow. White label, black lettering.

Estimate: 2,000–3,000 euros
Sold: 2,502 euros
Artcurial, Paris
January 30, 2012 (lot 195)
Specialist: PB Fashion

Estimate: 1,300–1,500 euros
Sold: 1,625 euros
Cornette de Saint Cyr, Paris
July 3, 2009 (lot 197)
Specialists: D. Chombert and F. Sternbach

CHRISTIAN DIOR

N ° I44302
COUTURE, 1968
by Marc Bohan

Ivory silk dress with check pattern; high collar; buttoned cuffs; tie belt; pleated skirt.

Estimate: 800–1,200 dollars
Sold: 1,037 dollars
Leslie Hindman Auctioneers, Chicago
April 17, 2012 (lot 97)
Specialist: Abigail Rutherford

YVES SAINT LAURENT

N ° 23029
COUTURE, Spring/Summer 1969

Purple organdy cocktail dress, entirely covered with layered rows of purple and white silk fringe; round neckline. White label, black lettering.

BIBLIOGRAPHY: Similar styles appear on p. 76 in the exhibition catalog *Yves Saint Laurent*, Metropolitan Museum of Art, New York, December 14, 1983–September 2, 1984, Clarkson N. Potter.

Estimate: 3,500–4,000 euros
Sold: 3,750 euros
Cornette de Saint Cyr, Paris
July 3, 2009 (lot 160)
Specialists: D. Chombert and F. Sternbach

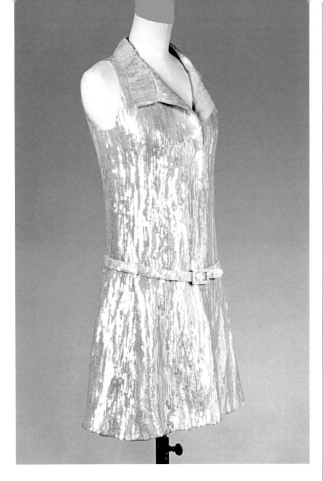

JEAN PATOU

JEAN PATOU

COUTURE
by Michel Goma

COUTURE
by Michel Goma

Ivory gazar evening mini dress entirely embroidered with star-shaped mother-of-pearl sequins; halter top armholes; turndown collar with small V-neckline; low waist; slightly flared skirt; thin belt with a buckle. White label, navy lettering.

Baby blue silk crepe evening gown with embroidered pearl and rhinestone trim; boat neckline; low square décolleté at the back enhanced with a bow; wraparound skirt.

Estimate: 800–1,200 euros
Sold: 1,487 euros
Artcurial, Paris
June 27, 2011 (lot 96)
Specialist: PB Fashion

Estimate: 1,000–2,000 dollars
Sold: 4,392 dollars
Leslie Hindman Auctioneers, Chicago
April 11–12, 2011 (lot 70)
Specialist: Abigail Rutherford

OSCAR DE LA RENTA

CHRISTIAN DIOR

N° 149228
COUTURE
by Marc Bohan

COUTURE

Orange and gold brocade ensemble; short sleeves; round neckline with geometric cutout at the neck; slightly flared skirt has mink trim, repeated on the collar of the zippered jacket.

Gold, yellow, and brown silk brocade cocktail dress in a psychedelic pattern; jewel neckline; single-breasted closure with ball-shaped buttons, repeated at the cuffs; slightly gathered low-waist skirt. Worn with a string tie belt ending with ostrich feathers attached to a gold clip. White label, black lettering.

Estimate: 300–500 dollars
Sold: 2,318 dollars
Leslie Hindman Auctioneers, Chicago
April 11–12, 2011 (lot 80)
Specialist: Abigail Rutherford

Estimate: 700–800 euros
Sold: 875 euros
Cornette de Saint Cyr, Paris
June 30, 2012 (lot 272)
Specialists: D. Chombert and F. Sternbach

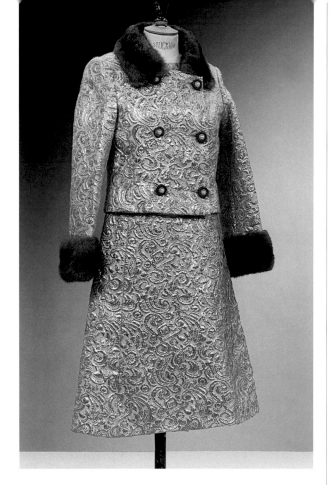

PIERRE BALMAIN

N° 145198
COUTURE

Cocktail ensemble in gold and silver brocade with stylized arabesque design; sleeveless A-line dress has boat neckline; bodice enhanced with openwork design; double-breasted short jacket with jeweled closure; turndown collar and cuffs adorned with wild mink. White label, black lettering.

Estimate: 400–600 euros
Sold: 475 euros
Cornette de Saint Cyr, Paris
June 30, 2012 (lot 61)
Specialists: D. Chombert and F. Sternbach

YVES SAINT LAURENT

N° 23705
COUTURE, Fall/Winter 1969

Brown panne velvet coat; round neckline; cuffs and hemline trimmed with rooster feathers; double-breasted closure; topstitching at the waist; skirt with small godets. White label, black lettering.

Estimate: 1,200–1,500 euros
Sold: 1,375 euros
Cornette de Saint Cyr, Paris
June 30, 2012 (lot 100)
Specialists: D. Chombert and F. Sternbach

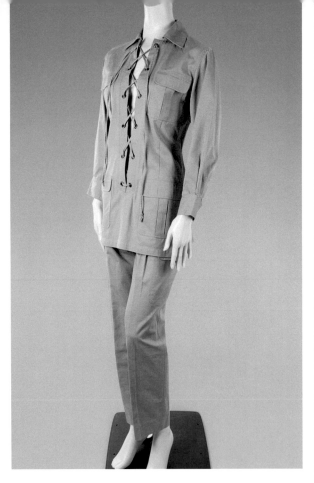

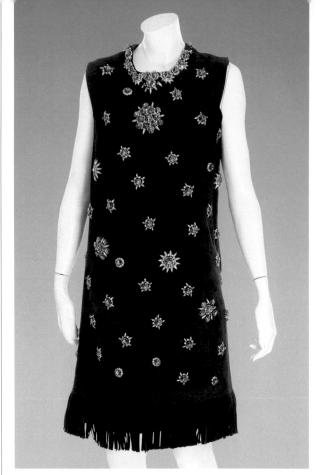

YVES SAINT LAURENT

PRÊT-À-PORTER, Spring/Summer 1968

Khaki cotton safari suit; tunic with front lacing down to waist; turndown collar; four patch pockets; cuffs; pants. Label "Saint Laurent Rive Gauche."

BIBLIOGRAPHY: Close-up of the tunic appears on p. 134 in the exhibition catalog *Saint Laurent Rive Gauche: Fashion Revolution*, Fondation Pierre Bergé-Yves Saint Laurent, March 5–July 17, 2011, Abrams, 2012.

Estimate: 1,000–2,000 dollars
Sold: 6,710 dollars
Leslie Hindman Auctioneers, Chicago
April 21, 2010 (lot 188)
Specialist: Abigail Rutherford

YVES SAINT LAURENT

N° 019926
COUTURE, Spring/Summer 1967
Model "Africaine"

Brown suede dress with stylized flower motifs of cabochons and rhinestones; geometric armholes; fringed hem. Label.

BIBLIOGRAPHY: The same dress appears on p. 191 in the exhibition catalog *Yves Saint Laurent*, Florence Müller, Farid Chenoune, Petit Palais, Musée des Beaux Arts de la Ville de Paris, March 11–August 29, 2010, Abrams, 2010.

Estimate: 7,000–8,000 pounds
Sold: 8,125 pounds
Christie's, London
December 1, 2011 (lot 46)
Specialist: Patricia Frost

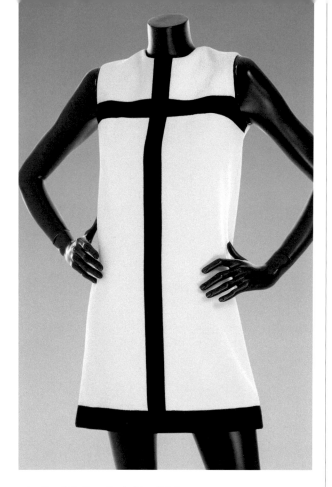

YVES SAINT LAURENT

N° 10576
COUTURE, Fall/Winter 1965–1966
Model "Mondrian"

Ivory wool dress; gold and black button. Label.

BIBLIOGRAPHY: The same dress in other colors appears on p. 84 and p. 85 in the exhibition catalog *Yves Saint Laurent*, Diana Vreeland, Metropolitan Museum of New York, December 4, 1983–September 2, 1984; in a sketch on p. 221 in the catalog *Yves Saint Laurent, 28 ans de creation*, Musée des Arts de la Mode, Paris, May 30–October 26, 1986, Herscher, 1986. A similar design is on p. 50 in *Yves Saint Laurent Images of Design, 1958-1988*, Ebury Press, 1988; on p. 71 in the exhibition catalog *Yves Saint Laurent*, Florence Müller and Farid Chenoune, Petit Palais, Musée des Beaux Arts de la Ville de Paris, March 11–August 29, 2010, Abrams, 2010.

Estimate: 25,000–30,000 pounds
Sold: 30,000 pounds
Christie's, London
December 1, 2011 (lot 45)
Specialist: Patricia Frost

YVES SAINT LAURENT

COUTURE, Fall/Winter 1966–1967
(Fabric: Racine)

Turquoise, red, green, and purple wool jersey dress; slightly asymmetric boat neckline; colorblock effect. White label, black lettering.

BIBLIOGRAPHY: The same style appears on p. 181 of *L'Art de la Mode*, no. 2835, September 1966 and on p. 85 of *Panorama des Collections—Jardin des Modes*, Fall/Winter 1966–1967.

Estimate: 7,000–7,500 euros
Sold: 22,499 euros
Cornette de Saint Cyr, Paris
July 3, 2009 (lot 220)
Specialists: D. Chombert and F. Sternbach

 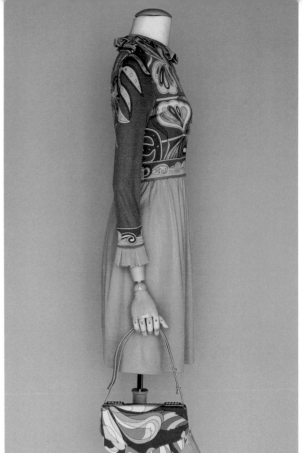

EMILIO PUCCI

EMILIO PUCCI

PRÊT-À-PORTER

PRÊT-À-PORTER

Silk jersey hostess dress in a stylized paisley print in shades of pink, red, white, and black; boat neckline; three-quarter sleeves.

Jersey dress; bodice in a yellow and orange stylized floral motif; pleated ruffles at the neck and cuffs; flowing yellow skirt, slightly gathered at the waist. Shown with a matching handbag.

Estimate: 400–600 dollars
Sold: 1,098 dollars
Leslie Hindman Auctioneers, Chicago
September 20, 2011 (lot 53)
Specialist: Abigail Rutherford

Estimate: 200–300 dollars
Sold: 720 dollars
Augusta Auctions, New York
March 21, 2010 (lot 98)
Specialist: Karen E. Augusta

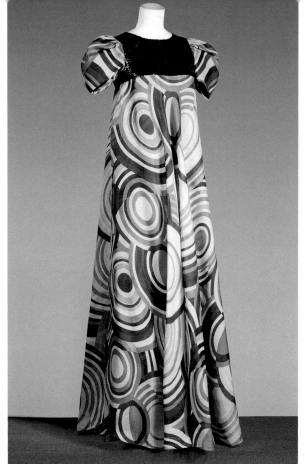

EMILIO PUCCI

PIERRE CARDIN

PRÊT-À-PORTER

COUTURE

Silk jersey print dress with a geometric pattern in shades of turquoise, cream, black, and indigo; boat neckline; three-quarter sleeves; self belt. Label "Emilio Pucci Florence—Italy."

Multicolored print gazar evening gown with a psychedelic pattern; black sequined panel at the top of the bodice gives the effect of an empire waistline; short baby-doll sleeves; body of dress embellished with two large full and floating panels. White label, black lettering.

Estimate: 200–300 dollars
Sold: 360 dollars
Charles A. Whitaker Auction Company, Philadelphia
April 27–28, 2012 (lot 899)
Specialist: Charles A. Whitaker

Estimate: 1,700–2,000 euros
Sold: 2,125 euros
Cornette de Saint Cyr, Paris
July 3, 2009 (lot 233)
Specialists: D. Chombert and F. Sternbach

NINA RICCI

COUTURE
by Gérard Pibyt

Evening gown of ivory linen embroidered with multicolored sequins in a fruit and flower pattern; rounded neckline with an opening and a button; short sleeves, waist, and hem trimmed with apple green inlay; long flared skirt with two slant pockets. No label.

Estimate: 200–400 dollars
Sold: 660 dollars
Augusta Auctions, New York
March 21, 2012 (lot 13)
Specialist: Karen A. Augusta

PIERRE BALMAIN

PRÊT-À-PORTER

Printed gazar gown in a floral psychedelic pattern against a pumpkin-colored background; V-neckline décolleté has pleated ruffle reminiscent of a jabot, repeated at the wrists; flared skirt; green satin belt. Label "Pierre Balmain Boutique."

Estimate: 300–350 euros
Sold: 625 euros
Cornette de Saint Cyr, Paris
April 4, 2012 (lot 552)
Specialists: D. Chombert and F. Sternbach

PIERRE BALMAIN

PRÊT-À-PORTER

Emerald green wool twill ensemble; bodice has round neckline embroidered with gold and silver metallic beads in a crisscross pattern, same trim is repeated at the edge of the three-quarter sleeves; long flared skirt. Label "Balmain Boutique."

Estimate: 600–800 dollars
Sold: 2,160 dollars
Christie's, New York
December 3–17, 2011 (lot 1727)
Specialist: Patricia Frost

PIERRE BALMAIN

GIVENCHY

N º 141502
COUTURE, 1967

PRÊT-À-PORTER

Gold brocade evening gown; stripes of geometric patterns in shades of pale blue, apricot, gray, and black embellished with gold lamé; empire waist, hem, and three-quarter sleeves are trimmed in black velvet; full flared skirt.

PROVENANCE: Brooklyn Museum.

Printed silk evening gown in a cherry and turquoise geometric print; small stand-up collar with an opening at the back; single cuff; skirt is slightly gathered. Worn with a matching belt with buckle. Label "Givenchy Nouvelle Boutique."

Estimate: 300–500 dollars
Sold: 900 dollars
Augusta Auctions, New York
March 21, 2012 (lot 288)
Specialist: Karen A. Augusta

Estimate: 40–60 euros
Sold: 217 euros
Bailly-Pommery & Voutier, Paris
September 26, 2011 (lot 192)
Specialist: PB Fashion

GIVENCHY

CHRISTIAN DIOR

N° 362413

PRÊT-À-PORTER

PRÊT-À-PORTER
by Marc Bohan

White piqué flared cotton skirt with a print of small red and green tulips.

Evening skirt of black duchess satin embroidered in a red and gold floral pattern; large bow at the waist. Label "Christian Dior Boutique."

Estimate: 30–50 euros
Sold: 240 euros
Bailly-Pommery & Voutier, Paris
April 23, 2012 (lot 164)
Specialist: PB Fashion

Estimate: 200–300 euros
Sold: 682 euros
Artcurial, Paris
June 27, 2011 (lot 128)
Specialist: PB Fashion

CHRISTIAN DIOR

N º I47229
COUTURE, 1969
by Marc Bohan

Pink and ivory floral-print silk ensemble; asymmetric single-shoulder crossover top with two floating panels; gold metal and white Bakelite belt; cropped flared pants.

Estimate: 500–700 dollars
Sold: 1,952 dollars
Leslie Hindman Auctioneers, Chicago
April 17, 2012 (lot 98)
Specialist: Abigail Rutherford

CARVEN

COUTURE, 1968

Coral silk crepe evening gown; stand-up collar; back zipper; geometric insert under the bustline; floral-pattern design of beads and sequins at the wrists; skirt with a slit on either side. White label, green lettering.

Estimate: 60–80 euros
Sold: 150 euros
Artcurial, Paris
June 11, 2012 (lot 107)
Specialist: PB Fashion

BIBA

PRÊT-À-PORTER

Bottle-green twill ensemble with a design of stylized red pirate ships; blouse with turndown collar; self-covered buttons; turnback cuffs; bell-bottom pants.

PROVENANCE: Brooklyn Museum.

Estimate: 300–500 dollars
Sold: 300 dollars
Augusta Auctions, New York
November 2, 2011 (lot 389)
Specialist: Karen E. Augusta

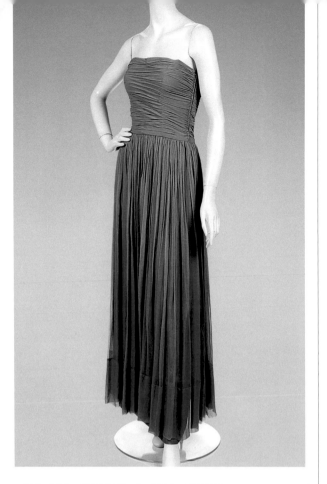

PHILIPPE VENET

CHRISTIAN DIOR

COUTURE

N º 120239
COUTURE, Spring/Summer 1963
by Marc Bohan

Emerald green silk chiffon evening gown; draped bustier over a gathered flowing skirt.

Black organza evening gown with four rows of small ruffles on bodice; rounded neckline embellished with a rose; full skirt with ruffled hem. Label "Christian Dior Paris."

Estimate: 400–600 dollars
Sold: 732 dollars
Leslie Hindman Auctioneers, Chicago
December 6, 2011 (lot 30)
Specialist: Abigail Rutherford

Estimate: 800–1,200 dollars
Sold: 10,800 dollars
Charles A. Whitaker Auction Company, Philadelphia
April 27–28, 2012 (lot 824)
Specialist: Charles A. Whitaker

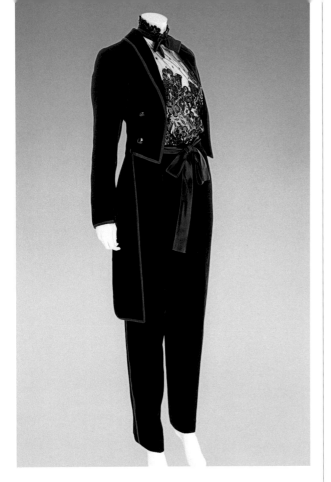

YVES SAINT LAURENT

N° 44743
COUTURE, 1968

Black velvet tuxedo, *le smoking*, with black braid trim; double-breasted tailcoat; shawl collar; trousers with satin stripe down the side. Worn with a sheer silk tulle blouse embroidered with sequins and satin tie-belt. Label.

Estimate: 5,000–8,000 pounds
Sold: 3,000 pounds
Christie's, London
December 1, 2011 (lot 98)
Specialist: Patricia Frost

JEANNE LANVIN

N° 38145
COUTURE
by Antonio Castillo

Black Chantilly lace cocktail dress; bustier visible under the bodice; bow and small gathers at the back of the skirt. White label, black lettering.

Estimate: 180–220 euros
Sold: 620 euros
Artcurial, Paris
June 27, 2011 (lot 93)
Specialist: PB Fashion

NORMAN NORELL

COUTURE, 1968

Ivory silk crepe evening gown; stand-up collar with faux-necklace made of four rows of emerald- and ruby-colored stones and rhinestones; cuffs; long skirt; belt with buckle. No label.

<u>PROVENANCE</u>: Brooklyn Museum.

Estimate: 300–500 dollars
Sold: 510 dollars
Augusta Auctions, New York
November 2, 2011 (lot 384)
Specialist: Karen E. Augusta

JEAN PATOU

COUTURE
(Embroidery: Lesage)

Nude-colored gazar evening gown entirely embroidered with rhinestones, sequins, tear-shaped beads, and gemstones rimmed in silver Lurex; low round décolleté; short sleeves; slightly flared skirt. White label, black lettering.

Estimate: 1,000–1,200 euros
Sold: 2,726 euros
Artcurial, Paris
June 27, 2011 (lot 236)
Specialist: PB Fashion

BALENCIAGA

COUTURE

White tulle sheath evening dress entirely embroidered with braiding, gold metallic thread, and coral, white, and gold beads in a floral pattern; boat neckline. Label "Balenciaga, 10 Avenue George V, Paris."

Estimate: 1,000–2,000 pounds
Sold: 7,500 pounds
Christie's, London
December 1, 2011 (lot 62)
Specialist: Patricia Frost

CARVEN

COUTURE

Multicolored Lurex evening gown in an arabesque pattern; halter neckline; halter-top sleeve; flared skirt. White label, green lettering.

Estimate: 400–600 euros
Sold: 500 euros
Cornette de Saint Cyr, Paris
June 30, 2012 (lot 332)
Specialists: D. Chombert and F. Sternbach

ROBERTO CAPUCCI

COUTURE

Beige chiffon evening gown; drape begins at the neckline; halter neckline; completely open back; flowing skirt; fringed and gold-beaded bolero with stand-up collar.

Estimate: 1,200–1,400 euros
Sold: 2,250 euros
Cornette de Saint Cyr, Paris
June 30, 2012 (lot 160)
Specialists: D. Chombert and F. Sternbach

CHRISTIAN DIOR

JEANNE LANVIN

N° 110561
COUTURE, Spring/Summer 1961
by Marc Bohan

COUTURE

Ivory silk satin evening gown; bustier has slight drape and a black panel that floats over the long flared skirt.
<u>PROVENANCE</u>: Brooklyn Museum.

Black silk velvet evening gown encrusted with taffeta on the front; jewel neckline; skirt slightly gathered at the waist. Worn with a belt with buckle. White label, black lettering.

Estimate: 600–800 dollars
Sold: 4,800 dollars
Augusta Auctions, New York
March 21, 2012 (lot 276)
Specialist: Karen E. Augusta

Estimate: 80–120 euros
Sold: 100 euros
Artcurial, Paris
November 25, 2011 (lot 270)
Specialist: PB Fashion

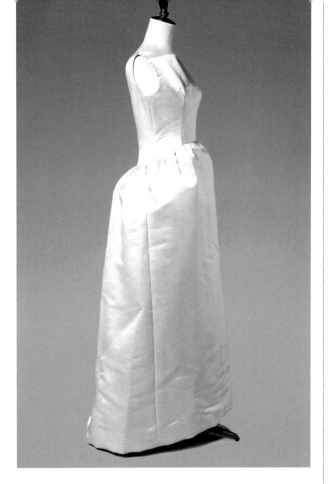

BALENCIAGA

N° 96455
COUTURE, Summer 1960

Ivory Duchess satin evening gown; boat neckline rounded in the back; asymmetric insert at the waist with small gathers over a long skirt. White label, black lettering.

Estimate: 600–800 euros
Sold: 2,726 euros
Artcurial, Paris
June 27, 2011 (lot 402)
Specialist: PB Fashion

CHRISTIAN DIOR

N° 113325
COUTURE, Fall/Winter 1961–1962
by Marc Bohan

Pastel pink moiré evening gown; empire-waist bodice gives the appearance of overlapping panels; over a long, slightly flared skirt. White label, black lettering.

Estimate: 600–800 euros
Sold: 1,627 euros
Artcurial, Paris
June 11, 2012 (lot 385)
Specialist: PB Fashion

Courrèges was revolutionary—he represented the 1960s, the future, a whole new order, a range of possibilities. But, in the recent past, the fashion house has taken a back seat. In late 2011, Frédéric Torloting and Jacques Bungert, former vice-presidents at Young & Rubicam France, took it upon themselves to awaken this sleeping beauty.

ANDRÉ BEFORE COURRÈGES

In the 1940s, while he was a student at the École Nationale des Ponts et Chaussées, André Courrèges could not decide whether to become an architect or a structural engineer. But, in 1950, he joined Balenciaga as a cutter and his decision was made. Like Cristóbal Balenciaga, Courrèges always approached couture with an architect's perspective. When he left the company eleven years later, he took with him a mastery of the craft and the woman who would become his wife, Coqueline. She was, in his words, his "creative complement." Together, they founded the company in 1961 and she would continue to run it long after her husband's retirement in 1994.

COURRÈGES TODAY

Coqueline Courrèges was very protective of the company she and her husband had run for so many years. Reluctant to sell it to the first buyer to come along, it was she who found Frédéric Torloting and Jacques Bungert. She approached them cautiously, and spent several months getting to know them. The two men were fashion novices, yet Madame Courrèges followed her instinct and chose them to take over the reins of the company in 2011.

The two entrepreneurs had found a treasure: a brand with an intact legacy and reputation, a brand that still stood for everything it had created or imposed. "My style," said André Courrèges, "accompanies a silhouette, a way of moving through life." As concerned with style as he was with function, his clothes offered women even more freedom, with new shapes, no waistline, hemlines above the knees, pants for every day, and flat boots. Just as "Le Corbusier brought light into homes," Courrèges said he wanted to "bring light into clothes." His shades of white were nearly iridescent and the color white became one of the fundamental markers of the brand.

Like Courrèges, Torloting and Bungert could see beyond the current trends. Working within a restricted budget, they decided against a star in-house designer, did not hold fashion shows—too costly—or follow the conventional calendar of collection seasons. Instead, they built a simple and playful website where one can browse though a book of monographs and order a classic dress or the mythic reissued vinyl jacket. Respectful of the brand's DNA, Frédéric Torloting and Jacques Bungert have made the most of its history. They have reissued designs that are perfectly suited to today and have announced the eventual sale of no less than 25,000 unsold Courrèges treasures. For the moment, the items are housed in their historic factory in Pau. Currently, they are focusing on fragrance, and have decided to relaunch the timeless Courrèges perfumes, including *Empreinte*, once a bestseller but forgotten today. They are also planning to release a new fragrance, *Blanc de Courrèges*.

— Striped Coat, 1968–1969
Photograph belongs to the Courrèges Archives.

COURRÈGES

LE SMO-KING

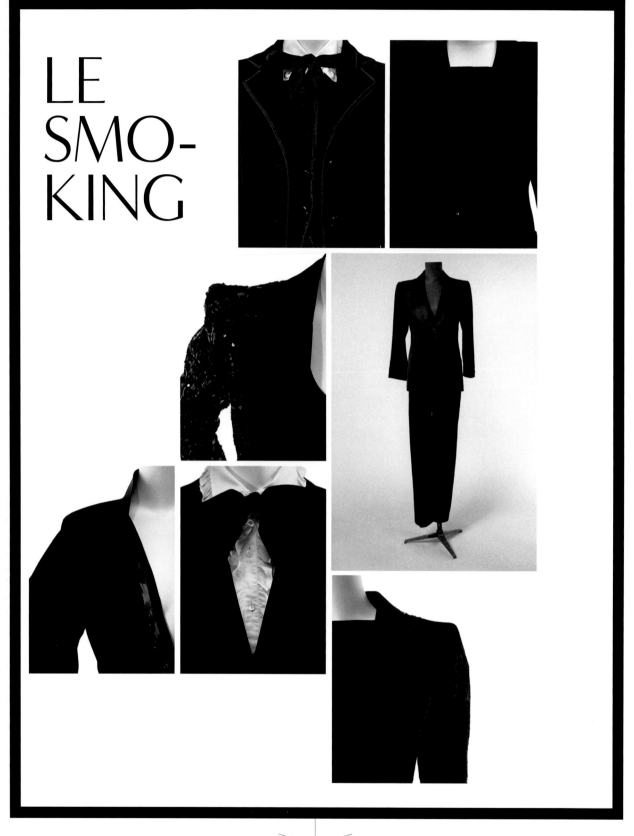

ICONS OF VINTAGE FASHION
Spotlight

LE SMOKING

A highlight at today's auctions, le smoking *has a fascinating past. Worn for special occasions or displayed in museums, the tuxedo has always played an important part in fashion history. When it was first presented as part of a woman's collection, it set off a revolution. One of the most famous depictions of the garment was captured by the photographer Helmut Newton (see book's jacket).*

THE TUXEDO, ONE HUNDRED YEARS BEFORE YSL

Originally, the tuxedo belonged exclusively to a man's wardrobe. Serving as both dressing gown and outerwear, the hybrid jacket was meant to protect a gentleman's clothing from the smoke and ash of cigars and cigarettes. The garment was not especially elegant, but its owner was. A gentleman would slip on the jacket over his evening clothes before entering the smoking room (hence its French name, *le smoking*) and remove it when he returned to the dinner table, free of any telltale smell or ashy residue.

It was only in the 1860s that the tuxedo began to look as it does today. Its distinguishing features, such as silk fabric and the tails, were applied to a regular man's jacket, lending it a new sophistication. This new version of the dinner jacket received the ultimate stamp of approval when it was adopted by the Prince of Wales, the future King Edward VII of England, and crafted by the tailors of Saville Row.

This dark black suit with satin lapels and a matching stripe running down the side of the pants, would become the traditional choice for evening wear, but only for men.

YVES SAINT LAURENT SHAKES THINGS UP

In 1966, Yves Saint Laurent made history, broke all the rules, and caused a multidimensional upheaval when he included the emblematic men's garment in his women's collection. Echoing the growing women's liberation movement, the appropriation of a man's garment by a woman represented a social upheaval. Moreover, the sartorial shift also implied a shift of power as century-old dress codes were shattered. Women now wore pants both when and where it would have previously been frowned upon.

According to Pierre Bergé, "Fashion is not trivial; it reflects society's temperament. Men's clothes represented power. By having women wear them, Saint Laurent passed along the attributes of power from one sex to the other." (From the *Smoking Forever* exhibition held at the Fondation Pierre Bergé—Yves Saint Laurent, October 5, 2005– April 23, 2006.)

VARIATIONS ON THE THEME OF THE TUXEDO

Yves Saint Laurent created many variations of the tuxedo, and featured it in every one of his haute couture collections from 1966 to 2002. *Le smoking* definitely deserved its own exhibition.

By including it in a woman's wardrobe, the couturier liberated the tuxedo from the tacit but nevertheless strict rules that applied to men's clothing. The process amused Yves Saint Laurent as he played with different fabrics and designs, replacing the pants with a skirt, the bow tie with a ribbon, the collar with a jabot, and even going as far as having his muses wear the tuxedo jacket over nothing! A man's garment, when worn by a woman, was suddenly infused with sensuality.

Quickly adopted by Catherine Deneuve, Lauren Bacall, and Betty Catroux, who each wore it in her own exceedingly feminine way, *le smoking* became a fashion icon.

The tuxedo is a mythic, magical piece of clothing. In Yves Saint Laurent's hands, it became a sensation. Its popularity endures and, because of Yves Saint Laurent, it continues to appeal to confident women who prefer a different form of sartorial femininity.

CELEBRITY AUCTIONS

When it comes to the success of auctions of objects belonging to movie stars, media icons, or other mythic celebrities from the world of show business, the sky is the limit.

— Elizabeth Taylor by Francesco Scavullo, 1984.
Silkscreen on canvas, private collection.

ICONS OF VINTAGE FASHION
Spotlight

WHEN SENTIMENTAL VALUE DEFIES THE EXPERTS

Once emotions are involved, irrationality sets in and it becomes impossible to estimate the price of an object. At celebrity auctions, an item is not acquired for what it is but for its ability to evoke the person who was the original owner.

Buyers often feel symbolically connected to the star they idolize by owning something that once belonged to the celebrity in question. Businesses often do the same with the hope that the celebrity's aura will extend to the company. Gérard Darel bought Jackie Kennedy's pearls from Sotheby's in 1998 and the cable-knit sweater Marilyn Monroe wore in *Let's Make Love* (1960) from Christie's in 1999. Not only did these acquisitions capture the headlines and generate publicity for the company, but it also allowed Gérard Darel to replicate the items and make them part of the brand's identity.

The actual value of these objects is more symbolic than monetary and celebrity auctions often set new records. On December 8, 2009, the Kerry Taylor auction house in London offered thirty-six outfits once belonging to Audrey Hepburn. A cocktail dress of Chantilly lace, a Hubert de Givenchy design worn by the actress both at the Oscars and in the film *How to Steal a Million Dollars*, was the highlight of the sale; estimated at between 15,000 and 20,000 pounds, it sold for 60,000 pounds. The auction house had expected global sales results to reach 100,000 pounds—the final figure was 270,000 pounds!

On May 7 and 8, 2011, Julien's Auctions in Beverly Hills presented the "Hollywood Legends" auction featuring two of Lady Diana's dresses (that sold for 144,000 and 132,000 dollars), a cocktail dress and bathing suit once worn by Marilyn Monroe (that sold for 348,000 and 84,000 dollars), a hat worn by Audrey Hepburn in *Funny Face* (15,360 dollars), Gloria Swanson's Louis Vuitton trunk (5,760 dollars), and a necklace that belonged to Angelina Jolie (38,400 dollars).

RECORDS SET BY ELIZABETH TAYLOR

In December 2011, Christie's organized a spectacular auction of Elizabeth Taylor's jewels, clothes, film memorabilia, and other objects.

Estimated at between two and three million dollars, La Peregrina, a pearl discovered by a Panamanian slave in the sixteenth century and offered to Elizabeth Taylor by Richard Burton, sold for 11.8 million dollars, shattering the record for the most expensive pearl jewel ever offered at auction. Records were also broken with the sale of the Taj Mahal, a ruby and gold necklace, and for Taylor's ever-present, famous diamond ring. Each item sold for 8.8 million dollars.

Besides the mythic jewelry, including the celebrated diamonds that were a gift from Richard Burton, other items included Louis Vuitton suitcases, embroidered jackets (one by Versace that featured a likeness of the movie star), evening gowns, and other pieces that bore the names of fashion's most illustrious designers: Christian Dior, Versace, Armani, Yves Saint Laurent, and Givenchy.

A stunning silver encrusted dress by Christian Dior from 1968 was estimated at between 4,000 and 6,000 dollars and

— Beaded evening sweater "The Face," Atelier Versace, circa 1992. Part of "The Collection of Elizabeth Taylor: The Icon and her Haute Couture, Evening Sale (III)" auction at Christie's, December 14, 2011 (sold: 128,500 dollars).

sold for 362,500 dollars. The dress Elizabeth Taylor wore when she married Richard Burton for the second time fetched 62,500 dollars. A black velvet cape worn in 1969 for Princess Grace of Monaco's fortieth birthday celebration sold for 60,000 dollars although it was estimated at 2,000 dollars. A black dress by the couturier Valentino, immortalized in a photograph taken of Elizabeth Taylor by Cecil Beaton in 1969, was estimated at 2,000 dollars but sold for 62,500 dollars.

American reality star Kim Kardashian is a great admirer of Elizabeth Taylor. She bought three jade bracelets (64,900 dollars) and offered her explanation for the auction's phenomenal success in the online magazine instyle.com: "These are more than just pieces of jewelry. [Taylor] wore them all the time during the last years of her life and I think they embody part of her spirit." Whether it is spirit, soul, aura, or power of seduction, each buyer feels that he or she takes away a small part of Taylor's essence—contained within a simple object is an intangible and precious treasure.

Christie's estimated the total sale at between 30 and 50 million dollars; the final number was 154.2 million dollars—the magic of Elizabeth Taylor.

PVC, wood, metal, Rhodoid, cardboard, stone, resin, aluminum, vinyl, rubber, paper…materials one would expect to find in a factory or a kitchen are instead the main features of a collection unlike any other. Jacobo Romano and Jorge Zulueta assembled more than 300 pieces by Paco Rabanne, selected from haute couture shows for the Grupo Accion Instrumental, a collective of artists founded in 1968 in Buenos Aires. The Grupo Accion Instrumental works to revitalize traditional opera.

Artcurial organized the auction of this exceptional collection of theatrical pieces at the Hôtel Drouot on January 30, 2012.

FASHION MATERIALS

Appropriately titled "Fashion Materials," the sale featured a sample of the work of Paco Rabanne, showcasing his avant-garde use of materials.

From his very first collection, cobbled together in his dorm room in 1965, Paco Rabanne surprised the world with his ingenious use of industrial materials, such as aluminum and Rhodoid, that had never before been used in fashion. The following year, he began working with what would become his signature material: small squares of metal, linked together and used to drape the body. At the "Fashion Materials" auction, the squares are featured on a guipure and leather tunic-dress embellished with little metallic bells, rings, and discs; on a spectacular pinafore dress made of metal discs and bells with a bead-trimmed skirt; and on a dress made of oval metal discs and swan feathers.

Using other experimental materials, Rabanne created a dress of Bakelite and aluminum discs with a skirt entirely constructed of silver plastic beads in a crisscross pattern, with a fringe that perfectly replicated the fall and flow of a traditional woven fabric; a dress that was a mosaic of PVC tiles; another dress, in the spirit of the Roaring Twenties, made of small aluminum plates; a headdress adorned with a laser disc; an iris-colored overcoat made of Rhodoid; a cardboard bustier covered in Rhodoid sequins; a bib necklace with corks and bottle necks instead of beads; and yet another dress made entirely of beads and wood cubes.

MUSIC, PLEASE!

Paco Rabanne's materials were shiny, noisy, and sensory. His designs belonged to the world of music; his models danced barefoot, their dresses swaying while the little pieces of metal clinked together, creating a rhythmic clatter.

Not surprisingly, his revolutionary creations lent themselves to the world of opera. They were inspirational and, according to Zulueta and Romano, "his costumes added a new dimension to our work. On stage, 'Haute Couture' became 'Haute Culture' and was at the core of a brand-new aesthetic. […] These 'uncomfortable' costumes became a source of inspiration for our operas that are always connected to the world of art."

Rabanne's creations evoke both fantasy and controversy and clearly belong to the world of art. He was the costume designer for several films, including *Two or Three Things I Know About Her* (Jean-Luc Godard, 1967), *Casino Royale* (John Huston, 1967), *Two for the Road* (Stanley Donen, 1966), and the iconic *Barbarella* (Roger Vadim, 1967).

From his very first collection, called "Twelve Unwearable Dresses in Contemporary Materials," Paco Rabanne defined himself as a provocateur, a precursor, and an avant-garde artist. But "unwearable" did not mean "impossible." The collection's title would become the guideline of his work as he continued to test the material limitations of couture.

— Auctions: "Paco Rabanne—Fashion Materials" at Artcurial, January 30, 2012, in collaboration with the experts from PB Fashion. *From top to bottom and left to right*:
- A dress made of aluminum squares and PVC discs.
- A pinafore dress, bib, and straps made of metal discs and bells, circa 1988.
- Bustier of molded cardboard, entirely covered in white Rhodoid sequins.
- Dress made of beads and small wood cubes.

PACO RABANNE

1970s

*Sweet
Liberty*

For fashion, the 1970s were years distinguished by affluence and eclecticism.

Evoking the style of past decades, the hostess dress was back in vogue. For formal occasions, women still wore long dresses. The cape, another echo from the past, was a favorite of designers and Halston's creations recalled the Belle Époque.

Freedom was in the air and prints were a staple: flowery bohemian styles at Dior and Chloé; geometric patterns and op art at Pucci, Valentino, Leonard, and Ossie Clark; and an ostentatious monogram pattern at Gucci.

The maxi and bell-bottoms replaced the mini. Fall colors were in style, offering a palette of chocolate brown, burgundy red, pumpkin, and mustard that either blended smoothly or clashed intentionally. All eyes turned to the East and Far East as ethnic styles influenced Western collections: a chic hippie look at Pucci and Thea Porter; dazzling Russian and Chinese collections at Yves Saint Laurent; Slavic and Oriental designs at Ungaro, Givenchy, Lanvin, Oscar de la Renta, and Guy Laroche.

The early 1970s marked the passing of Gabrielle Chanel, who died on Sunday, January 10, 1971, but her legacy of timeless fashion lived on. A dress with bouffant sleeves by Madame Grès confirmed her visionary talent. In the late 1970s, Azzaro and Mugler offered an inkling of what the next decade would bring.

GIVENCHY

N º 64970
COUTURE

Copper-colored silk chiffon evening gown with sunburst pleats sprinkled with gold lamé polka dots; square neckline; fitted velvet cuffs; puffy sleeves. Label.

<u>PROVENANCE</u>: Fashion Institute of Design & Merchandising.

Estimate: 300–500 dollars
Sold: 540 dollars
Augusta Auctions, New York
November 10, 2010 (lot 221)
Specialist: Karen E. Augusta

YVES SAINT LAURENT

N º 33469
COUTURE, Fall/Winter 1973–1974

Long satin shirtdress with multicolor flower print on navy blue background, each motif adorned with sequins; turndown collar; slightly gathered shoulders; flared skirt. White label, black lettering.

<u>BIBLIOGRAPHY</u>: The identical model is reproduced in *L'Officiel 1,000 Modèles, Yves Saint Laurent 1962–2002*, special issue no. 1, éditions Jalou.

Estimate: 700–800 euros
Sold: 1,000 euros
Cornette de Saint Cyr, Paris
June 30, 2012 (lot 65)
Specialists: D. Chombert and F. Sternbach

TAN GIUDICELLI

PRÊT-À-PORTER

Powder pink crepe jersey dress with a cape-like draping over the front; high draped neck with a sash at the back; cuffs with small buttons.

Estimate: 100–150 euros
Sold: 435 euros
Bailly-Pommery & Voutier, Paris
April 23, 2012 (lot 252)
Specialist: PB Fashion

SIMONETTA

VALENTINO

ANONYMOUS

PRÊT-À-PORTER

PRÊT-À-PORTER

PRÊT-À-PORTER

Coral jersey hostess dress; applied ivory braid in a lattice pattern; round neckline adorned with a double ruffle and a small tie; ruffle is repeated at the bottom of the mid-length sleeves; front zipper to the waist; flared skirt. Label "Simonetta et Fabiani Boutique."

Silk crepe evening gown with golden yellow and anise-green floral print on white background; sculpted round neckline; straight cuffs; slightly flared skirt. Label "Valentino Boutique."

Hostess dress with white, navy blue, and tangerine stripes; tight-fitting at the bottom; three-quarter sleeves with batwing look.

Estimate: 120–150 euros
Sold: 225 euros
Artcurial, Paris
November 25, 2011 (lot 475)
Specialist: PB Fashion

Estimate: 30–50 euros
Sold: 50 euros
Artcurial, Paris
June 11, 2012 (lot 290)
Specialist: PB Fashion

Estimate: 30–50 euros
Sold: 186 euros
Artcurial, Paris
June 27, 2011 (lot 259)
Specialist: PB Fashion

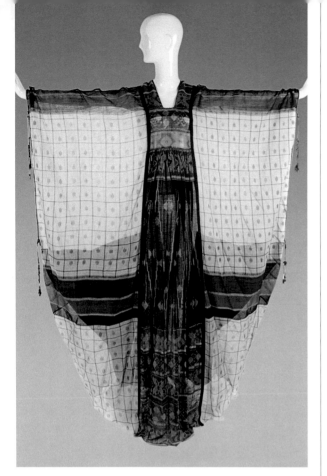

THEA PORTER

THEA PORTER

COUTURE

Silk and cotton caftan with multicolor ikat print; V-neckline; long sleeves with panels attached to the bottom of the dress. Label "Thea Porter Couture."

COUTURE

Silk chiffon caftan with ikat print in shades of purple and white adorned with gold Lurex and sequins. Label "Thea Porter Couture."

Estimate: 800–1,200 dollars
Sold: 7,930 dollars
Leslie Hindman Auctioneers, Chicago
September 16, 2010 (lot 115)
Specialist: Abigail Rutherford

Estimate: 1,000–2,000 dollars
Sold: 5,856 dollars
Leslie Hindman Auctioneers, Chicago
December 16, 2010 (lot 37)
Specialist: Abigail Rutherford

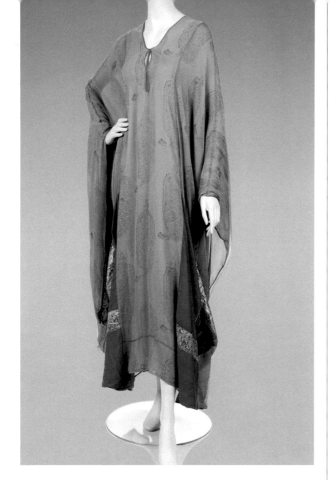 

THEA PORTER

CHRISTIAN DIOR

COUTURE

COUTURE
by Marc Bohan

Turquoise silk chiffon caftan with gold piping and patchwork inserts. Label "Thea Porter Couture."

Silk crepe dress with flower print and sienna, lavender, and mauve stripes on a red background; boat neckline; fringe on the bottom of the sleeves and the skirt.

Estimate: 1,000–2,000 dollars
Sold: 2,684 dollars
Leslie Hindman Auctioneers, Chicago
April 17, 2012 (lot 55)
Specialist: Abigail Rutherford

Estimate: 300–500 dollars
Sold: 1,037 dollars
Leslie Hindman Auctioneers, Chicago
December 6, 2011 (lot 243)
Specialist: Abigail Rutherford

VALENTINO

COUTURE

Evening ensemble with pleated ivory silk crepe top; high collar, décolleté, and bottom of sleeves adorned with scallops and sprinkled with small flowers; long pink taffeta skirt with layered pleated ruffles. Label "Valentino Couture."
PROVENANCE: Brooklyn Museum.

Estimate: 300–500 dollars
Sold: 720 dollars
Augusta Auctions, New York
March 21, 2012 (lot 15)
Specialist: Karen E. Augusta

GUY LAROCHE

COUTURE

Dress inspired by Russian folklore; cream silk satin pinafore partially embroidered with small orange, green, and yellow beads forming a geometric pattern; full long skirt with ruffled hem; emerald silk blouse; high gathered collar with tie; long puffy sleeves.

Estimate: 300–500 dollars
Sold: 183 dollars
Leslie Hindman Auctioneers, Chicago
April 21, 2010 (lot 106)
Specialist: Abigail Rutherford

GEOFFREY BEENE

COUTURE

Silk taffeta red, black, and green tartan plaid evening dress; bodice buttoned to the high neck, set off with a tie and a Bertha-collar look; full skirt with godets. Worn with a patent leather belt.

Estimate: 200–400 dollars
Sold: 366 dollars
Leslie Hindman Auctioneers, Chicago
September 20, 2011 (lot 284)
Specialist: Abigail Rutherford

YVES SAINT LAURENT

PRÊT-À-PORTER

Multicolored printed silk dress; pierrot collar; ruffled cuffs; skirt pleated from the hips. Label "Saint Laurent Rive Gauche."

Estimate: 100–150 euros
Sold: 186 euros
Eve, Paris
May 6, 2011 (lot M017)
Specialist: Sylvie Daniel

YVES SAINT LAURENT

PRÊT-À-PORTER

Silk crepe dress printed with small blue, green, purple, and white flowers on a red background; square neckline; bust with tucked pleats; slightly puffed sleeves; flowing skirt. Label "Saint Laurent Rive Gauche."

Estimate: 100–200 dollars
Sold: 195 dollars
Leslie Hindman Auctioneers, Chicago
September 16, 2010 (lot 189)
Specialist: Abigail Rutherford

YVES SAINT LAURENT

PRÊT-À-PORTER

Ivory silk crepe dress printed with small black polka dots; neck tie; mid-length balloon sleeves; tie belt; skirt pleated from the hips. Label "Saint Laurent Rive Gauche."

Estimate: 150–250 dollars
Sold: 397 dollars
Leslie Hindman Auctioneers, Chicago
September 16, 2010 (lot 334)
Specialist: Abigail Rutherford

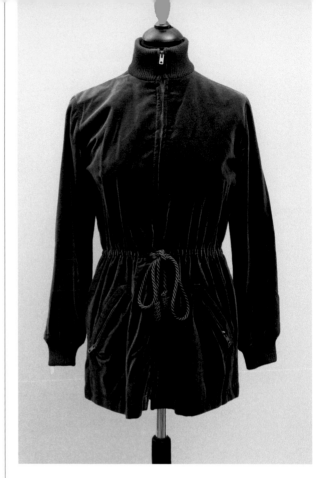

YVES SAINT LAURENT

PRÊT-À-PORTER

Light café au lait crepe jacket with ebony and praline trimming; round neckline; single-breasted closure with buttons under placket; two vertical pockets.

Estimate: 80–100 euros
Sold: 185 euros
Camard & Associés, Paris
March 18, 2012 (lot 116)

YVES SAINT LAURENT

PRÊT-À-PORTER

Sepia velvet parka; high neck with zipper and ribbing, repeated on the cuffs; waist fitted with drawstring tie; two zipped pockets. Label "Saint Laurent Rive Gauche."

Estimate: 80–120 euros
Sold: 183 euros
Bailly-Pommery & Voutier, Paris
April 23, 2012 (lot 170)
Specialist: PB Fashion

YVES SAINT LAURENT

PRÊT-À-PORTER

Olive green velvet jacket with black trim; round neckline adorned with a double taffeta ruffle, repeated on the cuffs; single-breasted closure with jet buttons; gathered shoulders. Label "Saint Laurent Rive Gauche."

Estimate: 150–200 euros
Sold: 188 euros
Artcurial, Paris
April 18, 2012 (lot 269)
Specialist: PB Fashion

HERMÈS

PRÊT-À-PORTER

Two-sided wool coat, green outside, plaid inside; greatcoat inspiration; small turndown collar; single-breasted closure; two pockets. Label "Hermès Sport."

Estimate: 400–500 euros
Sold: 625 euros
Gros & Delettrez, Paris
June 4, 2012 (lot 133)
Specialists: D. Chombert and F. Sternbach

EMANUEL UNGARO

VALENTINO

N º 4368
COUTURE, Fall/Winter 1976

PRÊT-À-PORTER

Chenille velvet coat with multicolored stripes trimmed with basket weaving; round collar; toggle buttons; two vertical pockets. Worn with a black doeskin belt trimmed with red leather. White label, black lettering.

Wool coat; size 9/10; with medium brown and chestnut herringbone pattern; small high collar adorned with velvet; single-breasted closure with buttons, repeated on the cuffs; long sleeves gathered at the shoulders; pleated back with half belt. Label "Valentino Boutique."

Estimate: 400–500 euros
Sold: 500 euros
Cornette de Saint Cyr, Paris
June 30, 2012 (lot 339)
Specialists: D. Chombert and F. Sternbach

Estimate: 100–150 euros
Sold: 125 euros
Artcurial, Paris
November 25, 2011 (lot 244)
Specialist: PB Fashion

YVES SAINT LAURENT

PRÊT-À-PORTER, Fall/Winter 1976–1977

Bronze pigskin suede coat; high collar; topstitching on the front facings and cuffs; loop buttons; gathered shoulders; two in-seam pockets; quilted lining. Label "Yves Saint Laurent Fourrures."

<u>BIBLIOGRAPHY</u>: Similar models are reproduced on p. 130 and p. 131 in *L'Officiel de la Couture et de la Mode de Paris*, no. 628, Winter 1976, éditions Jalou.

Estimate: 300–400 euros
Sold: 305 euros
Chayette & Cheval, Paris
February 5, 2012 (lot 303)
Specialist: PB Fashion

YVES SAINT LAURENT

PRÊT-À-PORTER

Mottled plum wool coat, some panels adorned with brown trim; wooden buttons with loop fasteners to the waist, repeated at the cuffs of the long, slightly gathered sleeves; two pockets. Label "Saint Laurent Rive Gauche."

Estimate: 100–150 euros
Sold: 219 euros
Chayette & Cheval, Paris
February 5, 2012 (lot 322)
Specialist: PB Fashion

LANVIN

PRÊT-À-PORTER

Pale yellow dress with green, blue, and tangerine floral print; round neckline; mid-length sleeves; gathered waist and A-line skirt; tie belt.

Estimate: 60–80 euros
Sold: 100 euros
Artcurial, Paris
June 11, 2012 (lot 407)
Specialist: PB Fashion

CHRISTIAN DIOR

N º 1565
COUTURE
by Marc Bohan

Gypsy-inspired white silk chiffon dress embroidered with multicolored butterflies and flowers; ruffled boat neckline, repeated on the short sleeves and wraparound skirt; pleated peplum-cut waist with corseted look.

Estimate: 600–800 dollars
Sold: 3,660 dollars
Leslie Hindman Auctioneers, Chicago
April 21, 2010 (lot 145)
Specialist: Abigail Rutherford

VALENTINO

PRÊT-À-PORTER

Red and white gingham checked dress; round neckline; small butterfly sleeves; front and long skirt cut on the bias; lace appliqués; two layers of ruffles at the hem; tie belt. Label "Valentino Boutique."

ICONOGRAPHY: Same dress is worn by Elizabeth Taylor on the cover of the *Ladies' Home Journal* in October 1975.

Estimate: 500–700 dollars
Sold: 6,600 dollars
Christie's, New York
December 3–17, 2011 (lot 1605)
Specialist: Patricia Frost

CHRISTIAN DIOR

Nº 154919
COUTURE, Spring/Summer 1971
by Marc Bohan

Ivory guipure lace silk evening gown with floral pattern; round neckline; powder-pink satin ribbon at the high waist; A-line skirt.

Estimate: 600–800 dollars
Sold: 1,464 dollars
Leslie Hindman Auctioneers, Chicago
December 6, 2011 (lot 238)
Specialist: Abigail Rutherford

CHLOÉ

PRÊT-À-PORTER

Ivory silk crepe evening gown with peasant inspiration; pleated bodice with turndown boat neckline; long skirt partially adorned with stylized floral design made of multicolored beads.

Estimate: 300–500 dollars
Sold: 519 dollars
Leslie Hindman Auctioneers, Chicago
April 21, 2010 (lot 117)
Specialist: Abigail Rutherford

OSSIE CLARK

PRÊT-À-PORTER
(Print: Celia Birtwell)

Chiffon dress printed with pastel shades of pink, blue, and green with a speckled stylized patchwork-like motif and diagonally overlaid ruffles; round neckline fastened with a button.

Estimate: 1,000–1,200 pounds
Sold: 1,188 pounds
Christie's, London
December 2, 2010 (lot 141)
Specialist: Patricia Frost

OSSIE CLARK

OSSIE CLARK

OSSIE CLARK

PRÊT-À-PORTER

PRÊT-À-PORTER

PRÊT-À-PORTER, 1974
(Print: Celia Birtwell)

Ivory and blue wool crepe dress; butterfly "disco" collar; small loop buttons to the lower hips, repeated on the cuffs of the long puffy sleeves; skirt with inverted pleats. Label "Ossie Clark for Radley."

Red, green, and black dress; faux double-pointed collar; pagoda sleeves; flowing skirt with alternating green and red panels forming godets. Label.

Black silk crepe dress with a wrap-around green and red floral print; V-neckline; balloon sleeves.

Estimate: 300–500 dollars
Sold: 671 dollars
Leslie Hindman Auctioneers, Chicago
April 11–12, 2011 (lot 151)
Specialist: Abigail Rutherford

Estimate: 1,000–2,000 dollars
Sold: 2,160 dollars
Christie's, New York
December 3–17, 2011 (lot 1651)
Specialist: Patricia Frost

Estimate: 800–1,200 pounds
Sold: 1,562 pounds
Christie's, London
December 2, 2010 (lot 142)
Specialist: Patricia Frost

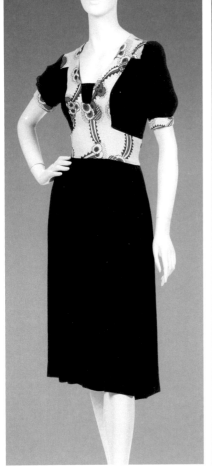  

OSSIE CLARK

PRÊT-À-PORTER
(Print: Celia Birtwell)

Black crepe dress; inserts with red and black print on ivory background; V-neckline with modesty panel; balloon sleeves; gathered flowing skirt. Label "Ossie Clark for Radley."

Estimate: 600–800 dollars
Sold: 457 dollars
Leslie Hindman Auctioneers, Chicago
September 20, 2011 (lot 74)
Specialist: Abigail Rutherford

RUDI GERNREICH

PRÊT-À-PORTER

Jersey evening dress with large black, white, gray, and camel-colored floral decorations; halter top with red background and open back; gathered skirt of gold and silver Lurex. Label "Rudi Gernreich For Harmon Knitwear."

Estimate: 200–400 dollars
Sold: 854 dollars
Leslie Hindman Auctioneers, Chicago
September 20, 2011 (lot 89)
Specialist: Abigail Rutherford

RUDI GERNREICH

PRÊT-À-PORTER

Purple jersey maxi dress with large multicolored floral motifs; crew neckline; cap sleeves; A-line skirt. Label "Rudi Gernreich For Harmon Knitwear."

Estimate: 200–400 dollars
Sold: 793 dollars
Leslie Hindman Auctioneers, Chicago
September 16, 2010 (lot 296)
Specialist: Abigail Rutherford

EMILIO PUCCI

LEONARD

PRÊT-À-PORTER

Silk jersey dress with vermilion, ivory, anise-green, and purple geometric print; black bodice adorned with a trompe-l'œil turndown collar, maxi skirt with pointed waistband. Label "Emilio Pucci Florence–Italy."

PRÊT-À-PORTER

Silk jersey dress with a tropical flower print on a black background; crew neckline; geometric pattern on cuffs, waist, and hem. Label "Leonard Fashion."

Estimate: 300–400 dollars
Sold: 360 dollars
Charles A. Whitaker Auction Company, Philadelphia
October 28–29, 2011 (lot 780)
Specialist: Charles A. Whitaker

Estimate: 300–400 dollars
Sold: 270 dollars
Charles A. Whitaker Auction Company, Philadelphia
October 28–29, 2011 (lot 796)
Specialist: Charles A. Whitaker

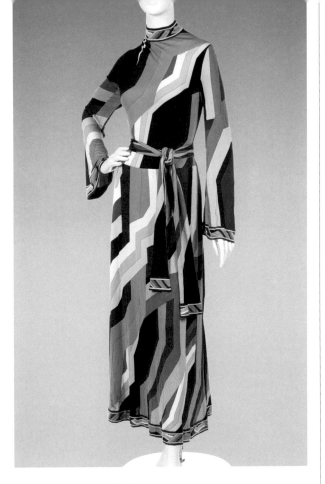

LEONARD

LEONARD

PRÊT-À-PORTER

PRÊT-À-PORTER

Maxi dress with geometric purple, lilac, blue, black, and white print; small high collar; long, slightly flared sleeves; waist with tie belt and flowing skirt.

Dress with multicolored psychedelic print; crew neckline; straight cuffs; belted look; flowing skirt.

Estimate: 200–400 dollars
Sold: 305 dollars
Leslie Hindman Auctioneers, Chicago
September 20, 2011 (lot 66)
Specialist: Abigail Rutherford

Estimate: 200–300 dollars
Sold: 210 dollars
Augusta Auctions, New York
March 21, 2012 (lot 350)
Specialist: Karen E. Augusta

EMILIO PUCCI

EMILIO PUCCI

PRÊT-À-PORTER

PRÊT-À-PORTER

Openwork silk jersey dress with purple, burgundy, orange, and black geometric print; crew neckline over cutout front.

Outfit with scrolling leaf print in shades of ochre, gray, black, and green on a raspberry red background; chocolate brown trim; blouse of wool bunting; turndown collar; single-breasted closure with buttons, repeated on the straight cuffs; wraparound velvet skirt. Label "Emilio Pucci Florence–Italy."

Estimate: 800–1,200 euros
Sold: 574 euros
Tajan, Paris
February 4, 2012 (lot 280)
Specialist: Jean-Jacques Wattel

Estimate: 300–500 dollars
Sold: 300 dollars
Charles A. Whitaker Auction Company, Philadelphia
October 28–29, 2011 (lot 795)
Specialist: Charles A. Whitaker

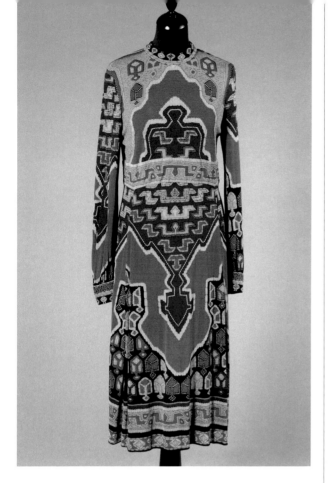

LEONARD

LEONARD

PRÊT-À-PORTER, Fall/Winter 1971–1972

PRÊT-À-PORTER

Loose jersey crepe dress with a multicolor red, blue, and ochre weaving-like print; round neckline; long sleeves with barrel cuffs adorned with small covered buttons. Label "Leonard Fashion."

Jersey outfit with green, blue, red, and white print; tunic top with straight neck and single-breasted closure with buttons; barrel cuffs; waist with tie belt; bell-bottom pants. Label "Leonard Fashion."

Estimate: 80–100 euros
Sold: 350 euros
Artcurial, Paris
June 11, 2012 (lot 20)
Specialist: PB Fashion

Estimate: 500–700 dollars
Sold: 3,120 dollars
Christie's, New York
December 3–17, 2011 (lot 1649)
Specialist: Patricia Frost

JEAN PATOU

PRÊT-À-PORTER
by Angelo Tarlazzi

Long dress with vibrant horizontal purple and burnt orange stripes; bias cut; tie sash at the back; plunging V-neckline; low V-cut back; spaghetti straps. Label "Jean Patou Boutique."

Estimate: 300–500 euros
Sold: 875 euros
Cornette de Saint Cyr, Paris
July 4, 2011 (lot 137)
Specialists: D. Chombert and F. Sternbach

LEONARD

N° 2470
PRÊT-À-PORTER

Wool jersey dress with patchwork black and white graphic print; high cowl collar; belted waist and A-line skirt. Label "Leonard Fashion."

Estimate: 200–300 euros
Sold: 375 euros
Cornette de Saint Cyr, Paris
June 30, 2012 (lot 412)
Specialists: D. Chombert and F. Sternbach

EMILIO PUCCI

HERMÈS

PRÊT-À-PORTER

PRÊT-À-PORTER

Silk jersey shirtdress with beaded geometric pistachio green, fuchsia, purple, and brown print on navy blue background; notched collar; single-breasted closure with covered buttons, repeated on the cuffs; full sleeves. Label "Emilio Pucci Florence–Italy."

Unbleached wool and silk brocade sweater decorated with cherry-tree branches; round collar with zipper on one shoulder. Label "Hermès Sport."

Estimate: 300–500 dollars
Sold: 330 dollars
Charles A. Whitaker Auction Company, Philadelphia
April 27–28, 2012 (lot 898)
Specialist: Charles A. Whitaker

Estimate: 150–200 euros
Sold: 190 euros
Artcurial, Paris
November 15, 2011 (lot 241)
Specialist: Cyril Pigot

JEAN MUIR

HERMÈS

PRÊT-À-PORTER

PRÊT-À-PORTER

Charcoal gray flannel dress trimmed in brandy-colored leather; bust decorated with topstitching in vertical stripes; square neckline; single-breasted closure with buttons on leather placket to the hips; waist adorned with a tie belt; partially pleated skirt. Label "Jean Muir London."

BIBLIOGRAPHY: The model is reproduced on p. 149 in *Vintage Fashion: Collecting and Wearing Designer Classics, 1900-1990*, Emma Baxter-Wright, Harper Collins USA, 2012.

Ochre wool coat trimmed in chocolate-colored lambskin; overlapping facings attached with two golden brass buckles. Label "Hermès Sport."

Estimate: 400–600 dollars
Sold: 570 dollars
Charles A. Whitaker Auction Company, Philadelphia
October 28–29, 2011 (lot 776)
Specialist: Charles A. Whitaker

Estimate: 200–300 euros
Sold: 765 euros
Artcurial, Paris
November 15, 2011 (lot 238)
Specialist: Cyril Pigot

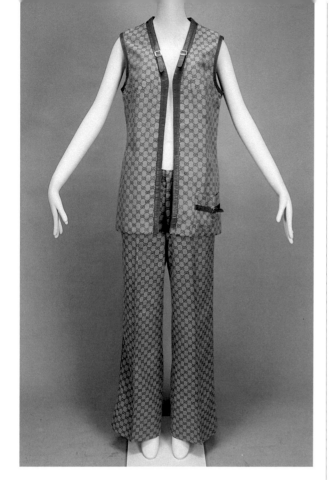

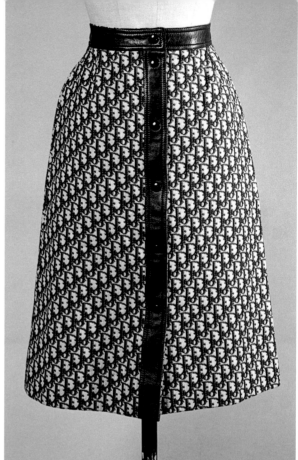

GUCCI

CHRISTIAN DIOR

PRÊT-À-PORTER

PRÊT-À-PORTER
by Philippe Guibourgé

Wool outfit with logo print; vest trimmed in hazelnut-brown leather; V-neckline adorned with two straps and gold metal buckles, repeated on the pocket; bell-bottom pants. No label.

Maxi skirt with blue and black logo print on beige background, trimmed with matching leather and buttoned in the front. Label "Miss Dior."

Estimate: 100–200 dollars
Sold: 540 dollars
Charles A. Whitaker Auction Company, Philadelphia
April 27–28, 2012 (lot 902)
Specialist: Charles A. Whitaker

Estimate: 80–120 euros
Sold: 250 euros
Artcurial, Paris
November 25, 2011 (lot 481)
Specialist: PB Fashion

GIVENCHY

RUDI GERNREICH

PRÊT-À-PORTER

PRÊT-À-PORTER, 1973

Burnt sienna wool dress; high rolled neck; buttoned epaulettes, repeated on the two vertical pockets; hem insert. Label "Givenchy Nouvelle Boutique."

Gingerbread wool knit mini dress; front vertical bands with inserted checked belt. Label "Rudi Gernreich For Harmon Knitwear."

<u>PROVENANCE</u>: Leon Bing, model and muse of Rudi Gernreich, Pasadena, California.

Estimate: 200–300 dollars
Sold: 270 dollars
Charles A. Whitaker Auction Company, Philadelphia
October 28–29, 2011 (lot 774)
Specialist: Charles A. Whitaker

Estimate: 400–600 dollars
Sold: 610 dollars
Leslie Hindman Auctioneers, Chicago
April 21, 2010 (lot 87)
Specialist: Abigail Rutherford

DOROTHÉE BIS
E. & J. JACOBSON

PRÊT-À-PORTER

Jacquard wool dress, striped herringbone pattern with shades of brown, caramel, orange, and plum; turndown collar with small points; barrel cuffs; A-line maxi skirt. White label, red lettering.

Estimate: 60–80 euros
Sold: 125 euros
Artcurial, Paris
October 3, 2011 (lot 130)
Specialist: PB Fashion

MISSONI

PRÊT-À-PORTER

Wool tulle pantsuit with beige and brown mosaic print; high bust. Worn with a reversible coat, black wool on one side and identical print on the other; turndown collar; double-breasted closure; in-seam pockets. Rust labels, black lettering.

Estimate: 250–300 euros
Sold: 313 euros
Cornette de Saint Cyr, Paris
July 4, 2011 (lot 225)
Specialists: D. Chombert and F. Sternbach

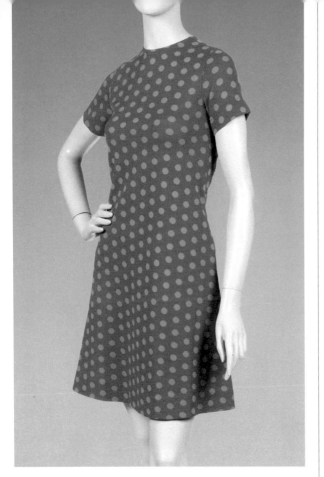

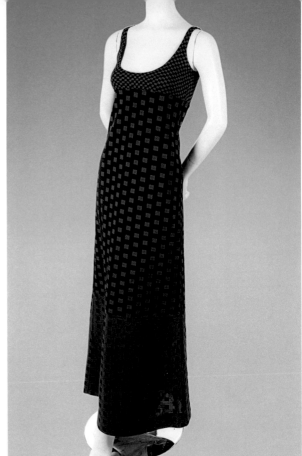

RUDI GERNREICH

RUDI GERNREICH

PRÊT-À-PORTER

PRÊT-À-PORTER, 1973

Flared wool knit dress with gold polka dots on a hot pink background. Label "Rudi Gernreich For Harmon Knitwear."

Wool knit A-line maxi dress with alternating pattern of red and black checks. Label "Rudi Gernreich For Harmon Knitwear."

PROVENANCE: Leon Bing, model and muse of Rudi Gernreich, Pasadena, California.

Estimate: 100–200 dollars
Sold: 195 dollars
Leslie Hindman Auctioneers, Chicago
December 6, 2011 (lot 109)
Specialist: Abigail Rutherford

Estimate: 400–600 dollars
Sold: 336 dollars
Leslie Hindman Auctioneers, Chicago
April 21, 2010 (lot 86)
Specialist: Abigail Rutherford

RUDI GERNREICH

PIERRE CARDIN

PRÊT-À-PORTER, 1971

COUTURE

Black and white wool knit mini dress; long puffy sleeves and gathered skirt with wavy decoration. Label "Rudi Gernreich For Harmon Knitwear."

<u>PROVENANCE</u>: Leon Bing, model and muse of Rudi Gernreich, Pasadena, California.

Black wool crepe tunic dress with fringes from the bust; round neckline.

Estimate: 100–200 dollars
Sold: 244 dollars
Leslie Hindman Auctioneers, Chicago
April 21, 2010 (lot 79)
Specialist: Abigail Rutherford

Estimate: 300–400 euros
Sold: 1,053 euros
Coutau-Begarie, Paris
December 10, 2011 (lot 100)

CHANEL

N° 53161, N° 53162, and N° 53163
COUTURE

Mottled tweed suit with shades of chocolate brown, green, peacock blue, and raw sienna; jacket with notched lapel; single-breasted closure; two flap pockets; skirt pleated from the hips. Worn with a matching green cardigan with cap sleeves.

Estimate: 400–600 euros
Sold: 750 euros

Cornette de Saint Cyr, Paris
February 13, 2012 (lot 117)

Specialists: D. Chombert and F. Sternbach

CHANEL

N° 46917
COUTURE

Multicolor silk dress with pink piping; turndown collar and a removable tie; short sleeves; skirt pleated from the hips; belt tied in the back; jacket with round collar; single-breasted closure with gold metal buttons; four flat pockets. Black label, white lettering.

Estimate: 350–400 euros
Sold: 725 euros

Cornette de Saint Cyr, Paris
April 4, 2012 (lot 335)

Specialists: D. Chombert and F. Sternbach

VALENTINO

COUTURE

Green wool herringbone suit; jacket with wide notched lapel adorned with Tanuki fur, repeated at the cuffs; double-breasted closure; skirt with inverted pleats. Label "Valentino Couture."

Estimate: 500–600 euros
Sold: 1,875 euros
Cornette de Saint Cyr, Paris
June 30, 2012 (lot 181)
Specialists: D. Chombert and F. Sternbach

YVES SAINT LAURENT

N° 30201
COUTURE, Fall/Winter 1972

Black lacquered silk outfit; quilted jacket decorated with bias topstitching and trimmed with Canadian sable; cowl neck; skirt pleated from the hips. White label, black lettering.

BIBLIOGRAPHY: A similar model is reproduced on p. 99 under number 101 of the exhibition catalog *Yves Saint Laurent*, Metropolitan Museum of Art, New York, December 14, 1983–September 2, 1984, Clarkson N. Potter. This model was donated by Lauren Bacall. *L'Officiel 1,000 Modèles, Yves Saint Laurent 1962–2002*, special issue no. 1, éditions Jalou.

Estimate: 800–1,000 euros
Sold: 7,500 euros
Cornette de Saint Cyr, Paris
June 30, 2012 (lot 411)
Specialists: D. Chombert and F. Sternbach

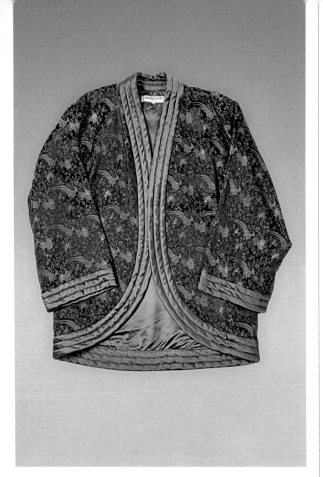

YVES SAINT LAURENT

PRÊT-À-PORTER

Chinese-inspired jacket in brocaded silk with red and purple floral pattern on a black background trimmed with quilted bottle-green satin; V-neckline; no buttons. Label "Yves Saint Laurent Rive Gauche."

Estimate: 200–400 dollars
Sold: 336 dollars
Leslie Hindman Auctioneers, Chicago
April 17, 2012 (lot 154)
Specialist: Abigail Rutherford

KENZO

PRÊT-À-PORTER

Embossed cotton shirtdress with black, purple, blue, and brown stripes; small high collar and asymmetric buttons, repeated on the cuffs; multicolor floral decoration on what looks like a shirt dickey; waist with tie belt; straight skirt with side slits. White label, red lettering, and portrait of Kenzo Takada, "Kenzo Jap."

Estimate: 80–120 euros
Sold: 313 euros
Artcurial, Paris
July 6, 2012 (lot 62)
Specialist: PB Fashion

KENZO

PRÊT-À-PORTER

Wraparound light café au lait mottled wool coat; size 7/8; quilted cotton inserts with a floral motif; trimmed V-neckline; waist with tie belt; two pockets. Label "Kenzo Jap."

Estimate: 80–120 euros
Sold: 563 euros
Artcurial, Paris
July 6, 2012 (lot 151)
Specialist: PB Fashion

YVES SAINT LAURENT

PRÊT-À-PORTER

Chinese-inspired silk dress with ochre, brown, and orange print on black background; small mandarin collar; asymmetric gold metal buttons; skirt with side slits. Label "Saint Laurent Rive Gauche."

Estimate: 150–250 dollars
Sold: 976 dollars
Leslie Hindman Auctioneers, Chicago
December 6, 2011 (lot 125)
Specialist: Abigail Rutherford

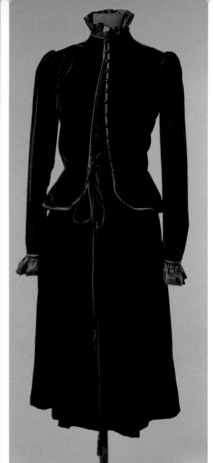

YVES SAINT LAURENT

PRÊT-À-PORTER

Peasant-inspired black cotton outfit with gold metallic trimming; peplum-cut camisole laced at the front; gathered skirt with ruffled taffeta hem. Label "Saint Laurent Rive Gauche."

Estimate: 600–800 dollars
Sold: 793 dollars
Leslie Hindman Auctioneers, Chicago
December 6, 2011 (lot 123)
Specialist: Abigail Rutherford

JEAN-LOUIS SCHERRER

N ° 00576
COUTURE
(Embroidery: Lesage)

Charcoal gray evening ensemble; jacket trimmed with glossy chocolate brown fox; embroidered with gold metallic thread and small white beads; full skirt forming godets.

Estimate: 700–900 dollars
Sold: 1,464 dollars
Leslie Hindman Auctioneers, Chicago
December 6, 2011 (lot 209)
Specialist: Abigail Rutherford

YVES SAINT LAURENT

**PRÊT-À-PORTER, Fall/Winter 1976
Collection "Ballets Russes"**

Cossack-inspired black velvet suit; small high collar adorned with a matching taffeta ruffle, repeated on the cuffs; single-breasted closure with buttons with loop fasteners; fitted waist with a peplum cut; skirt slightly gathered at the waist; camisole laced at the front. Label "Saint Laurent Rive Gauche."

Estimate: 300–400 euros
Sold: 867 euros
Artcurial, Paris
February 7, 2011 (lot 402)
Specialist: PB Fashion

YVES SAINT LAURENT

COUTURE

Gypsy-inspired muslin evening ensemble with Indian print; round collar with drawstring; flounced cuffs; full skirt with brown and white polka dots on black background. Worn with a quilted silk jacket with cashmere print trimmed with gold and red braid; single-breasted closure with buttons with loop fasteners; two flat pockets. White label, black lettering.

LANVIN

N º 89124
COUTURE
by Jules-François Crahay

Russian-inspired black linen dress with multicolor brocade trim; round gathered neck with slit; long raglan sleeves; cuffs with lace ruffles; full skirt. Worn with a patent leather belt. White label, black lettering.

Estimate: 500–600 euros
Sold: 1,125 euros
Cornette de Saint Cyr, Paris
June 30, 2012 (lot 152)
Specialists: D. Chombert and F. Sternbach

Estimate: 300–400 euros
Sold: 145 euros
Lafon Castandet, Paris
October 10, 2011 (lot 158)
Specialists: D. Chombert and F. Sternbach

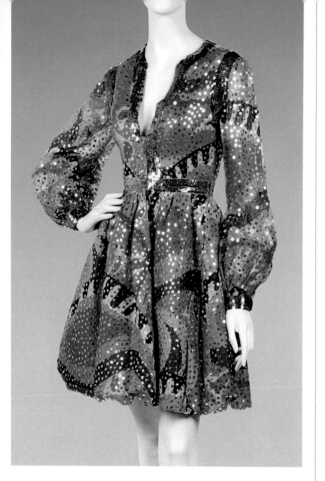

OSCAR DE LA RENTA

OSCAR DE LA RENTA

COUTURE

COUTURE

Chiffon silk cocktail dress printed with a multicolor abstract pattern and sprinkled with gold sequins; round neckline with plunging zipper; long puffy sleeves; short gathered full skirt.

Red silk crepe dress; gold brocaded braid trim with geometric pattern; V-neckline; maxi skirt gathered at the high waist.

Estimate: 300–500 dollars
Sold: 793 dollars
Leslie Hindman Auctioneers, Chicago
April 17, 2012 (lot 182)
Specialist: Abigail Rutherford

Estimate: 100–200 dollars
Sold: 198 dollars
Leslie Hindman Auctioneers, Chicago
September 20, 2011 (lot 181)
Specialist: Abigail Rutherford

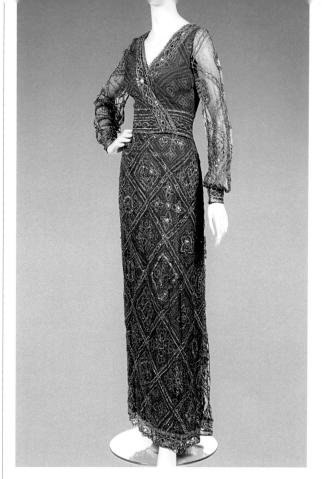

OSCAR DE LA RENTA

THEA PORTER

COUTURE

COUTURE

Green, red, and taupe silk brocade evening gown with a scroll and flower pattern; small high collar; high waist and cuffs with gold trim appliqué; gathered skirt.

<u>PROVENANCE</u>: Norma Seidman, Lincolnwood, Illinois.

Red silk chiffon evening gown printed with small geometric pattern and embroidered with gold beads, sequins, and small mirrors; V-neckline; straight cuffs and long transparent sleeves. Label "Thea Porter Couture."

Estimate: 100–200 dollars
Sold: 458 dollars
Leslie Hindman Auctioneers, Chicago
April 21, 2010 (lot 166)
Specialist: Abigail Rutherford

Estimate: 500–700 dollars
Sold: 1,098 dollars
Leslie Hindman Auctioneers, Chicago
December 6, 2011 (lot 95)
Specialist: Abigail Rutherford

CHLOÉ

CHRISTIAN DIOR

N° 009787
COUTURE, Spring/Summer 1978
by Marc Bohan

PRÊT-À-PORTER
by Karl Lagerfeld

Bottle-green silk evening dress with black lace inlays; turndown high collar above a design that creates the appearance of a shirt; bust adorned with darts; long skirt pleated from the hips.

Dotted Swiss cocktail dress; strapless look under transparent tulle; mid-length sleeves with satin bows; skirt gathered at the waist.

Estimate: 150–250 dollars
Sold: 336 dollars
Leslie Hindman Auctioneers, Chicago
April 17, 2012 (lot 65)
Specialist: Abigail Rutherford

Estimate: 200–400 dollars
Sold: 976 dollars
Leslie Hindman Auctioneers, Chicago
September 16, 2010 (lot 330)
Specialist: Abigail Rutherford

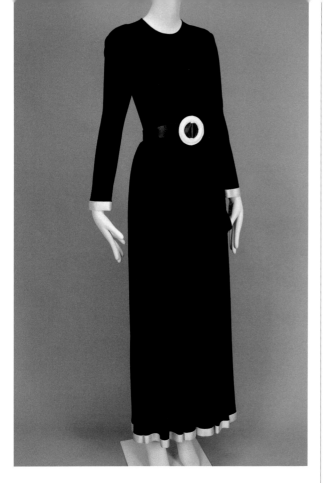

GEOFFREY BEENE

GIVENCHY

COUTURE

COUTURE

Navy blue jersey dress; round neckline; white satin band on cuffs and hem; long vertical pockets.

Black velvet and dotted Swiss tulle evening gown; ruffled neckline with Bertha look; ruffled cuffs; full gathered skirt.

Estimate: 200–300 dollars
Sold: 330 dollars
Charles A. Whitaker Auction Company, Philadelphia
April 27–28, 2012 (lot 904)
Specialist: Charles A. Whitaker

Estimate: 500–700 dollars
Sold: 305 dollars
Leslie Hindman Auctioneers, Chicago
September 20, 2011 (lot 201)
Specialist: Abigail Rutherford

CHANEL

HERMÈS

N° 40017
COUTURE

PRÊT-À-PORTER

Navy blue wool bouclé suit with matching topstitch; jacket with small straight collar and removable white cotton insert, repeated at the cuffs; cuff tabs; four gold metal buttons; two false flap pockets; flared skirt pleated from the hips at the front. White labels, black lettering.

Red glossy suede overcoat; size 9/10; turndown collar with logo trim, repeated on the cuffs; single-breasted closure; tie belt. Label "Hermès Sport."

Estimate: 500–600 euros
Sold: 625 euros
Cornette de Saint Cyr, Paris
February 13, 2012 (lot 408)
Specialists: D. Chombert and F. Sternbach

Estimate: 200–400 dollars
Sold: 868 dollars
Leslie Hindman Auctioneers, Chicago
September 20, 2011 (lot 353)
Specialist: Abigail Rutherford

CHANEL

CHANEL

COUTURE

COUTURE

Blue tweed dress suit trimmed with tone-on-tone and raspberry red wool braiding; sleeveless dress with round neckline; long jacket with military collar; single-breasted closure with Bakelite buttons inserted with gold metal, repeated on the cuffs; four flat pockets. Black labels, white lettering.

Ivory wool bouclé outfit trimmed in blue and fuchsia wool braid; size 9/10; coat lined with matching lambswool; round collar; single-breasted closure with gold metal buttons with lion heads; straight skirt. Label.

Estimate: 800–1,200 euros
Sold: 1,115 euros

Artcurial, Paris
November 15, 2010 (lot 187)
Specialist: PB Fashion

Estimate: 700–1,000 pounds
Sold: 2,000 pounds

Christie's, London
December 3, 2009 (lot 235)
Specialist: Patricia Frost

VALENTINO

VICKY TIEL

COUTURE

PRÊT-À-PORTER

Predominately beige tweed suit; jacket with notched lapel; double-breasted closure; two piped bias-cut pockets; A-line skirt. Worn with a fringed shawl. Label "Valentino Couture."

Oatmeal wool jersey pants outfit with multicolor jasper; flared tunic with hood transforming into a sash tied at the front; bell-bottom pants. Label.

Estimate: 500–700 euros
Sold: 938 euros
Cornette de Saint Cyr, Paris
June 30, 2012 (lot 173)
Specialists: D. Chombert and F. Sternbach

Estimate: 400–600 dollars
Sold: 2,400 dollars
Christie's, New York
December 3–17, 2011 (lot 1624)
Specialist: Patricia Frost

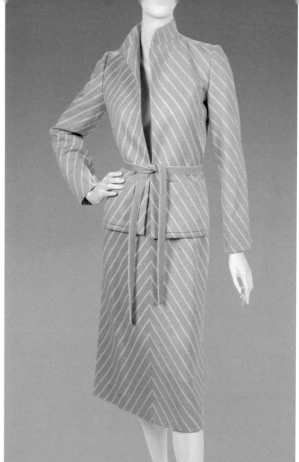

CHRISTIAN DIOR

CHRISTIAN DIOR

N° 02554
COUTURE, Spring/Summer 1973
by Marc Bohan

N° 004236
COUTURE, Spring/Summer 1974
by Marc Bohan

Black and cream striped embossed wool outfit; short-sleeve dress; false buttons; partially pleated skirt; single-breasted jacket with turndown collar; straight cuffs with buttons; two chest pockets; tie belt. Label "Christian Dior Paris."

Wool jersey outfit with café au lait and ivory diagonal stripes; open jacket with small high collar; two flat pockets; tie belt; A-line maxi skirt.

Estimate: 250–350 dollars
Sold: 300 dollars
Charles A. Whitaker Auction Company, Philadelphia
October 28–29, 2011 (lot 775)
Specialist: Charles A. Whitaker

Estimate: 200–400 dollars
Sold: 220 dollars
Leslie Hindman Auctioneers, Chicago
December 16, 2010 (lot 301)
Specialist: Abigail Rutherford

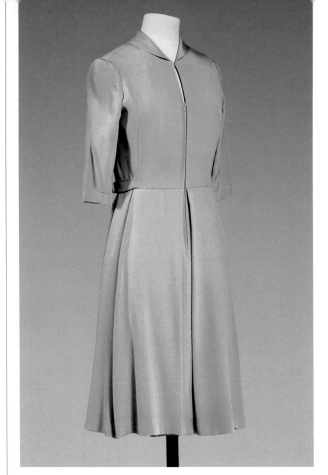

GIVENCHY

GRÈS

PRÊT-À-PORTER

COUTURE

Black wool skirted coat; wide turndown collar with tone-on-tone topstitching; single-breasted closure; long raglan sleeves; two vertical pockets; tie belt. Label "Givenchy Nouvelle Boutique."

Mustard silk crepe dress; turndown round collar and front zipper; three-quarter sleeves; inverted and knife pleats; half belt at the back. White label, black lettering.

Estimate: 100–150 euros
Sold: 200 euros
Artcurial, Paris
November 25, 2011 (lot 73)
Specialist: PB Fashion

Estimate: 300–400 euros
Sold: 375 euros
Cornette de Saint Cyr, Paris
July 4, 2011 (lot 211)
Specialists: D. Chombert and F. Sternbach

PIERRE CARDIN

COUTURE

Black vinyl jacket with rounded aileron armholes; waist adorned with circular applications closing the jacket with two ties; two inseam pockets.

Estimate: 100–120 euros
Sold: 508 euros

Artcurial, Paris
November 15, 2010 (lot 176)
Specialist: PB Fashion

YVES SAINT LAURENT

N ° 42471
COUTURE, Fall/Winter 1977

Black silk kimono jacket; cable ribbing look; sleeves adorned with cords and tassels; seams hidden under braid trim. White label, black lettering.

BIBLIOGRAPHY: A similar model is reproduced in another color on p. 176 in *Yves Saint Laurent et la photographie de mode*, preface by Marguerite Duras, photographs by Lothar Schmid, Albin Michel, 1988.

Estimate: 1,000–1,200 euros
Sold: 2,438 euros

Cornette de Saint Cyr, Paris
June 30, 2012 (lot 107)
Specialists: D. Chombert and F. Sternbach

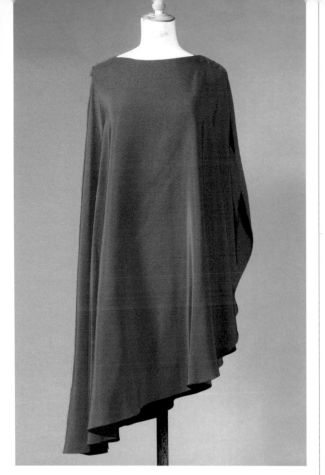

GRÈS

LANVIN

COUTURE

COUTURE, 1970

Tangerine silk crepe cape, open on both sides; boat neckline; asymmetric length. No label.

Camouflage-print cape; small straight collar; four leather buttons. Label "Lanvin, 22 Faubg St Honoré, Paris."

Estimate: 400–500 euros
Sold: 500 euros
Cornette de Saint Cyr, Paris
June 30, 2012 (lot 106)
Specialists: D. Chombert and F. Sternbach

Estimate: 500–700 pounds
Sold: 375 pounds
Christie's, London
December 3, 2009 (lot 97)
Specialist: Patricia Frost

CHRISTIAN DIOR

N ° 0491203302
PRÊT-À-PORTER

Silk bayadere dress with orange, purple, navy blue, and white stripes; high neckline and button cuffs; A-line skirt with a few pleats adorned with three buttons on the left side. Label "Christian Dior Boutique."

Estimate: 150–200 euros
Sold: 173 euros
Camard & Associés, Paris
March 18, 2012 (lot 130)

COURRÈGES

PRÊT-À-PORTER

Tangerine wool crepe jumper; snaps to the waist; A-line skirt with two pockets; vinyl belt with chrome-plated buckle with logo. Label "Courrèges Hyperbole."

Estimate: 80–120 euros
Sold: 350 euros
Artcurial, Paris
June 11, 2012 (lot 155)
Specialist: PB Fashion

YVES SAINT LAURENT

PRÊT-À-PORTER

Wool muslin shirtdress with a stylized floral print on a chocolate brown background; small high ruffled collar with buttoned opening, repeated on the cuffs; gathered shoulders; two inseam pockets. Worn with a matching thin pigskin suede belt. Label "Saint Laurent Rive Gauche."

Estimate: 70–90 euros
Sold: 100 euros
Artcurial, Paris
November 25, 2011 (lot 378)
Specialist: PB Fashion

HALSTON

GRÈS

COUNTURE

COUNTURE

Amber seersucker silk dress with asymmetric neckline; belted waist and asymmetric wraparound skirt forming godets. Worn with a stole.

Ruby red silk taffeta evening gown; high collar; large puffy sleeves; tailored waistline.

BIBLIOGRAPHY: The identical model is reproduced in another color on p. 143 in *Madame Grès: Sphinx of Fashion*, Patricia Mears, Yale University Press, New Haven, CT, 2008; p. 22, *Madame Grès*, Laurence Benaïm, Assouline, 1999.

Estimate: 600–800 dollars
Sold: 2,280 dollars
Charles A. Whitaker Auction Company, Philadelphia
April 27–28, 2012 (lot 893)
Specialist: Charles A. Whitaker

Estimate: 1,000–2,000 euros
Sold: 326 euros
Tajan, Paris
February 4, 2012 (lot 264)
Specialist: Jean-Jacques Wattel

GRÈS

ISSEY MIYAKE

COUTURE, Fall/Winter 1979–1980

COUTURE

Asymmetric gown made of two navy and royal blue crepe panels; long slit on one leg; one sloping shoulder. Label "Grès 1 rue de la Paix Paris."

Poppy red and green silk jersey sheath; asymmetric neckline with one strap holding a green sash at the front. No label.

Estimate: 600–800 euros
Sold: 2,478 euros
Thierry de Maigret, Paris
November 22, 2011 (lot 315)
Specialist: Séverine Experton-Dard

Estimate: 50–80 euros
Sold: 1,251 euros
Artcurial, Paris
July 6, 2012 (lot 258)
Specialist: PB Fashion

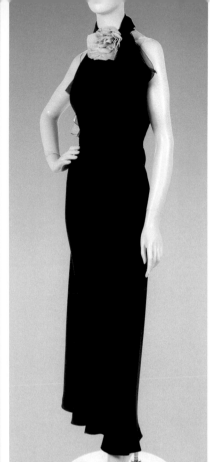

CHANEL

COURRÈGES

VALENTINO

PRÊT-À-PORTER

COUTURE

COUTURE

Black silk chiffon evening dress; round neckline; gathered sloping shoulders; waist adorned with two braid trimmings with floral decoration also holding in place the small gatherings of the flowing slit skirt. Label "Chanel Créations."

Navy blue wool crepe dress; round neckline halter top with logo imprinted on an ivory bib; A-line skirt. Label "Courrèges Couture Future."

Black silk crepe evening sheath; chiffon halter top with a frilled look, adorned with an ivory flower. Label "Valentino Couture."

Estimate: 600–800 dollars
Sold: 620 dollars

Leslie Hindman Auctioneers, Chicago
April 17, 2012 (lot 213)

Specialist: Abigail Rutherford

Estimate: 400–600 dollars
Sold: 732 dollars

Leslie Hindman Auctioneers, Chicago
September 16, 2010 (lot 294)

Specialist: Abigail Rutherford

Estimate: 1,000–2,000 dollars
Sold: 2,440 dollars

Leslie Hindman Auctioneers, Chicago
April 17, 2012 (lot 194)

Specialist: Abigail Rutherford

ICONS OF VINTAGE FASHION
1970s

YVES SAINT LAURENT

PRÊT-À-PORTER

Evening ensemble; top entirely embroidered with gold sequins; round neckline with asymmetric rhinestone buttons; sleeves crimped from the elbows; long black checked wraparound skirt; gold and silver metalized leather appliqué with geometric pattern. Label "Saint Laurent Rive Gauche."

Estimate: 800–1,200 dollars
Sold: 2,640 dollars
Christie's, New York
December 3–17, 2011 (lot 1688)
Specialist: Patricia Frost

YVES SAINT LAURENT

PRÊT-À-PORTER

Black and gold reptile-embossed Lurex evening gown; wraparound blouse with turndown collar; button cuffs on long full sleeves; flowing skirt; tie belt. Label "Saint Laurent Rive Gauche."

Estimate: 400–600 dollars
Sold: 1,037 dollars
Leslie Hindman Auctioneers, Chicago
April 21, 2010 (lot 187)
Specialist: Casey Monda

LORIS AZZARO

COUTURE

Evening ensemble; black and gold Lurex mesh crochet top adorned with small chains; trim embellished with tassels; boat neckline; open back; straight draped black jersey skirt with slit on one side.

Estimate: 500–600 euros
Sold: 750 euros
Cornette de Saint Cyr, Paris
December 12, 2011 (lot 338)
Specialists: D. Chombert and F. Sternbach

GRÈS

COUTURE

Shimmering blue and plum taffeta
evening gown; bow on the round
neckline and at the waist; full skirt
on layered slips that simulates the
appearance of a train. White label, black
lettering.

Estimate: 120–150 euros
Sold: 1,053 euros
Bailly-Pommery & Voutier, Paris
September 26, 2011 (lot 465)
Specialist: PB Fashion

SCAASI

COUTURE, Fall 1979

Fuchsia tulle ball gown with purple
chenille polka-dot appliqué; draped
bustier adorned with an upside-down
ruffle; waist set off with a matching silk
belt; full flared layered skirt worn with a
petticoat. Label.
PROVENANCE: Brooklyn Museum.

Estimate: 400–600 dollars
Sold: 1,320 dollars
Augusta Auctions, New York
November 2, 2011 (lot 109)
Specialist: Karen E. Augusta

BILL GIBB

PRÊT-À-PORTER

Black silk chiffon dress; plunging
V-neckline with pleated, ruffled camisole
look; turquoise and burgundy ribbon
appliqué and gold braiding; matching
long flowing skirt with a tulle apron
embroidered with plant motifs. White
label, black lettering.

Estimate: 300–400 euros
Sold: 938 euros
Cornette de Saint Cyr, Paris
July 4, 2011 (lot 140)
Specialists: D. Chombert and
F. Sternbach

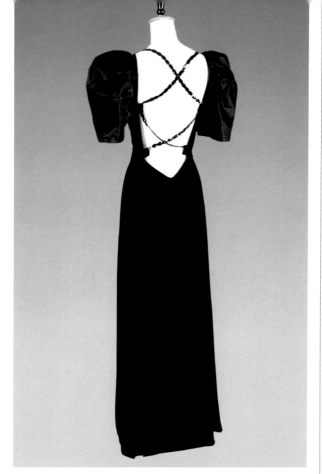

COURRÈGES

CHRISTIAN DIOR

COUTURE

N° 09271
COUTURE, Fall/Winter 1977
by Marc Bohan

Black velvet evening gown; boat neckline and open back adorned with crisscrossing sequined straps; mid-length black taffeta balloon sleeves; A-line skirt. Label "Courrèges Couture Future."

Black silk evening gown; bustier decorated with a silk pongee floral pattern; full gazar skirt. Worn with a jacket inspired by a traveling cape with a ruffle-like collar and sash tie; sleeves and bottom adorned with guipure lace. White label, black lettering.

Estimate: 400–500 euros
Sold: 500 euros
Gros & Delettrez, Paris
December 19, 2011 (lot 120)
Specialists: D. Chombert and F. Sternbach

Estimate: 500–600 euros
Sold: 1,500 euros
Cornette de Saint Cyr, Paris
December 12, 2011 (lot 175)
Specialists: D. Chombert and F. Sternbach

VALENTINO

COUTURE

Tricolored ivory, pearl, and light charcoal gray dress with draped look; halter top set off with satin and adorned with a bow on the open back; full flowing skirt with gathered waist framing a taupe panel. Label "Valentino Couture."

Estimate: 1,000–1,200 euros
Sold: 3,000 euros

Cornette de Saint Cyr, Paris
June 30, 2012 (lot 195)

Specialists: D. Chombert and F. Sternbach

AZZEDINE ALAÏA

COUTURE

1930s-inspired black silk evening gown; V-neckline trimmed with descending band of sequins crossing at the hips to set off the waist; back with same openwork; flowing skirt. White label, black lettering.

Estimate: 1,300–1,500 euros
Sold: 5,625 euros

Cornette de Saint Cyr, Paris
July 2, 2010 (lot 90)

Specialists: D. Chombert and F. Sternbach

AZZEDINE ALAÏA

COUTURE

Ivory silk satin evening gown; crew neckline; back with apron look and a tie. White label, black lettering.

Estimate: 1,200–1,500 euros
Sold: 1,750 euros

Cornette de Saint Cyr, Paris
July 2, 2010 (lot 155)

Specialists: D. Chombert and F. Sternbach

GIVENCHY

COUTURE

Black gazar dress; asymmetric neckline; one shoulder enhanced with a large ruffle and adorned with a bow; full short skirt with a long train. Black label, white lettering.

Estimate: 500–600 euros
Sold: 1,188 euros
Cornette de Saint Cyr, Paris
June 30, 2012 (lot 66)
Specialists: D. Chombert and F. Sternbach

SIMONETTA

COUTURE, 1970

Voluminous pink silk gazar evening cape; round neckline; gathered two-layer cape; asymmetric length. Label "Simonetta-Rome."

Estimate: 800–1,500 pounds
Sold: 1,125 pounds
Christie's, London
December 3, 2009 (lot 312)
Specialist: Patricia Frost

LORIS AZZARO

LORIS AZZARO

COUTURE

COUTURE

Gold lamé evening gown; pleated top with molded bra; high waist over wide skirt with sunburst pleats. White label, black lettering.

White silk jersey gown; draped bustier set off with a gold lamé stylized snake necklace-collar; flowing skirt. White label, black lettering.

Estimate: 1,000–1,200 euros
Sold: 1,750 euros
Cornette de Saint Cyr, Paris
July 4, 2011 (lot 260)
Specialists: D. Chombert and F. Sternbach

Estimate: 1,100–1,200 euros
Sold: 2,000 euros
Cornette de Saint Cyr, Paris
July 2, 2010 (lot 75)
Specialists: D. Chombert and F. Sternbach

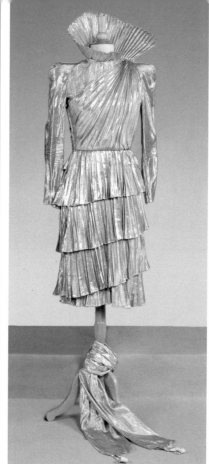

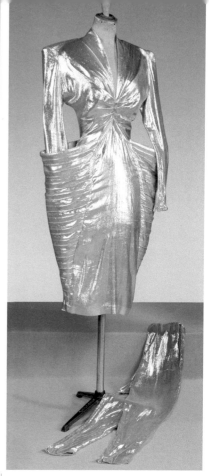

THIERRY MUGLER

PRÊT-À-PORTER, Spring/Summer 1979

Beige jersey sequined translucent pants outfit; half-siren and half-cosmonaut inspiration; slight V-neckline; breasts set off with two shells made of mother-of-pearl coated acetate; long sleeves and calves with decorative barbs. No label.

BIBLIOGRAPHY: The model is reproduced on p. 6 and p. 7 in *Thierry Mugler: Fashion Fetish Fantasy*, Claude Deloffre, ed. Marylou Luther, General Pub Group, 1998, photographs by Helmut Newton.

Estimate: 2,000–2,200 euros
Sold: 2,875 euros

Cornette de Saint Cyr, Paris
July 2, 2010 (lot 270)

Specialists: D. Chombert and
F. Sternbach

THIERRY MUGLER

PRÊT-À-PORTER, Spring/Summer 1979

Gold lamé dress; pleated rigid asymmetric collar like a millstone ruff; diagonally draped bust; skirt with four pleated ruffles; straight shoulders with shoulder pads. Worn over stretch pants. Brown label, gold lettering.

BIBLIOGRAPHY: A similar model is reproduced on p. 48 and p. 49 in *Histoire idéale de la mode contemporaine, les plus beaux défilés de 1971 à nos jours*, Olivier Saillard, éditions Textuel, 2009.

Estimate: 2,500–3,000 euros
Sold: 8,125 euros

Cornette de Saint Cyr, Paris
July 2, 2010 (lot 185)

Specialists: D. Chombert and
F. Sternbach

THIERRY MUGLER

PRÊT-À-PORTER

Silver lamé dress with plunging neckline; bust set off with draped fabric; sleeves and straight shoulders with shoulder pads; pencil skirt adorned with two wide amphora-like hip pockets with the impression of tucked pleats. Worn with very tight pants. Brown label, gold lettering.

BIBLIOGRAPHY: An identical model is reproduced on p. 336 in *Dictionnaire international de la mode, ouvrage collectif*, eds. Bruno Remaury and Lydia Kamitsis, éditions Regard, 2004.

Estimate: 2,500–3,000 euros
Sold: 3,500 euros

Cornette de Saint Cyr, Paris
July 2, 2010 (lot 66)

Specialists: D. Chombert and
F. Sternbach

— Cameron Silver, founder and owner of Decades, the illustrious vintage shop located in Los Angeles.

A Conversation with Cameron Silver of DECADES

Tell us about Decades and about your passion for vintage.
I have always loved fashion, and as far back as I can remember I have been interested in history. It seemed natural to combine these two passions and I opened Decades in 1997. I don't have a favorite decade but I am particularly drawn to the aesthetics of the 1970s.

How would you define vintage?
The definition of vintage is always evolving, especially because of the seismic changes in twenty-first-century fashion. Many of the great twentieth-century designers have retired or died and today's designers move from company to company: Phoebe Philo left Chloé for Céline, Raf Simons left Jil Sander for Dior, Stefano Pilati left Yves Saint Laurent for Zegna, and so on. Because of this phenomenon, their earlier creations become especially interesting. While they are not considered vintage in terms of their age, they have suddenly become collectible. This is similar to what happened after the tragic death of Alexander McQueen—his work increased in value overnight. In other words, there is no simple and easy definition of vintage. Let's say that the term applies to items of clothing from the past that are valuable and deemed collectible.

What is the typical story behind an item sold at Decades?
Nothing is typical at Decades. We get our clothes from many different sources: from celebrities (living or deceased), from auctions, flea markets, or retailers. I look for something that speaks to me in one way or another and that will appeal to our clients.

— Decades, the ultimate destination for luxury vintage.

Who are your clients?

We have a truly global and international clientele ranging from Hollywood celebrities to Arab princesses as well as Asian socialites. All of them dictate rather than follow fashion and like the idea of owning something special and unique.

Because of prêt-à-porter and the evolution of fashion, do you think that today's clothes will be tomorrow's vintage? Will there be as many clothes worth collecting as in the past?

Of course, there are many excellent twenty-first-century designers who will undoubtedly create collectible pieces. When a contemporary designer can accurately capture the zeitgeist of a moment in fashion, his creations stand a good chance of becoming collector's items. Look at Tom Ford: His time at Gucci is a perfect example of how fashion is cyclical. His inspired 1970s designs have all become collector's pieces. The essence of the past ten years in terms of fashion is illustrated in the work of Alber Elbaz at Lanvin, Karl Lagerfeld at Chanel, Rick Owens and Mary Katrantzou. I collect men's vintage and, each season, I focus on a few designers who are pushing men's fashion forward.

How would you define vintage?

The term *vintage* usually refers to an older item of clothing or an object with a brand name, but it can also apply to an item without a label that evokes a specific era or couturier.

To qualify as vintage, an item must have the following characteristics:

- – Be al least twenty years old
- – Reflect the style of a specific designer or couturier
- – Be in its original condition, without any alterations
- – Represent a period in fashion or design
- – Be in good condition

Why are people attracted to vintage?

Nostalgia buffs are drawn to certain periods for the culture and lifestyle. There is a sociological aspect to this phenomenon as people search for identity. They want to stand out at a time when fashion has become more uniform. And there is always something reassuring about turning toward the past, toward happier times, especially when we are going through a period of crisis. For others, buying and wearing secondhand clothes represents a more responsible lifestyle—vintage has unexpectedly become linked to the "slow fashion" movement.

Is there a real vintage "market," in the economic sense of the word?

I think we are indeed witnessing an economic phenomenon. Prices have skyrocketed and the number of vintage stores has grown exponentially. The interest in vintage is highlighted on the red carpet and in the media. Today, vintage has become more than about style; it's also about money. The market will have to stabilize as far as prices are concerned—they have risen enormously in the past five years, even though it is normal for an item to increase in value because of its unique nature and age.

Who are the vendors at the Marché de la Mode Vintage?

Professional vendors, antique dealers, collectors, or individuals who come to sell everything related to fashion and design from the 1950s to the 1980s.

They are European, from France of course, but also from Italy, Belgium, Ireland, Switzerland, Spain, and England. There were thirty vendors in 2002. For the 2012 fair, we had 350 vendors. Some vendors concentrate on a specific century or a particular item.

A pioneer in its field, the Marché de la Mode Vintage in Lyon has come to symbolize both vintage and large crowds. Ever since its first show in 2002, the Marché has become the not-to-be-missed event for enthusiasts who come to shop and bask in the past. They are also drawn by the old-fashioned entertainment: a hula-hoop show, rockabilly music, and a banana split–making contest. Cécile Liard, the mastermind of this multi-faceted fair, spoke to us about the appeal of vintage.

A Conversation with
Cécile Liard of the MARCHÉ DE LA MODE VINTAGE, *Lyon*

Are there atypical vendors whose offerings have surprised you?

This year we had vendors from Paris who specialized in corsets and bathing suits; there was a magnificent collection of pieces from the 1950s that had never been worn and really symbolized the changes that were taking place during that decade—especially for women, as the 1960s approached. We also had a vendor selling cigarette holders, an unusual item.

Who are the customers?

Specialists and aficionados who show up early to get the best items; young people, between the ages of 12 and 18, who are looking for that special piece that will make them stand out; stylists who come for inspiration; interior designers shopping for their clients; and the nostalgic who want to revisit the past. We welcomed 23,000 visitors in 2012 (compared to 800 in 2002).

Increasingly popular and well attended, the Marché de la Mode Vintage now partners with prestigious names such as Bensimon and Jalouse magazine. The future of this vintage market is looking very bright.

"We organized another sale, then another . . . and that was that!"

But fur, like bathing suits, was a seasonal item and they began to look for something else to sell during the off-season. Sternbach suggested leather goods, luxury brands of course. Another success. Maître Jutheau, for whom they worked exclusively, asked them to organize a sale of accessories. Again, a triumph! Their ambitions were constrained, however, by this exclusive arrangement and, in 1993, they opened their own firm in the office they still occupy today. At the time, the fashion-appraising field was just developing and there were only a handful of specialists, including Françoise Auguet, the fashion historian who specializes in twentieth-century couture and Sylvie Daniel, a specialist in fashion as well as lace, vintage textiles, and fans. Chombert and Sternbach began to establish their areas of specialty and expertise.

It was difficult at first. When Maître Le Fur asked them to organize the sale of a collection of costume jewelry, Dominique Chombert and Françoise Sternbach bought several books on the subject and studied them tirelessly. Soon, costume jewelry sales were added to their repertoire. Every year they schedule a jewelry rendezvous, an auction that has become so popular, clients mark their calendars well in advance.

The two women have been credited with the creation of thematic sales. In 1993, they asked Maître Le Fur if they could take over a small part of the auction he was organizing. They

CHOMBERT *and* STERNBACH

The office of Chombert and Sternbach, nestled between stamp and ephemera shops, is situated at 16 Rue de Provence, just a few steps away form the Hôtel Drouot.

Their story began in 1989 when both Dominique Chombert and Françoise Sternbach were out of work. Although the friends had fashion backgrounds (Chombert's family was in the fur business and Sternbach's managed a boutique), they were struggling to get back into the field. Chombert and Sternbach soon realized that "if [they] were going to do something [they] would have to do it on [their] own." Following a fortuitous meeting with an auctioneer and a clerk (who would direct them along the path that would ultimately become theirs), the women organized their first fur sale "for the fun of it." What happened next? The sale generated one million francs in receipts.

wanted to sell fifty items made by Hermès. Based on the auction's resounding success, they organized several more, each time on a larger scale. They took over "Room 8," the smallest of Drouot's rooms for their first auction devoted exclusively to Hermès: The sale turned into a spectacle, complete with shoving, fainting spells, and calls to the EMS. As a result, the subsequent sales grew in size, from 50 lots to 300, to 900 until they passed the 1,000-lot mark. Vuitton and Chanel sales followed, as well as those devoted to a specific designer (Schiaparelli, Poiret, Mugler, Cardin, and the extraordinary auction of Saint Laurent Rive Gauche clothes held simultaneously with the sale of furniture and art objects belonging to Pierre Bergé) and, more recently, "L'homme, son univers, ses icônes," an auction devoted entirely to Yves Saint Laurent.

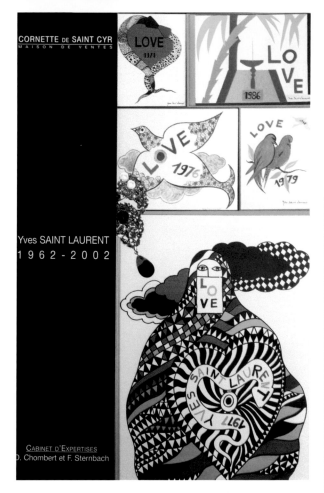

The trajectory of their story is unique, as are they. They have brought a new dimension to a field that is constantly changing. They are responsible for the growing number of couture and costume jewelry sales listed in the *Gazettes,* the weekly auction magazines. They have added aesthetic features to their own publications and print announcements of their upcoming sales—another novelty in the world of auctions. Chombert and Sternbach are determined to see couture achieve the same status as art at Drouot.

They are passionate about their work and both agree that the most extraordinary item they have ever come across was the "Cocteau jacket by Elsa Schiaparelli," sold in 2009. They also like to recount the story of a modest older couple who, shyly, brought in a few items uncovered in their attic: The dresses were by Vionnet and fetched more than 30,000 euros, a sum that was certain to enrich their golden years! These tales are the treasures of their business.

- *Opposite*: Françoise Sternbach and Dominique Chombert, in their Rue de Provence office in Paris.
- *Above*: Flyers and catalogs published by Chombert and Sternbach.

1980s

Glamour and the Avant-Garde

The 1980s have long been criticized, even reviled.

While they have been described as the ultimate incarnation of bad taste, the flashy style of the 1980s is beginning to get some recognition. Designs from the period are slowly making their way into museum collections, and the decade is seen as the last one to have strong fashion codes that are easily identified.

The 1980s style reflected the insouciance of the period. Anything goes, even the most outlandish eccentricities: primary and wild colors combined with sequins and lamé, leather everywhere, padded shoulders, and fuller hips. Jean Paul Gaultier's famous corsets, with their protruding breasts, remain the ultimate symbol of the decade, the emblem of extravagance.

There was a strong focus on the shape of the body. Azzedine Alaïa, a favorite of vintage enthusiasts, created form-fitting clothes made of Lycra and other stretch fabrics that hugged the body. Body-consciousness set in. Thierry Mugler and Claude Montana played with proportions; their designs are structured, with very exaggerated lines.

Karl Lagerfeld reignited Chanel while the Japanese entered the world of Western high fashion with avant-garde designs that are unstructured and oversized. Early Japanese designs are very much in demand today with entire auctions devoted to the period: "Mode Nippone" (October 4, 2010) and "Mode Nippone II" (July 6, 2012) at Artcurial.

JEAN-CHARLES DE CASTELBAJAC

PRÊT-À-PORTER

Multicolored tartan plaid wool coat on ivory background with blue and red band appliqués; collar hood; fringed facings; two flat pockets. Label "Jean-Charles de Castelbajac pour Ko and Co."

Estimate: 120–150 euros
Sold: 125 euros
Artcurial, Paris
April 18, 2012 (lot 94)
Specialist: PB Fashion

JEAN-CHARLES DE CASTELBAJAC

PRÊT-À-PORTER

Multicolored wool tartan jacket on ivory background with collar hood; fringed facings; long sleeves with green and red faux fur; etamine back printed with inscriptions and figurative drawings; two zipped pockets. Label "Jean-Charles de Castelbajac pour Ko and Co."

Estimate: 200–300 euros
Sold: 1,053 euros
Artcurial, Paris
February 7, 2011 (lot 457)
Specialist: PB Fashion

JEAN-CHARLES DE CASTELBAJAC

PRÊT-À-PORTER, Fall/Winter 1988–1989

Plaid-inspired embossed wool coat; size 3/4; in shades of bright yellow, orange, red, and violet; turndown collar adorned with a teddy bear; fringed arms and bottom; one flat pocket. Label "Jean-Charles de Castelbajac pour Ko and Co."

Estimate: 200–400 dollars
Sold: 510 dollars
Augusta Auctions, New York
November 2, 2011 (lot 263)
Specialist: Karen E. Augusta

JEAN-CHARLES DE CASTELBAJAC

PRÊT-À-PORTER

Plaid-inspired embossed wool coat, size 3/4, in a pattern predominantly of green, blue, and purple; turndown fur collar; flat pockets with bottom fringe and fringe at the hem. Label "Jean-Charles de Castelbajac pour Ko and Co."

Estimate: 150–200 euros
Sold: 375 euros
Artcurial, Paris
October 3, 2011 (lot 136)
Specialist: PB Fashion

POPY MORENI

PRÊT-À-PORTER

Bright yellow and black vinyl cloak; drawstring hood; snaps in the front and on each side; two flat pockets. Label "Catricepar Popy Moreni."

BIBLIOGRAPHY: Similar models are reproduced in other colors on p. 22 and p. 23 in *Elle Style: The 1980s*, François Baudot, Jean Demarchy, Filipacchi, 2003.

Estimate: 70–90 euros
Sold: 175 euros
Artcurial, Paris
April 18, 2012 (lot 473)
Specialist: PB Fashion

JEAN-CHARLES DE CASTELBAJAC

PRÊT-À-PORTER

Quilted saffron cotton coat trimmed with brown, red, and blue leather; turndown collar and asymmetric snaps; two flat pockets; peacock appliqué on the back; fanned tail in multicolored suede and leather. White label, silver lettering.

Estimate: 250–350 euros
Sold: 375 euros
Artcurial, Paris
October 3, 2011 (lot 389)
Specialist: PB Fashion

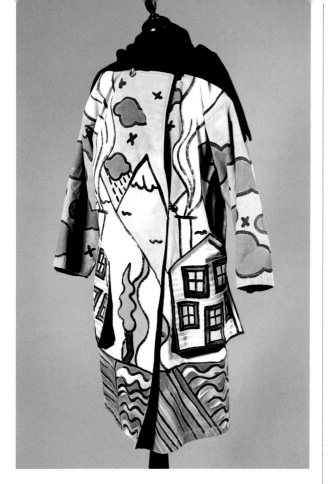

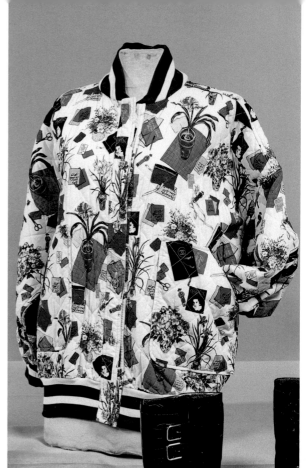

JEAN-CHARLES DE CASTELBAJAC

PRÊT-À-PORTER, Fall/Winter 1988–1989

Hand-painted cotton coat by Corinne Jacq; size 9/10; decorated with primitive patterns; collar hood; pockets decorated with houses; single-breasted closure with asymmetric buttons with loop fasteners; black wool lining. Label "Jean-Charles de Castelbajac pour Ko and Co."

Estimate: 400–600 euros
Sold: 3,503 euros
Artcurial, Paris
April 18, 2012 (lot 441)
Specialist: PB Fashion

CHANEL

PRÊT-À-PORTER
by Karl Lagerfeld

Varsity-inspired quilted cotton jacket with multicolor print, collar, and cuffs, and bottom with black and white stripes; single-breasted closure with gold metal logo buttons; two flat pockets. Label "Chanel Boutique."

Estimate: 150–200 euros
Sold: 250 euros
Cornette de Saint Cyr, Paris
February 13, 2012 (lot 240)
Specialists: D. Chombert and F. Sternbach

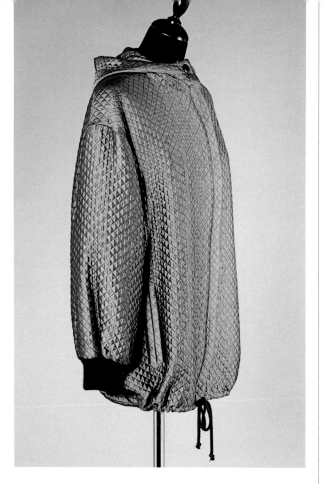

YVES SAINT LAURENT

PRÊT-À-PORTER

Teal hooded wool and quilted silk jacket with zipper; black cuffs; drawstring bottom. Label "Yves Saint Laurent Rive Gauche."

Estimate: 70–90 euros
Sold: 100 euros
Artcurial, Paris
April 18, 2012 (lot 439)
Specialist: PB Fashion

GIANNI VERSACE

PRÊT-À-PORTER

Quilted leather and bottle-green houndstooth embossed wool suit; jacket with high collar and two metallic buttons; straight skirt.

Estimate: 80–120 euros
Sold: 876 euros
Artcurial, Paris
April 18, 2012 (lot 449)
Specialist: PB Fashion

YVES SAINT LAURENT

PRÊT-À-PORTER

Black, midnight blue, mauve, and celadon green wool jacket with a harlequin-inspired pattern; cutout panels adorned with trim; round neck single-breasted with jet buttons. Label "Saint Laurent Rive Gauche."

BIBLIOGRAPHY: A similar model is reproduced on p. 412 in *Designers History 10 Years: YSL 1985–1995*, Yashiaki Yanada, Gap, Japan, 1996.

Estimate: 70–90 euros
Sold: 434 euros
Artcurial, Paris
February 7, 2011 (lot 395)
Specialists: D. Chombert and F. Sternbach

ROMEO GIGLI

PRÊT-À-PORTER

Garnet red "jesters" outfit cut in pointed angles; notched collar; single-breasted; sparkling gold lamé vest; high collar with upright points; belt.

Estimate: 150–250 dollars
Sold: 732 dollars
Leslie Hindman Auctioneers, Chicago
April 21, 2010 (lot 245)
Specialist: Abigail Rutherford

THIERRY MUGLER

PRÊT-À-PORTER

Turquoise wool crepe pants outfit; high collar set off with bias cut; long raglan sleeves with aileron shape decorated with piping; zipped front; two chest pockets; waist adorned with a belt and enamel buckle; blousy back with inverted pleats. Blue label, silver lettering.

Estimate: 1,200–1,300 euros
Sold: 15,000 euros
Cornette de Saint Cyr, Paris
July 2, 2010 (lot 170)
Specialists: D. Chombert and F. Sternbach

THIERRY MUGLER

PRÊT-À-PORTER,
Spring/Summer 1986

Gold lamé pants outfit; strapless; molded bra with cutout look; snaps on the back; zippered ankles. Blue label, silver lettering.

Estimate: 1,000–1,200 euros
Sold: 2,625 euros
Cornette de Saint Cyr, Paris
July 2, 2010 (lot 115)
Specialists: D. Chombert and F. Sternbach

PACO RABANNE

COUTURE

Multicolored blistered lamé dress sprinkled with covered bulbs; bodice top made of gold metallic oval sequins; round neck with opening in the back fastened with several ties; full flared skirt. White label, black lettering.

Estimate: 1,500–2,000 euros
Sold: 1,877 euros
Artcurial, Paris
January 30, 2012 (lot 282)
Specialist: PB Fashion

LOUIS FÉRAUD

COUTURE

Gold and blue silk evening gown with oriental inspiration; completely trimmed in tubular beads and sequins with a pinstriped pattern; crossed-bodice look with shallow V-neckline; short sleeves, one of which is draped; wraparound skirt; belt.

Estimate: 300–500 euros
Sold: 2,875 euros
Cornette de Saint Cyr, Paris
July 2, 2010 (lot 305)
Specialists: D. Chombert and F. Sternbach

THIERRY MUGLER

PRÊT-À-PORTER,
Fall/Winter 1986–1987

Gold lamé faux two-piece evening gown; bustier with sunburst pleats to the hips; bias-cut skirt forming a train. Blue label, silver lettering.

Estimate: 1,500–1,700 euros
Sold: 6,500 euros
Cornette de Saint Cyr, Paris
July 4, 2011 (lot 63)
Specialists: D. Chombert and F. Sternbach

LORIS AZZARO

COUTURE

Gold lamé Cleopatra-inspired evening sheath with permanent sunburst pleats; look of a pointed yoke to the waist setting off the V-neckline and shoulders. White label, black lettering.

Estimate: 1,100–1,200 euros
Sold: 5,000 euros
Cornette de Saint Cyr, Paris
July 2, 2010 (lot 142)
Specialists: D. Chombert and F. Sternbach

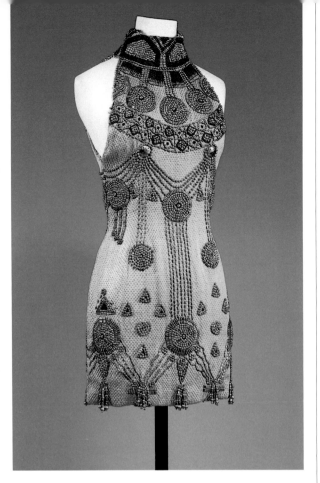

GIANNI VERSACE

GIANNI VERSACE

COUTURE

COUTURE

Apple green woven silk cocktail dress trimmed with antique gold metal beads and black glass round and tubular beads; halter top with high neck with ethnic designs; straight skirt. Label "Atelier Versace."

Golden chain mail cocktail dress; halter neckline and high collar; skirt with asymmetric length cut on the bias. Label "Gianni Versace Couture."

Estimate: 1,500–1,700 euros
Sold: 3,750 euros
Cornette de Saint Cyr, Paris
July 4, 2011 (lot 219)
Specialists: D. Chombert and F. Sternbach

Estimate: 1,300–1,400 euros
Sold: 3,125 euros
Cornette de Saint Cyr, Paris
June 30, 2012 (lot 340)
Specialists: D. Chombert and F. Sternbach

GIANNI VERSACE

GIANNI VERSACE

COUTURE

COUTURE

Gray tulle top lined with black silk and trimmed with beads, rhinestones, and sequins on multicolored chains with dominant red and gold colors and ethnic designs that transform into tassels; halter-cut with high collar. White label, black lettering, "Atelier Versace."

Gray tulle top with gold trim appliqué setting off a V-neckline; open cross patterns and loops; black silk back; long raglan sleeves. Label "Atelier Versace."

Estimate: 800–1,000 euros
Sold: 2,000 euros
Cornette de Saint Cyr, Paris
July 4, 2011 (lot 351)
Specialists: D. Chombert and F. Sternbach

Estimate: 800–900 euros
Sold: 1,375 euros
Cornette de Saint Cyr, Paris
July 4, 2011 (lot 164)
Specialists: D. Chombert and F. Sternbach

YVES SAINT LAURENT

PRÊT-À-PORTER

Black silk velvet dress; draped bodice with neckline plunging to the waist set off with silver taffeta tie belt; puffy mid-length sleeves; straight skirt. Label "Saint Laurent Rive Gauche."

Estimate: 120–150 euros
Sold: 347 euros
Artcurial, Paris
February 7, 2011 (lot 472)
Specialist: PB Fashion

DIAMANT NOIR

PRÊT-À-PORTER
by Claude Pétin

Black velvet dress partially adorned with sequined silver appliqué; round neckline fastened with a jewel button in the back; front adorned with two large padded embellishments, repeated on the two pockets; A-line skirt.

Estimate: 150–180 euros
Sold: 188 euros
Artcurial, Paris
October 3, 2011 (lot 323)
Specialist: PB Fashion

ICONS OF VINTAGE FASHION
1980s

PACO RABANNE

COUTURE

Black silk velvet evening gown; trompe-l'œil bolero; Medici-inspired collar and lace gigot sleeves embroidered with white soutache and sequins in a stylized floral pattern; double-breasted closure; skirt with small train. White label, black lettering.

Estimate: 1,000–1,500 euros
Sold: 1,251 euros
Artcurial, Paris
January 30, 2012 (lot 93)
Specialist: PB Fashion

THIERRY MUGLER

PRÊT-À-PORTER

Silver lamé partially draped long dress; right shoulder adorned with a hanging panel like a half cape; gathered skirt of asymmetric length. No label.

Estimate: 1,500–2,000 euros
Sold: 1,875 euros
Cornette de Saint Cyr, Paris
July 2, 2010 (lot 342)
Specialists: D. Chombert and F. Sternbach

YVES SAINT LAURENT

N° 069985
COUTURE, Fall/Winter 1987

Silver lamé wraparound evening gown with reptile embossed print; draped V-neckline set off with a bow at the waist; flowing skirt. White label, black lettering.

BIBLIOGRAPHY: The identical model is reproduced in *L'Officiel de la Couture et de la Mode de Paris, Yves Saint Laurent Collections 1957–2002—2,500 Modèles,* special issue, éditions Jalou.

Estimate: 1,000–1,200 euros
Sold: 2,125 euros
Cornette de Saint Cyr, Paris
June 30, 2012 (lot 92)
Specialists: D. Chombert and F. Sternbach

MOSCHINO

ANGELO TARLAZZI

COUTURE

PRÊT-À-PORTER

Black crepe cocktail dress; gold fringe on straps, bust, and hips; adorned with a tassel; straight skirt. Label "Moschino Couture."

Black satin and gold lamé stretch sheath with a horizontal puckered look; wide boat neckline.

Estimate: 120–150 euros
Sold: 150 euros
Cornette de Saint Cyr, Paris
June 30, 2012 (lot 147)
Specialists: D. Chombert and F. Sternbach

Estimate: 120–150 euros
Sold: 434 euros
Artcurial, Paris
February 7, 2011 (lot 468)
Specialist: PB Fashion

FRANCE ANDREVIE

YVES SAINT LAURENT

PRÊT-À-PORTER

PRÊT-À-PORTER

Gray, black, and brown striped satin jacket with velvet appliqué of buildings; notched collar; one button; long cuffed sleeves.

Gold metalized-leather jacket; notched lapel; one button; chest pocket and two front flap pockets. Label "Saint Laurent Rive Gauche."

Estimate: 50–80 euros
Sold: 288 euros
Artcurial, Paris
April 18, 2012 (lot 443)
Specialist: PB Fashion

Estimate: 100–150 euros
Sold: 146 euros
Chayette & Cheval, Paris
February 5, 2012 (lot 293)
Specialist: PB Fashion

ANGELO TARLAZZI

PACO RABANNE

PRÊT-À-PORTER

Black silk taffeta mini dress with gold abstract print; entirely draped with a lateral gathered look; left side adorned with half bows enhanced with raffia.

COUTURE

Sienna asymmetric dress with gold sequin appliqué; transversal ruffle forming a small sleeve on the right shoulder; draped skirt. No label.

Estimate: 150–180 euros
Sold: 620 euros
Artcurial, Paris
February 7, 2011 (lot 475)
Specialist: PB Fashion

Estimate: 800–1,200 euros
Sold: 938 euros
Artcurial, Paris
January 30, 2012 (lot 113)
Specialist: PB Fashion

ANGELO TARLAZZI

PACO RABANNE

PRÊT-À-PORTER

COUTURE, Spring/Summer 1981

Green and blue Lurex jersey strapless mini dress adorned with gold metal coin-like charms; short indigo silk crepe ruffled skirt with a matching taffeta half slip.

Dress with top made of linked oval silver metallic sequins; skirt of glossy swan feathers in vivid stripes; V-neckline and low back. No label.

BIBLIOGRAPHY: A similar model is reproduced on p. 142 in *Paco Rabanne*, Lydia Kamitsis, éditions Michel Lafon, 1996.

Estimate: 180–200 euros
Sold: 248 euros
Artcurial, Paris
February 7, 2011 (lot 456)
Specialist: PB Fashion

Estimate: 2,000–3,000 euros
Sold: 10,009 euros
Artcurial, Paris
January 30, 2012 (lot 251)
Specialist: PB Fashion

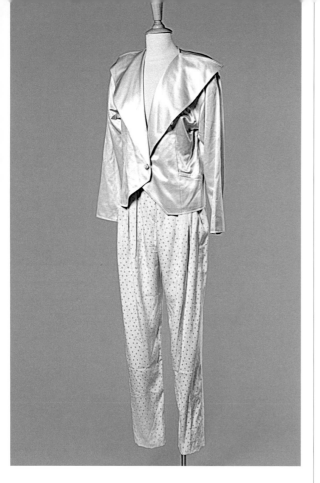

EMANUEL UNGARO

YVES SAINT LAURENT

PRÊT-À-PORTER

PRÊT-À-PORTER

Ivory silk pants outfit; jacket with wide lapel; one button, repeated on the cuffs; gathered pants with a polka-dot pattern. Label "Emanuel Ungaro Parallèle."

Black silk tailored jacket trimmed with gold and silver stars and sprinkled with sequins; round neckline; single-breasted closure. Label "Saint Laurent Rive Gauche."

Estimate: 70–90 euros
Sold: 74 euros
Artcurial, Paris
February 7, 2011 (lot 288)
Specialist: PB Fashion

Estimate: 900–1,000 euros
Sold: 1,000 euros
Cornette de Saint Cyr, Paris
June 30, 2012 (lot 135)
Specialists: D. Chombert and F. Sternbach

YVES SAINT LAURENT

PRÊT-À-PORTER

Woven ribbed silk eton evening jacket sprinkled with sequins; V-neckline; gathered shoulders. Label "Saint Laurent Rive Gauche."

Estimate: 400–500 euros
Sold: 1,125 euros
Cornette de Saint Cyr, Paris
July 2, 2010 (lot 163)
Specialists: D. Chombert and F. Sternbach

SONIA RYKIEL

PRÊT-À-PORTER, Spring/Summer 1982

Ivory crepe pants outfit; jacket without lining; loose front panel trimmed with hammered gold metal coins; long sleeves with same decoration; V-neckline; single-breasted closure; short, wide pants.

BIBLIOGRAPHY: The same model is reproduced in black on p. 221 in the exhibition catalog *Sonia Rykiel Exhibition*, presented at Arts décoratifs, Musée de la Mode et du Textile à Paris, November 19, 2008–April 19, 2009.

Estimate: 80–120 euros
Sold: 186 euros
Artcurial, Paris
June 27, 2011 (lot 97)
Specialist: PB Fashion

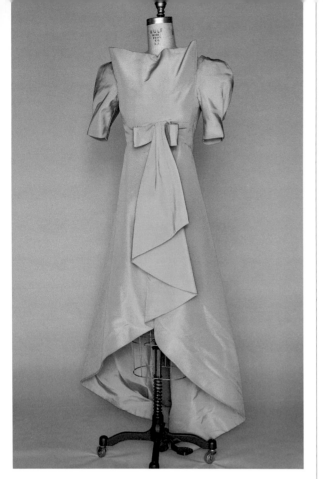

SCAASI

PIERRE CARDIN

COUTURE, Spring 1980

PRÊT-À-PORTER

Golden yellow silk faille evening gown; upright panel on the front; short gigot sleeves; bow at the waist securing a draped panel of the long asymmetric skirt. Label.

<u>PROVENANCE</u>: Brooklyn Museum.

Cherry red silk evening gown; bust with oversized turndown collar forming a short cape fastened with one tie on the open back and one tie at the waist; straight skirt. Label "Pierre Cardin Boutique."

Estimate: 300–500 dollars
Sold: 1,200 dollars
Augusta Auctions, New York
November 2, 2011 (lot 381)
Specialist: Karen E. Augusta

Estimate: 300–400 dollars
Sold: 580 dollars
Augusta Auctions, New York
March 30, 2011 (lot 190)
Specialist: Karen E. Augusta

SCAASI

JAMES GALANOS

COUTURE, 1982

COUTURE

Black tulle cocktail dress embossed with large polka dots; transparent sheath at the top of the bust and on the arms; ruffled collaret and cuffs; three-tiered skirt.

PROVENANCE: Brooklyn Museum.

Black silk evening gown; muslin bodice adorned with lace and enhanced with black beads in overlaid scallops, repeated on the long puffy sleeves; barrel cuffs; straight crepe skirt.

Estimate: 300–500 dollars
Sold: 1,200 dollars
Augusta Auctions, New York
November 2, 2011 (lot 121)
Specialist: Karen E. Augusta

Estimate: 600–800 dollars
Sold: 515 dollars
Augusta Auctions, New York
March 30, 2011 (lot 194)
Specialist: Karen E. Augusta

VALENTINO

ROBERTO CAPUCCI

COUTURE

COUTURE

Evening gown; black ottoman silk bodice with velvet appliqué trimmed in jet beads and soutache adorned with marcasite; boat neckline; wing sleeves; slightly gathered red satin skirt. Label "Valentino Couture."

Blue silk cocktail dress; multicolored shantung bias trim running along the boat neckline and into the Renaissance-inspired wings over the sleeves; straight skirt with slightly gathered waist; matching belt. Black label, white lettering.

Estimate: 3,000–4,000 euros
Sold: 8,750 euros
Cornette de Saint Cyr, Paris
July 4, 2011 (lot 216)
Specialists: D. Chombert and F. Sternbach

Estimate: 8,000–10,000 euros
Sold: 10,625 euros
Cornette de Saint Cyr, Paris
July 4, 2011 (lot 165)
Specialists: D. Chombert and F. Sternbach

PACO RABANNE

PIERRE BALMAIN

COUTURE

Gala evening dress; bustier draped in electric blue silk; black skirt completely covered with blue and light gray appliqués in a wavy design trimmed with silver Lurex threads and enhanced with matching glass cabochons; asymmetric length forming a small train at the back. Black label, white lettering.

COUTURE
by Erik Mortensen

Gala evening dress; ivory silk satin bodice adorned with rhinestones and white, translucent, and black beads forming an abstract pattern; fitted waist and hips on a full midnight blue skirt of asymmetric length. White label, black lettering.

Estimate: 1,500–2,000 euros
Sold: 6,881 euros
Artcurial, Paris
January 30, 2012 (lot 74)
Specialist: PB Fashion

Estimate: 200–300 euros
Sold: 313 euros
Cornette de Saint Cyr, Paris
July 2, 2010 (lot 74)
Specialists: D. Chombert and F. Sternbach

CHANEL

NINA RICCI

COUTURE, Spring/Summer 1989
by Karl Lagerfeld

COUTURE
by Gérard Pibyt

Black lace evening gown; square neckline and short sleeves trimmed with silk ribbon forming picot edging, repeated in rows at the neckline, on the bodice, at the hips, and at the bottom of the full skirt; satin bow at the bust. No label.

Bright green gala evening gown; bodice covered with small beads, rhinestones, and sequins; boat neckline set off with a bouquet of flowers; very full gathered tulle skirt adorned with arabesque patterns made of Lurex; full petticoat. White label, gold lettering and logo.

Estimate: 700–800 euros
Sold: 1,063 euros
Cornette de Saint Cyr, Paris
February 13, 2012 (lot 130)
Specialists: D. Chombert and F. Sternbach

Estimate: 300–500 euros
Sold: 500 euros
Cornette de Saint Cyr, Paris
July 2, 2010 (lot 109)
Specialists: D. Chombert and F. Sternbach

NINA RICCI

COUTURE
by Gérard Pibyt

Strapless evening gown; white linen top adorned with soutaches trimmed with small mother-of-pearl beads and white glass paste; full black silk shantung skirt with darts forming round pleats; horsehair-stiffened slip. White label, gold lettering and logo.

Estimate: 400–500 euros
Sold: 500 euros
Cornette de Saint Cyr, Paris
June 30, 2012 (lot 266)
Specialists: D. Chombert and F. Sternbach

YVES SAINT LAURENT

N º 50872
COUTURE, Fall/Winter 1983

Black velvet strapless mini sheath with draped look; asymmetric tulle skirt; dotted Swiss ruffle at the hips forming a train; adorned with a large bow at the back. White label, black lettering.

Estimate: 1,000–1,200 euros
Sold: 1,625 euros
Cornette de Saint Cyr, Paris
December 12, 2011 (lot 403)
Specialists: D. Chombert and F. Sternbach

GEOFFREY BEENE

COUNTURE

Black seersucker embossed organza gown; halter top with large bow on the open back; belted waist; ample skirt forming godets.

Estimate: 300–500 dollars
Sold: 671 dollars
Leslie Hindman Auctioneers, Chicago
April 11–12, 2011 (lot 124)
Specialist: Abigail Rutherford

VALENTINO

COUTURE

Strapless formal gown; black velvet top with trimmed open back plunging to the hips; green silk tulip skirt embossed with a floral pattern; fuchsia taffeta lining; large bow at the waist. White label, brown lettering.

Estimate: 700–800 euros
Sold: 1,125 euros
Cornette de Saint Cyr, Paris
July 4, 2011 (lot 263)
Specialists: D. Chombert and F. Sternbach

CHLOÉ

PRÊT-À-PORTER
by Karl Lagerfeld

Black silk crepe dress; high collar; single-breasted closure; asymmetric skirt; multicolored long sleeves; long straight skirt.

Estimate: 80–120 dollars
Sold: 122 dollars
Leslie Hindman Auctioneers, Chicago
April 17, 2012 (lot 69)
Specialist: Abigail Rutherford

THIERRY MUGLER

GEOFFREY BEENE

PRÊT-À-PORTER, Fall/Winter 1982–1983

COUTURE

Cherry red tulip-shaped satin cocktail dress; bustier set off with a turndown facing, continued on the back with ribbon lacing; corset look finishing with a V-cut at the waist; gathered skirt with voluminous hips; tight fitted hemline and slit at the back. Blue label, silver lettering.

Black silk satin and dotted Swiss tulle evening gown sprinkled with small, multicolored tassels; bodice with cutout work and open back; partially gathered full skirt.

Estimate: 1,300–1,500 euros
Sold: 4,000 euros
Cornette de Saint Cyr, Paris
July 2, 2010 (lot 173)
Specialists: D. Chombert and F. Sternbach

Estimate: 700–900 dollars
Sold: 457 dollars
Leslie Hindman Auctioneers, Chicago
April 11–12, 2011 (lot 126)
Specialist: Abigail Rutherford

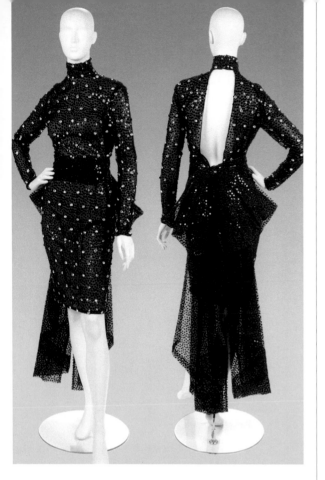

CHRISTIAN DIOR

GIVENCHY

COUTURE, Fall/Winter 1986–1987
by Marc Bohan

Black sequined evening dress sprinkled with silver sequins; high neckline and openwork back enhanced with a large bow with long sashes that form a train; straight skirt; wide draped belt.

COUTURE

Black silk satin and velvet evening dress; openwork back adorned with two large bows; gathered skirt.

Estimate: 600–800 dollars
Sold: 1,952 dollars
Leslie Hindman Auctioneers, Chicago
December 16, 2010 (lot 290)
Specialist: Abigail Rutherford

Estimate: 200–400 dollars
Sold: 122 dollars
Leslie Hindman Auctioneers, Chicago
April 11–12, 2011 (lot 219)
Specialist: Abigail Rutherford

CLAUDE MONTANA

GIANNI VERSACE

Ebony jersey sheath; round neckline; snaps between the shoulder blades; openwork on the back and waist; slit in the back of the skirt gives the appearance of a small train.

COUTURE

Black crepe cocktail dress; back with geometric openwork; back of the skirt adorned with metallic eyelets. Label "Gianni Versace Couture."

Estimate: 1,000–2,000 dollars
Sold: 2,074 dollars
Leslie Hindman Auctioneers, Chicago
April 11–12, 2011 (lot 165)
Specialist: Abigail Rutherford

Estimate: 300–500 dollars
Sold: 918 dollars
Leslie Hindman Auctioneers, Chicago
April 21, 2010 (lot 222)
Specialist: Abigail Rutherford

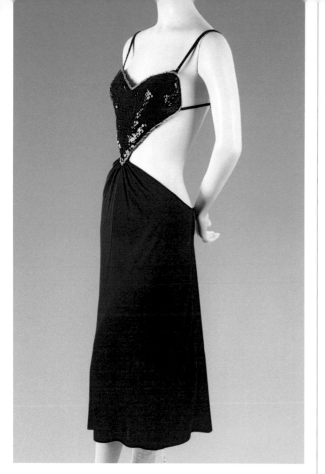

LORIS AZZARO

GUY LAROCHE

COUTURE

COUTURE

Evening dress with a sequined heart-shaped top connected to a flowing silk skirt cut very low in the back. Label.

Cocktail outfit; bolero with small, high neck and black velvet bustier with gold brocaded bias trim; jewel buttons; taffeta bubble skirt.

Estimate: 400–600 dollars
Sold: 1,342 dollars
Leslie Hindman Auctioneers, Chicago
April 21, 2010 (lot 130)
Specialist: Abigail Rutherford

Estimate: 300–500 dollars
Sold: 207 dollars
Leslie Hindman Auctioneers, Chicago
April 11–12, 2011 (lot 161)
Specialist: Abigail Rutherford

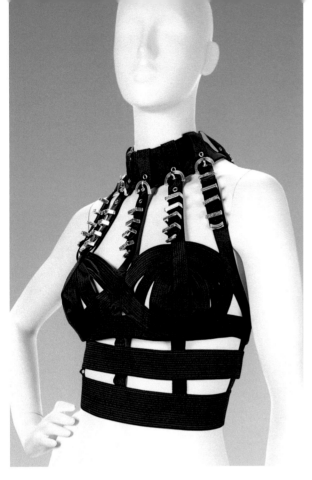

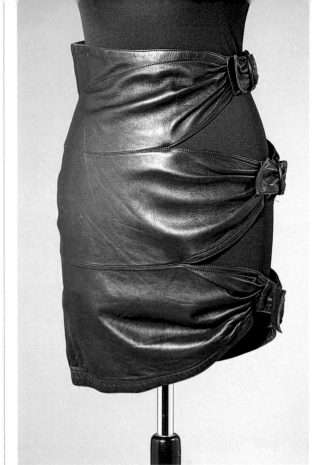

GIANNI VERSACE

AZZEDINE ALAÏA

COUTURE

PRÊT-À-PORTER

Bondage top made of black topstitched satin bands, some adorned with gold metal loops and attached to the neck with a belt buckle; halter look. Label "Gianni Versace Couture."

Black leather skirt fastened on the left side with three buckles, giving a draped look. No label.

BIBLIOGRAPHY: The identical skirt is illustrated by Thierry Perez on p. 45 in *Alaïa*, François Baudot, Assouline, 1996. The identical model is reproduced on p. 125 in *L'Officiel de la Mode*, no. 697, 1983.

Estimate: 1,000–2,000 dollars
Sold: 3,172 dollars
Leslie Hindman Auctioneers, Chicago
September 16, 2010 (lot 399)
Specialist: Abigail Rutherford

Estimate: 150–200 euros
Sold: 1,251 euros
Artcurial, Paris
April 18, 2012 (lot 419)
Specialist: PB Fashion

AZZEDINE ALAÏA

AZZEDINE ALAÏA

PRÊT-À-PORTER

PRÊT-À-PORTER

Copper linen dress; boat neckline with snap at the back over large triangle cutout to the waist; short sleeves with snaps; full gathered skirt with snaps at the back, adorned with two loose pockets. White label, black lettering.

Blue jean outfit; jacket with tight bottom; turndown collar; front zipper; two flap pockets; barrel cuffs; adjustable waist tabs; high-waisted pants with tight, zippered ankles. White labels, black lettering.

Estimate: 100–150 euros
Sold: 2,002 euros
Artcurial, Paris
June 11, 2012 (lot 150)
Specialist: PB Fashion

Estimate: 120–150 euros
Sold: 744 euros
Artcurial, Paris
June 27, 2011 (lot 421)
Specialist: PB Fashion

AZZEDINE ALAÏA

AZZEDINE ALAÏA

PRÊT-À-PORTER

PRÊT-À-PORTER, Fall/Winter 1984–1985

Black jean dress; turndown notched lapel; diagonal zipper to the bottom of the A-line skirt; zippers also at the bottom of the long sleeves and on the pockets; contoured cut. White label, black lettering.

BIBLIOGRAPHY: The identical model in leather is worn by Grace Jones, reproduced on p. 148 and p. 149 in *Alaïa*, Steidl, 1998; the identical model is also reproduced on p. 99 in *Elle Style: The 1980s*, François Baudot, Jean Demarchy, Filipacchi, 2003.

Cinnamon ribbed knit wool and alpaca outfit; short full jacket with large shawl collar; long batwing sleeves, tighter at the cuffs; two flat pockets; straight skirt. White labels, black lettering.

BIBLIOGRAPHY: The identical jacket is reproduced in another color on p. 65 in *Alaïa*, Steidl, 1998.

Estimate: 100–150 euros
Sold: 1,735 euros
Artcurial, Paris
June 27, 2011 (lot 458)
Specialist: PB Fashion

Estimate: 120–150 euros
Sold: 500 euros
Artcurial, Paris
October 3, 2011 (lot 391)
Specialist: PB Fashion

AZZEDINE ALAÏA

AZZEDINE ALAÏA

PRÊT-À-PORTER

PRÊT-À-PORTER

Black wool asymmetric peplum-cut jacket; small, high collar over lapels; double-breasted closure with buttons repeated on the cuffs of the long raglan sleeves. White label, black lettering.

Dusty brown blistered pigskin suede bolero; wide shawl collar transforming into a tie belt; two pockets. White label, black lettering.

Estimate: 120–150 euros
Sold: 225 euros
Artcurial, Paris
October 3, 2011 (lot 195)
Specialist: PB Fashion

Estimate: 150–180 euros
Sold: 867 euros
Artcurial, Paris
June 27, 2011 (lot 223)
Specialist: PB Fashion

AZZEDINE ALAÏA

JEAN PAUL GAULTIER

PRÊT-À-PORTER

PRÊT-À-PORTER

Taupe cotton skirted trench coat; size 7/8; large back flap; belted waist and godets. Worn with jersey pedal pushers.

Black and purple tartan plaid wool pants outfit; crossover jacket with a pleated panel forming a peplum at the back; notched lapel; waist with two tie sashes; chest pocket; high-waisted pants cinched at the ankles. Label "Jean Paul Gaultier pour Bogy's."

Estimate: 1,200–1,500 euros
Sold: 1,611 euros
Eve, Paris
July 12, 2011 (lot M036)
Specialist: Sylvie Daniel

Estimate: 300–400 euros
Sold: 2,753 euros
Artcurial, Paris
October 3, 2011 (lot 300)
Specialist: PB Fashion

JEAN PAUL GAULTIER

JEAN PAUL GAULTIER

PRÊT-À-PORTER

PRÊT-À-PORTER

Teal serge wool shorts outfit; halter top; high collar with two tuck clasps, repeated on the adjustable waist tabs; two inseam pockets. Label "Jean Paul Gaultier pour Kashinawa."

Preppy wool jacket with burgundy, green, and light blue stripes; notched lapel; double-breasted closure with buttons repeated on the cuffs; two flap pockets and one chest pocket; contoured peplum look. Label "Jean Paul Gaultier pour Bogy's."

Estimate: 250–350 euros
Sold: 313 euros
Artcurial, Paris
October 3, 2011 (lot 375)
Specialist: PB Fashion

Estimate: 100–150 euros
Sold: 125 euros
Artcurial, Paris
October 3, 2011 (lot 235)
Specialist: PB Fashion

JEAN PAUL GAULTIER

JEAN PAUL GAULTIER

PRÊT-À-PORTER, Fall/Winter 1986–1987

PRÊT-À-PORTER, Fall/Winter 1986–1987

Pants outfit with zippered red and black nylon top adorned with satiny bottle-green inserts and lead gray, black, and almond striped cotton ribbing; logo topstitching on sleeves; black and purple jodhpur–inspired pants with matching buckskin inserts. Label "Jean Paul Gaultier pour Gibo."

Black cotton dress with front zipper; molded red quilted bra cups; navy blue and bottle-green inserts; sides set off with black and copper striped ribbing. Label "Jean Paul Gaultier pour Gibo."

BIBLIOGRAPHY: A similar dress is reproduced on p. 29 in *L'Officiel 1,000 Modèles, Jean Paul Gaultier—30 ans de création, 1977–2007*, éditions Jalou, January 2007.

Estimate: 180–220 euros
Sold: 13,763 euros
Artcurial, Paris
April 18, 2012 (lot 120)
Specialist: PB Fashion

Estimate: 1,000–1,500 pounds
Sold: 1,250 pounds
Christie's, London
December 3, 2009 (lot 307)
Specialist: Patricia Frost

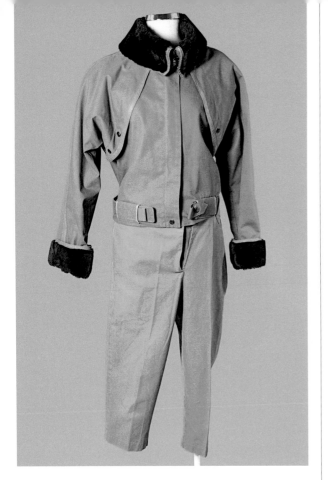

JEAN PAUL GAULTIER

JEAN PAUL GAULTIER

PRÊT-À-PORTER, Fall/Winter 1981–1982

Carmel-colored cotton pants outfit trimmed with leather; jacket with hidden zipper and round neckline; raglan sleeves and front flaps with eyelets, cuffs, and removable collar of chocolate faux fur; waist with side loops holding a belt; short pants. Label "Jean Paul Gaultier pour Kashinawa."

<u>BIBLIOGRAPHY</u>: The identical pants in another color and coat with the same inspiration are reproduced on p. 169 in *L'Officiel de la Mode*, no. 676, 1981.

Estimate: 300–400 euros
Sold: 1,752 euros

Artcurial, Paris
April 18, 2012 (lot 230)
Specialist: PB Fashion

PRÊT-À-PORTER, Fall/Winter 1986–1987

Double black and white tartan plaid bubble skirt; elastic waist holding small pleats. Label "Jean Paul Gaultier pour Gibo."

<u>BIBLIOGRAPHY</u>: The identical skirt is on p. 297 in the exhibition catalog *The Fashion World of Jean Paul Gaultier: From the Sidewalk to the Catwalk*, Thierry-Maxime Loriot, Abrams, 2011, presented at the Montreal Museum of Fine Arts, June 17–October 2, 2011; p. 161, *L'Officiel 1,000 Modèles, Jean Paul Gaultier—30 ans de création, 1977–2007*, éditions Jalou, 2007.

Estimate: 120–150 euros
Sold: 150 euros

Artcurial, Paris
April 18, 2012 (lot 69)
Specialist: PB Fashion

JEAN PAUL GAULTIER

JEAN PAUL GAULTIER

PRÊT-À-PORTER

Black and red plaid cotton dress; shirt look with notched collar and single-breasted closure with buttons; three-quarter sleeves; pareo skirt with two tying panels. Label "Jean Paul Gaultier pour Gibo."

PRÊT-À-PORTER, Fall/Winter 1985–1986
Collection "Le charme coincé de la bourgeoisie"

Quilted cherry satin evening coat with bathrobe inspiration; shawl collar; two flat pockets.

BIBLIOGRAPHY: The identical model is reproduced on p. 25 in *L'Officiel 1,000 Modèles, Jean Paul Gaultier—30 ans de création, 1977-2007*, éditions Jalou, 2007.

Estimate: 200–300 dollars
Sold: 600 dollars
Augusta Auctions, New York
November 2, 2011 (lot 259)
Specialist: Karen E. Augusta

Estimate: 400–500 euros
Sold: 1,239 euros
Eve, Paris
July 12, 2011 (lot M075)
Specialist: Sylvie Daniel

JEAN PAUL GAULTIER

PRÊT-À-PORTER, Spring/Summer 1987
Collection "Trois fois rien pour un bon
à rien"

Black embossed cotton blend corset
slip; molded bra adorned with zigzag
topstitching; zipper; mesh sides; laced at
the back. Label "Junior Gaultier."

BIBLIOGRAPHY: Similar and identical
models are reproduced on p. 614 and
p. 615 in *Fashion: A History from the 18th to
the 20th Century (Collection from the Kyoto
Costume Institute)*, Akiko Fukai, Taschen,
2002; p. 191, *Mode vintage, Les Plus Beaux
Modèles des grands créateurs*, Zandra
Rhodes, éditions de Lodi, 2007.

Estimate: 180–220 euros
Sold: 688 euros
Artcurial, Paris
April 18, 2012 (lot 241)
Specialist: PB Fashion

JEAN PAUL GAULTIER

PRÊT-À-PORTER, Fall/Winter
1984–1985, Collection "Barbès"

Black velvet sheath dress with blistered
look; cone-shaped bra; laced back;
shirring at the bottom of the skirt. Label
"Junior Gaultier."

BIBLIOGRAPHY: The identical models in
other colors are reproduced on p. 20
in *L'Officiel 1,000 Modèles, Jean Paul
Gaultier—30 ans de création, 1977–2007*,
éditions Jalou, January 2007; p. 126,
*The Fashion World of Jean Paul Gaultier:
From the Sidewalk to the Catwalk*, T. Loriot,
Abrams, 2011.

Estimate: 3,000–4,000 pounds
Sold: 13,750 pounds
Christie's, London
December 3, 2009 (lot 313)
Specialist: Patricia Frost

JEAN PAUL GAULTIER

PRÊT-À-PORTER

Blue nylon corset dress adorned with
white topstitching; black mesh on the
sides; molded bra; front zipper. Label
"Junior Gaultier."

Estimate: 180–220 euros
Sold: 2,753 euros
Artcurial, Paris
April 18, 2012 (lot 377)
Specialist: PB Fashion

JEAN PAUL GAULTIER

JEAN PAUL GAULTIER

PRÊT-À-PORTER, Spring/Summer 1988
Collection "La concierge est dans l'escalier"

PRÊT-À-PORTER, Spring/Summer 1989
Collection "Voyage autour du monde en 168 tenues"

Short black jean jacket with open neckline showing the shoulders, partially adorned with two ribbon appliqués and a tie at the front; two adjustable waist tabs; barrel cuffs at the bottom of long sleeves. Label "Junior Gaultier."

BIBLIOGRAPHY: Similar models are reproduced on p. 34 in *L'Officiel 1,000 Modèles, Jean Paul Gaultier—30 ans de création, 1977–2007*, éditions Jalou, 2007.

Cotton gabardine blue jean "cage" jacket; single-breasted closure with metal snaps with logo; two flap pockets; barrel cuffs. Label "Junior Gaultier."

Estimate: 80–120 euros
Sold: 8,133 euros
Artcurial, Paris
April 18, 2012 (lot 183)
Specialist: PB Fashion

Estimate: 200–300 euros
Sold: 4,004 euros
Artcurial, Paris
April 18, 2012 (lot 364)
Specialist: PB Fashion

 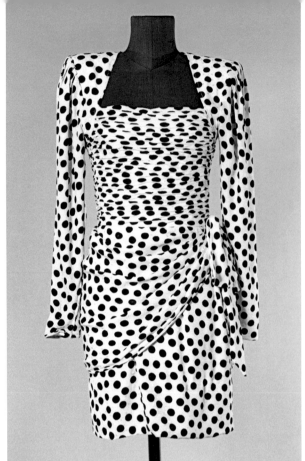

CHRISTIAN LACROIX

EMANUEL UNGARO

COUTURE, Spring/Summer 1988

PRÊT-À-PORTER

Green embossed cotton strapless dress with white polka dots; bust adorned with black grosgrain bows; concealed zipper; separate removable balloon sleeves; waist set off with a V-cut; skirt with wide pleats; nylon mesh slip. No label.

BIBLIOGRAPHY: The identical models in other fabrics are reproduced in *Joyce*, no. 7, January–February 1988, and in *L'Officiel de la Couture et de la Mode de Paris*, no. 737, February 1988.

Ivory embossed silk crepe cocktail dress with black polka dots; square neckline with geometric cut in the back; draped bust; bow on the skirt for a wraparound look; gathered shoulders. Label "Emanuel Ungaro Parallèle."

Estimate: 80–120 euros
Sold: 867 euros
Artcurial, Paris
June 27, 2011 (lot 485)
Specialist: PB Fashion

Estimate: 120–150 euros
Sold: 434 euros
Artcurial, Paris
February 7, 2011 (lot 417)
Specialist: PB Fashion

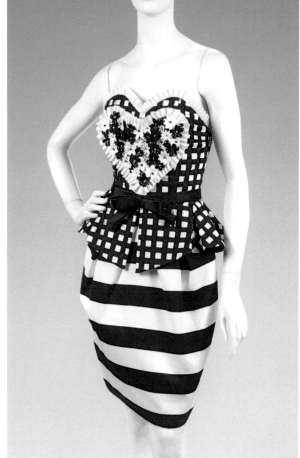

CHRISTIAN LACROIX

CHRISTIAN LACROIX

PRÊT-À-PORTER

Pink silk satin dress printed with black polka dots; V-neckline set off with a double half-bow; skirt with striped panel at the back for slight bustle effect. Label "Christian Lacroix–Bergdorf Goodman."

PRÊT-À-PORTER

Outfit of black and white silk satin; cross-hatched peplum–cut bustier; heart-shaped neckline with a frill trim; heart-shaped flower bouquet on the bust; striped straight skirt; belt tied with a bow. Label "Christian Lacroix–Amen Wardy."

Estimate: 300–500 dollars
Sold: 366 dollars
Leslie Hindman Auctioneers, Chicago
December 16, 2010 (lot 321)
Specialist: Abigail Rutherford

Estimate: 700–900 dollars
Sold: 1,952 dollars
Leslie Hindman Auctioneers, Chicago
December 16, 2010 (lot 313)
Specialist: Abigail Rutherford

ANNABELLE

SCAASI

PRÊT-À-PORTER

COUTURE

Navy blue silk crepe outfit printed with multicolored polka dots; red ribbing; short-sleeve top with round neckline; jacket; pleated skirt.

Blue and white organdy dress with white, red, and blue polka dots; bow at the neck; three-quarter puffy sleeves; skirt with three layers of ruffles.

Estimate: 40–60 euros
Sold: 50 euros
Artcurial, Paris
October 3, 2011 (lot 78)
Specialist: PB Fashion

Estimate: 100–200 dollars
Sold: 64 dollars
Augusta Auctions, New York
March 30, 2011 (lot 89)
Specialist: Karen E. Augusta

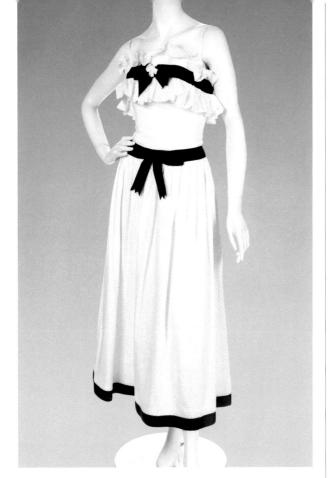

CHANEL

PRÊT-À-PORTER
by Karl Lagerfeld

Long dress of white English lace; ruffled bust and waist set off with black silk ribbon and a bow; full skirt with black ribbon hem. Label "Chanel Boutique."

Estimate: 600–800 dollars
Sold: 732 dollars
Leslie Hindman Auctioneers, Chicago
April 11–12, 2011 (lot 199)
Specialist: Abigail Rutherford

JEAN-LOUIS SCHERRER

N º 008057
COUTURE
(Embroidery: Lesage)

Formal strapless gown; black velvet and white gazar bodice trimmed with plant motif made of beads and silk thread; ivory gazar skirt with black polka dots; asymmetric length forming a train and white ruffle along the hem; dotted black muslin petticoat trimmed with lace. White label, black lettering.

Estimate: 1,300–1,500 euros
Sold: 1,625 euros
Cornette de Saint Cyr, Paris
July 2, 2010 (lot 243)
Specialists: D. Chombert and F. Sternbach

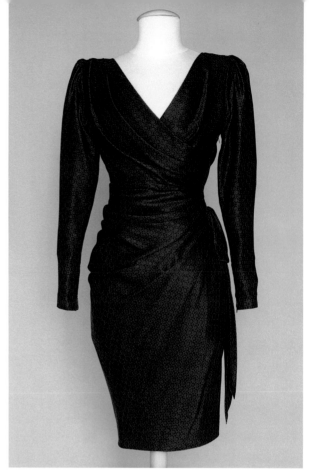

ANONYMOUS

PRÊT-À-PORTER

Ivory silk dress with large black polka dots; V-neckline; two matching buttons at the waist securing the small folds on the bodice and the draped skirt.

YVES SAINT LAURENT

N° 63947
COUTURE, 1985

Purple silk dress with black polka dots and wraparound look; crossed bodice and draped waist set off with a bow on the left side; gathered shoulders; straight skirt. Label.
<u>PROVENANCE</u>: Brooklyn Museum.

Estimate: 15–30 euros
Sold: 99 euros
Artcurial, Paris
June 27, 2011 (lot 321)
Specialist: PB Fashion

Estimate: 300–500 dollars
Sold: 1,680 dollars
Augusta Auctions, New York
November 2, 2011 (lot 315)
Specialist: Karen E. Augusta

ANGELO TARLAZZI

PRÊT-À-PORTER

Strapless black silk taffeta dress with white polka dots; draped and fitted to the hips; drop gathered skirt; large bow on the back.

Estimate: 120–150 euros
Sold: 188 euros
Artcurial, Paris
April 18, 2012 (lot 426)
Specialist: PB Fashion

EMANUEL UNGARO

PRÊT-À-PORTER

Silk crepe dress printed with a stylized floral pattern in beige, black, and red; small, high collar; buttons at the back; tight cuffs; waist set off with a draped sash tied as a belt; straight skirt. Label "Ungaro Solo Donna."

Estimate: 50–80 euros
Sold: 49 euros
Bailly-Pommery & Voutier, Paris
September 26, 2011 (lot 40)
Specialist: PB Fashion

YVES SAINT LAURENT

COUTURE, Spring/Summer 1986

Embossed silk dress printed with a black plant motif on ivory background; round neckline in front; low V-cut in the back set off with two sashes tied in a bow; mid-length puffy sleeves; straight, slightly pleated skirt. Worn with a glossy black snakeskin belt. White label, black lettering.

BIBLIOGRAPHY: An identical model is reproduced in *L'Officiel de la Couture et de la Mode de Paris, Yves Saint Laurent— Collections 1957–2002, 2,500 Modèles,* special issue, éditions Jalou.

Estimate: 80–120 euros
Sold: 313 euros
Artcurial, Paris
June 11, 2012 (lot 368)
Specialist: PB Fashion

GIVENCHY

COUTURE

Bubblegum pink crepe cocktail dress; draped bodice; round neckline; wraparound skirt set off with a bow and trimmed with matching rooster feathers. White label, black lettering.

Estimate: 200–250 euros
Sold: 150 euros
Cornette de Saint Cyr, Paris
June 30, 2012 (lot 98)
Specialists: D. Chombert and F. Sternbach

CHANEL

N° 66382
COUTURE
by Karl Lagerfeld

Velvet and black silk taffeta skater dress; round neckline; gathered skirt with a bow at the back.

Estimate: 600–800 dollars
Sold: 915 dollars
Leslie Hindman Auctioneers, Chicago
April 21, 2010 (lot 178)
Specialist: Abigail Rutherford

VALENTINO

COUTURE

Black wild silk wraparound dress with white trim in scrolling patterns; V-neckline; short kimono sleeves; A-line skirt with three white buttons; matching belt. Label "Valentino Couture."

Estimate: 500–700 euros
Sold: 625 euros
Cornette de Saint Cyr, Paris
June 30, 2012 (lot 300)
Specialists: D. Chombert and F. Sternbach

YVES SAINT LAURENT

COUTURE, Fall/Winter 1983–1984

Black silk velvet and bubblegum pink taffeta cocktail dress; bodice with stays draped to give a look of vertical folds; straight skirt; large bow at the hip. White label, black lettering.

BIBLIOGRAPHY: An identical model is reproduced in *L'Officiel de la Couture et de la Mode de Paris, Yves Saint Laurent— Collections 1957–2002, 2,500 Modèles*, special issue, éditions Jalou.

Estimate: 200–300 euros
Sold: 286 euros
Bailly-Pommery & Voutier, Paris
April 23, 2012 (lot 310)
Specialist: PB Fashion

YVAN & MARZIA

ANGELO TARLAZZI

PRÊT-À-PORTER

PRÊT-À-PORTER

Black cocktail dress; blistered jersey bodice; round neckline; drop waist; gathered nylon bubble skirt over ruffled slip, repeated on the cuffs.

Black lace and taffeta cocktail dress; boat neckline set off with fur collar; draped waist forming a corselet and adorned with two large bows at the back; scalloped at the bottom of the three-quarter sleeves and the hem. No label.

Estimate: 60–80 euros
Sold: 99 euros
Artcurial, Paris
November 15, 2010 (lot 54)
Specialist: PB Fashion

Estimate: 220–250 euros
Sold: 496 euros
Artcurial, Paris
February 7, 2011 (lot 435)
Specialist: PB Fashion

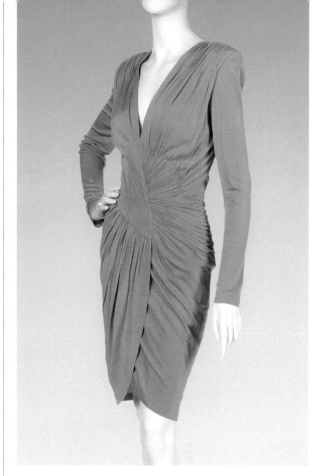

BILL BLASS

VICKY TIEL

PRÊT-À-PORTER

Midnight blue silk taffeta cocktail dress; round neckline and open back trimmed with a ruffle, repeated on the cuffs and the hem; gathered skirt.

PRÊT-À-PORTER

Coral silk jersey draped cocktail dress with a wraparound look and V-neckline.

Estimate: 300–500 dollars
Sold: 198 dollars
Leslie Hindman Auctioneers, Chicago
April 17, 2012 (lot 115)
Specialist: Abigail Rutherford

Estimate: 150–250 dollars
Sold: 97 dollars
Leslie Hindman Auctioneers, Chicago
April 11–12, 2011 (lot 182)
Specialist: Abigail Rutherford

PIERRE CARDIN

CHRISTIAN LACROIX

PRÊT-À-PORTER

PRÊT-À-PORTER

Fuchsia embossed silk dress; boat neckline with pleated front; skirt with wraparound pleated floating panel; right shoulder and waist adorned with a bow. Label "Création Pierre Cardin."

Cocktail outfit; purple velvet top; high neck with diamond-like rhinestone brooch; cap sleeves; raspberry red silk skirt with godets; wide matching belt.

Estimate: 100–150 euros
Sold: 112 euros
Artcurial, Paris
February 7, 2011 (lot 119)
Specialist: PB Fashion

Estimate: 500–1,000 pounds
Sold: 563 pounds
Christie's, London
December 2, 2010 (lot 135)
Specialist: Patricia Frost

YVES SAINT LAURENT

PRÊT-À-PORTER

Gown with asymmetric neckline and pink, purple, orange, and red floral print on an ivory background; left shoulder adorned with two sashes forming a strap when tied; bias-cut gathered skirt. Label "Saint Laurent Rive Gauche."

Estimate: 80–120 euros
Sold: 372 euros
Artcurial, Paris
June 27, 2011 (lot 261)
Specialist: PB Fashion

YVES SAINT LAURENT

PRÊT-À-PORTER, Spring/Summer 1986

Cotton outfit with floral print on blue background; criss-crossed blouse; gathered skirt and quilted, single-breasted jacket with V-neckline. Label "Saint Laurent Rive Gauche."

BIBLIOGRAPHY: An identical jacket is reproduced on p. 577 in *Designers History, 10 Years: YSL 1985–1995*, Yashiaki Yanada, Gap, Japan, 1996.

Estimate: 100–200 dollars
Sold: 220 dollars
Leslie Hindman Auctioneers, Chicago
April 17, 2012 (lot 138)
Specialist: Abigail Rutherford

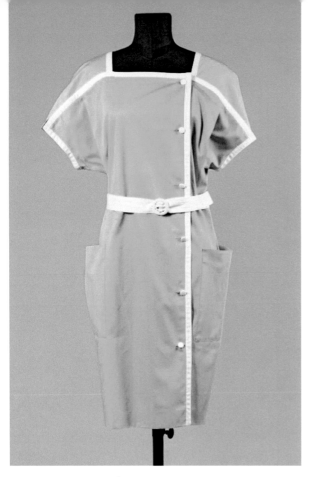 

COURRÈGES

JEAN-RÉMY DAUMAS

PRÊT-À-PORTER

PRÊT-À-PORTER

Bubblegum pink straight cotton dress with white trim; square neckline and buttons on the left side; low armholes; two flat pockets. Worn with a matching white buckled belt.

White cotton pinafore dress inspired by a maid's uniform, with a tie in the back; round collar and edges enhanced with a pleated ruffle.

Estimate: 50–80 euros
Sold: 50 euros
Artcurial, Paris
June 27, 2011 (lot 87)
Specialist: PB Fashion

Estimate: 40–60 euros
Sold: 805 euros
Artcurial, Paris
June 27, 2011 (lot 163)
Specialist: PB Fashion

CHRISTIAN LACROIX

LORIS AZZARO

PRÊT-À-PORTER

COUTURE

Seersucker outfit with rose print; peplum top; heart-shaped neckline enhanced with a frill and a heart-shaped bouquet of roses; straight skirt.

Strapless silk dress with a flower and fruit motif in green, pink, and blue; ruffled bust and high draped waist; straight skirt adorned with a peplum of asymmetric length, pleated at the back. No label.

Estimate: 400–600 dollars
Sold: 1,342 dollars
Leslie Hindman Auctioneers, Chicago
April 21, 2010 (lot 169)
Specialist: Abigail Rutherford

Estimate: 120–150 euros
Sold: 150 euros
Artcurial, Paris
April 18, 2012 (lot 29)
Specialist: PB Fashion

YVES SAINT LAURENT

PRÊT-À-PORTER

Black ottoman wool wraparound dress with satin trim; asymmetric jewel buttons; slightly gathered straight skirt; waist set off with a ribbon tie belt. Label "Saint Laurent Rive Gauche."

Estimate: 100–150 euros
Sold: 149 euros
Artcurial, Paris
February 7, 2011 (lot 359)
Specialist: PB Fashion

YVES SAINT LAURENT

PRÊT-À-PORTER

Black grain de poudre and satin tuxedo coatdress; notched lapel; double-breasted closure with buttons repeated on the cuffs; chest pocket and two vertical pockets. Label "Saint Laurent Rive Gauche."

Estimate: 150–250 dollars
Sold: 122 dollars
Leslie Hindman Auctioneers, Chicago
April 17, 2012 (lot 143)
Specialist: Abigail Rutherford

YVES SAINT LAURENT

N° 45065
COUTURE

Black grain de poudre and velvet coat; notch lapel; two buttons at the waist and cuffs; flap pockets; small slit at the back. White label, black lettering.

Estimate: 500–700 euros
Sold: 620 euros
Artcurial, Paris
February 7, 2011 (lot 188)
Specialist: PB Fashion

VALENTINO

PRÊT-À-PORTER

Black silk velvet and muslin evening ensemble; bodice with elastic waist forming a peplum; square neckline with quilted modesty panel, with same material repeated on the shoulders and the barrel cuffs; straight skirt. Label "Valentino Boutique."

Estimate: 70–90 euros
Sold: 75 euros
Artcurial, Paris
October 3, 2011 (lot 241)
Specialist: PB Fashion

CHANEL

PRÊT-À-PORTER
by Karl Lagerfeld

Cream and navy blue fantasy tweed suit with matching wool trim in both colors; navy circular designs; open jacket with round neckline; two flat pockets; straight skirt. Label "Chanel Boutique."

Estimate: 300–500 dollars
Sold: 671 dollars
Leslie Hindman Auctioneers, Chicago
April 11–12, 2011 (lot 206)
Specialist: Abigail Rutherford

YVES SAINT LAURENT

PRÊT-À-PORTER

Black and white striped cotton blend jacket; grosgrain trim; round collar; single-breasted closure with buttons; ruffled peplum. Label "Saint Laurent Rive Gauche."

Estimate: 80–120 euros
Sold: 188 euros
Artcurial, Paris
April 18, 2012 (lot 136)
Specialist: PB Fashion

YVES SAINT LAURENT

PRÊT-À-PORTER, Fall/Winter 1987–1988

Ruby red silk satin jacket with quilted lining; round neckline; crossed facings; padded cuffs and edging; double-breasted closure with covered buttons; two pockets. Label "Saint Laurent Rive Gauche."

BIBLIOGRAPHY: An identical model is reproduced in other colors on p. 479 in *Designers History, 10 Years: YSL 1985-1995*, Yashiaki Yanada, Gap, Japan, 1996.

Estimate: 200–400 dollars
Sold: 244 dollars
Leslie Hindman Auctioneers, Chicago
December 6, 2011 (lot 126)
Specialist: Abigail Rutherford

YVES SAINT LAURENT

N º 481(...)7
COUTURE

Navy blue blazer; notched lapel; double-breasted closure with buttons; chest pocket. White label, black lettering.

Estimate: 80–120 euros
Sold: 250 euros
Artcurial, Paris
November 25, 2011 (lot 199)
Specialist: PB Fashion

YVES SAINT LAURENT

Nº 52689
COUTURE

Navy blue wool gabardine open jacket; gold buttons on the cuffs; two vertical pockets. White label, black lettering.

Estimate: 70–90 euros
Sold: 100 euros
Artcurial, Paris
November 25, 2011 (lot 452)
Specialist: PB Fashion

CHANEL

PRÊT-À-PORTER
by Karl Lagerfeld

Black and green tweed crisscross bolero with a crosshatch pattern; two flat pockets with gold metal logo buttons, repeated on the cuffs; twisted buckle. Label "Chanel Boutique."

Estimate: 100–150 euros
Sold: 248 euros
Artcurial, Paris
February 7, 2011 (lot 266)
Specialist: PB Fashion

CHANEL

N º 70775
COUTURE
by Karl Lagerfeld

Navy blue tweed tailored jacket with braid trim; round neckline; gold metal buttons on a button placket that forms a modesty panel; four flat pockets. Black label, white lettering.

Estimate: 500–600 euros
Sold: 1,188 euros
Cornette de Saint Cyr, Paris
June 30, 2012 (lot 221)
Specialists: D. Chombert and F. Sternbach

YVES SAINT LAURENT

PRÊT-À-PORTER

Tailored black velvet jacket embroidered with gold thread and trimmed with an inlaid spiked floral pattern of orange, indigo, and purple crepe, adorned with studs; small, high collar; single-breasted closure with looped buttons. Label "Saint Laurent Rive Gauche."

Estimate: 150–200 euros
Sold: 250 euros
Artcurial, Paris
April 18, 2012 (lot 62)
Specialist: PB Fashion

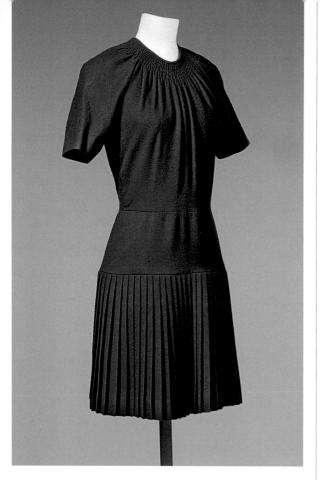

VALENTINO

PIERRE CARDIN

COUTURE

COUTURE

Navy blue cashmere and wool dress; neck set off with smocking; short raglan sleeves; drop waist and pleated skirt. Label "Valentino Couture."

Vermilion crepe cocktail dress; boat neckline; long batwing sleeves; skirt with four overlaid bands.

Estimate: 300–400 euros
Sold: 188 euros
Cornette de Saint Cyr, Paris
July 4, 2011 (lot 42)
Specialists: D. Chombert and F. Sternbach

Estimate: 80–120 euros
Sold: 74 euros
Artcurial, Paris
June 27, 2011 (lot 24)
Specialist: PB Fashion

CHLOÉ

PRÊT-À-PORTER
by Karl Lagerfeld

Blue organza dress with fine white crosshatch; boat neckline in front, V-cut at the back; small buttons to the waist; sloping shoulders; gathered, layered skirt. White label, black lettering.

Estimate: 60–80 euros
Sold: 438 euros
Artcurial, Paris
June 11, 2012 (lot 127)
Specialist: PB Fashion

JEAN-LOUIS SCHERRER

N º 269090
PRÊT-À-PORTER

Red silk crepe cocktail dress; mid-length lace balloon sleeves adorned with flowers; drop waist and gathered lace skirt. Label "Scherrer Boutique."

Estimate: 30–50 euros
Sold: 25 euros
Artcurial, Paris
June 27, 2011 (lot 267)
Specialist: PB Fashion

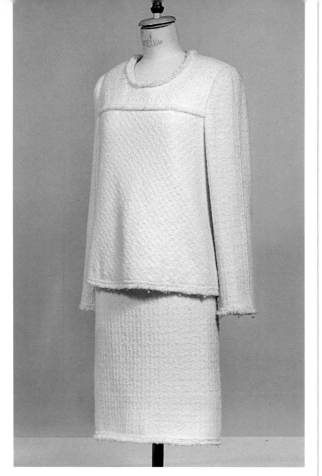

CHANEL

JEAN MUIR

N º 082672
COUTURE
by Karl Lagerfeld

PRÊT-À-PORTER

Ivory wool faux two-piece with mosaic pattern trimmed with fringe; tunic with round neckline buttoned in the back; straight skirt. White label, black lettering.

Beige wool cape-coat; round neckline set off with a bow; barrel cuffs.

Estimate: 400–450 euros
Sold: 625 euros
Cornette de Saint Cyr, Paris
February 13, 2012 (lot 607)
Specialists: D. Chombert and F. Sternbach

Estimate: 100–200 dollars
Sold: 220 dollars
Leslie Hindman Auctioneers, Chicago
April 17, 2012 (lot 80)
Specialist: Abigail Rutherford

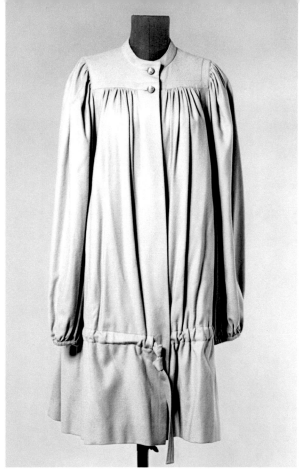

NINA RICCI

LANVIN

PRÊT-À-PORTER

PRÊT-À-PORTER

Café au lait wool gabardine mini dress; slit neckline and cuffs; two loose pockets.

Gray unlined wool serge coat; round neckline fastened with two buttons; long puffy sleeves; drop waist with drawstring and small gatherings.

Estimate: 80–120 euros
Sold: 74 euros
Coutau-Begarie, Paris
December 10, 2011 (lot 129)

Estimate: 60–80 euros
Sold: 186 euros
Artcurial, Paris
February 7, 2011 (lot 96)
Specialist: PB Fashion

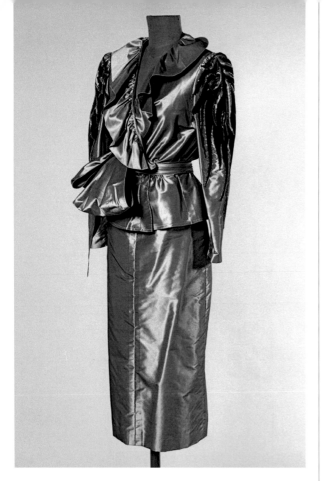

JEAN-LOUIS SCHERRER

PRÊT-À-PORTER

Shimmering bronze silk taffeta evening ensemble; peplum cut; slightly gathered bodice; V-neckline set off with a ruffle fastened with a clasp at the waist; gathered sleeves tight at the cuffs and adorned with green velvet appliqué and small beads; pencil skirt. Worn with a sash belt tied into a large bow. Label "Scherrer Boutique."

Estimate: 80–100 euros
Sold: 500 euros
Artcurial, Paris
October 3, 2011 (lot 240)
Specialist: PB Fashion

SYBILLA

PRÊT-À-PORTER

Olive green linen dress with piping in a lattice pattern of diamonds and squares; round neckline; short raglan sleeves; belted waist and gathered skirt. Label "Sybilla pour Gibo."

Estimate: 200–300 euros
Sold: 1,001 euros
Artcurial, Paris
July 6, 2012 (lot 224)
Specialist: PB Fashion

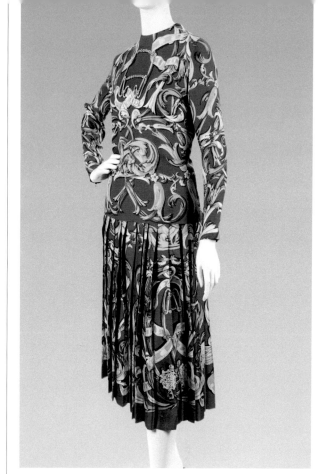

JEAN PAUL GAULTIER HERMÈS

PRÊT-À-PORTER, Spring/Summer 1988
Collection "La concierge est dans l'escalier"

Crepe outfit printed with shades of pink, greenish-gray, and ivory; blouse with turndown collar and barrel cuffs; bib; lace apron with a ruffled peplum look.

BIBLIOGRAPHY: The identical skirt is reproduced on p. 34 in *L'Officiel 1,000 Modèles, Jean Paul Gaultier—30 ans de création 1977–2007*, éditions Jalou.

PRÊT-À-PORTER, Spring/Summer 1987

Silk outfit with gilding print on red background; round collar; pleated skirt.

Estimate: 1,800–2,000 euros
Sold: 2,354 euros
Eve, Paris
June 18, 2012 (lot M011)
Specialist: Sylvie Daniel

Estimate: 400–600 dollars
Sold: 793 dollars
Leslie Hindman Auctioneers, Chicago
September 16, 2010 (lot 390A)
Specialist: Abigail Rutherford

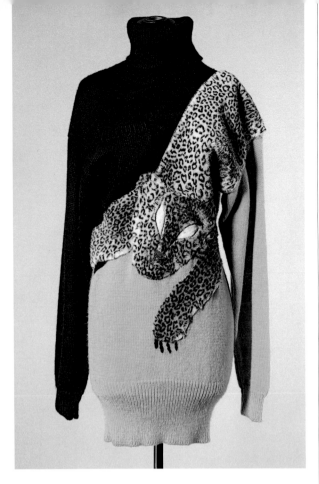 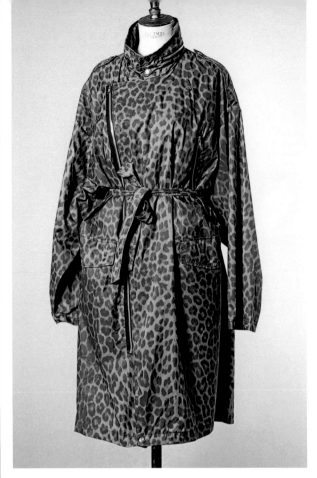

JEAN-CHARLES DE CASTELBAJAC

K-WAY

PRÊT-À-PORTER, Spring/Summer 1987

PRÊT-À-PORTER
by Jean-Charles de Castelbajac

Black and mustard knit dress; wool and mohair blend with faux fur leopard appliqué; rolled neck; chest pocket. White label, silver lettering, "Jean-Charles de Castelbajac pour Ko and Co."

BIBLIOGRAPHY: A similar model is reproduced in *Vogue*, August 1987.

Panther-print nylon raincoat with perfecto jacket inspiration; high collar containing a hood; asymmetric zipper; multiple pockets; epaulets; long batwing-inspired sleeves; back storm flap; tie belt.

Estimate: 300–400 euros
Sold: 1,501 euros
Artcurial, Paris
October 3, 2011 (lot 134)
Specialist: PB Fashion

Estimate: 100–150 euros
Sold: 125 euros
Artcurial, Paris
April 18, 2012 (lot 174)
Specialist: PB Fashion

PATRICK KELLY

ANONYMOUS

Panther-print cotton suit; fitted waist and notched lapel; one button; chest pocket; peplum forming godets; straight skirt.

Panther-print crepe evening gown; asymmetric neckline; one ruffled wing sleeve; draped bodice; drop waist; slit; gathered and layered skirt.

Estimate: 150–250 dollars
Sold: 335 dollars
Leslie Hindman Auctioneers, Chicago
September 20, 2011 (lot 330)
Specialist: Abigail Rutherford

Estimate: 40–60 euros
Sold: 100 euros
Artcurial, Paris
October 3, 2011 (lot 181)
Specialist: PB Fashion

THIERRY MUGLER

ISSEY MIYAKE

PRÊT-À-PORTER, Resort 1988

PRÊT-À-PORTER

Gray cotton muslin dress; snaps all the way down the front; bustier with an asymmetric cuff; waist secures the small gatherings of the full skirt; two loose hip pockets; tie belt.

Black and charcoal gray cotton outfit; blouse with turndown collar; zipper at the back and on the cuffs; mid-calf length skirt, folded over and adorned with a circular cuff forming loose asymmetric pockets on each side; elastic waist with small gatherings. Mauve and charcoal gray label, pale yellow lettering.

Estimate: 80–120 euros
Sold: 125 euros
Artcurial, Paris
October 3, 2011 (lot 447)
Specialist: PB Fashion

Estimate: 250–300 euros
Sold: 313 euros
Artcurial, Paris
July 6, 2012 (lot 386)
Specialist: PB Fashion

ISSEY MIYAKE

PRÊT-À-PORTER

Polyester, cotton, and linen outfit with permanent pleats; beige, white, and gray print; full sweater with single-breasted closure with buttons; sloping shoulders; mid-calf length skirt gathered at the waist forming godets. Mauve and charcoal gray label, pale yellow lettering.

Estimate: 300–400 euros
Sold: 438 euros
Artcurial, Paris
July 6, 2012 (lot 76)
Specialist: PB Fashion

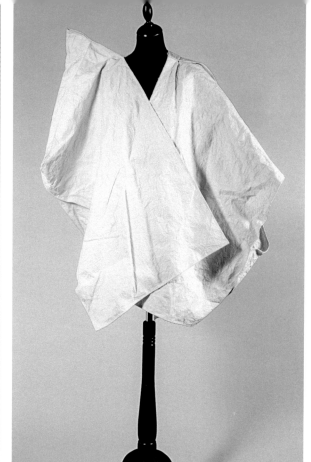

ISSEY MIYAKE

PRÊT-À-PORTER, 1985

Asymmetric unstructured jacket with kimono inspiration in crinkled ivory paper cloth called "kamiko." Ivory label, gray lettering, "Issey Miyake International Council."

BIBLIOGRAPHY: A coat with same inspiration is reproduced on pp. 26–27, *Issey Miyake*, *Mémoire de la mode*, Laurence Benaïm, Assouline, 1997; p. 322, *Histoire de la mode au XXe siècle*, Y. Deslandres, F. Müller, Somogy, 1986; under no. 23 *Issey Miyake, photographies de Irving Penn*, published for the exhibition "Issey Miyake A Un," Musée des Arts Décoratifs, October 15–December 31, 1988, Pont Royal, 1988; p. 68, *Histoire idéale de la mode contemporaine—Les plus beaux défilés de 1971 à nos jours*, Olivier Saillard, Textuel, 2009.

Estimate: 500–800 euros
Sold: 6,256 euros
Artcurial, Paris
July 6, 2012 (lot 277)
Specialist: PB Fashion

THIERRY MUGLER

THIERRY MUGLER

PRÊT-À-PORTER, Resort 1988

PRÊT-À-PORTER, Fall/Winter 1987–1988

Gray linen blend dress with wine-colored topstitching; halter look; neckline set off with a cuff; snaps at the back; full gathered skirt; two pockets. Blue label, silver lettering.

Black velvet and silver lamé cocktail dress; heart-shaped neckline with modesty panel and draped straps; A-line skirt. Blue label, silver lettering.

Estimate: 100–150 euros
Sold: 150 euros
Artcurial, Paris
June 11, 2012 (lot 399)
Specialist: PB Fashion

Estimate: 80–120 euros
Sold: 500 euros
Artcurial, Paris
October 3, 2011 (lot 369)
Specialist: PB Fashion

THIERRY MUGLER

THIERRY MUGLER

PRÊT-À-PORTER, Fall/Winter 1988–1989

PRÊT-À-PORTER, Fall/Winter 1989–1990

Black wool gabardine suit; tailored waist; neckline with asymmetric notched facings; snaps; two bias-cut pockets; slit pencil skirt. Blue label, silver lettering.

Black wool gabardine suit; tailored jacket; asymmetric notched neckline adorned with polyester satin; front snaps; two pockets; long sleeves with piping; straight skirt. Blue label, silver lettering.

Estimate: 80–120 euros
Sold: 1,000 euros
Cornette de Saint Cyr, Paris
April 4, 2012 (lot 460)
Specialists: D. Chombert and F. Sternbach

Estimate: 150–200 euros
Sold: 250 euros
Cornette de Saint Cyr, Paris
June 30, 2012 (lot 129)
Specialists: D. Chombert and F. Sternbach

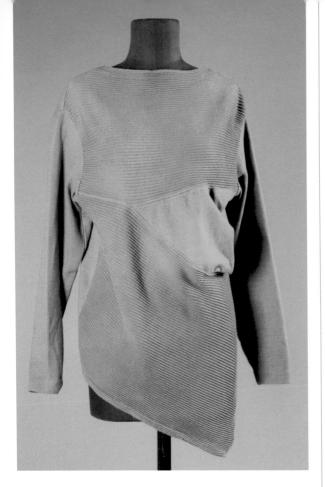

ISSEY MIYAKE

PRÊT-À-PORTER

Old rose jersey cotton blend unstructured sweater with boat neckline. Gray label, beige lettering.

Estimate: 80–120 euros
Sold: 225 euros
Artcurial, Paris
July 6, 2012 (lot 400)
Specialist: PB Fashion

ISSEY MIYAKE

PRÊT-À-PORTER

Faux fur coat with black coating forming scales; size 7/8; oversized turndown collar; double-breasted closure with snaps; long sleeves with cuffs. Mauve and charcoal gray label, pale yellow lettering.

Estimate: 300–400 euros
Sold: 938 euros
Artcurial, Paris
July 6, 2012 (lot 105)
Specialist: PB Fashion

YOHJI YAMAMOTO

COMME DES GARÇONS

PRÊT-À-PORTER

PRÊT-À-PORTER

Orange wool velvet asymmetric coat; wide turndown collar; crossed facings; belted waist. Label.

Black embossed linen outfit; unstructured dress with high waist; smocked strap on the left side; curved bone support in the back; frock coat with notched collar and single-breasted closure with buttons; bone stays in the back slit. Black labels, white lettering.

Estimate: 1,000–2,000 pounds
Sold: 1,250 pounds
Christie's, London
December 3, 2009 (lot 261)
Specialist: Patricia Frost

Estimate: 400–600 euros
Sold: 3,253 euros
Artcurial, Paris
July 6, 2012 (lot 153)
Specialist: PB Fashion

YOHJI YAMAMOTO

PRÊT-À-PORTER

Dark blue wool hooded coat with burnoose inspiration; single-breasted closure; long raglan sleeves; two flat flap pockets. Gray label, black lettering.

Estimate: 150–200 euros
Sold: 288 euros
Artcurial, Paris
July 6, 2012 (lot 208)
Specialist: PB Fashion

YOHJI YAMAMOTO

PRÊT-À-PORTER

Unstructured navy blue wool overcoat; back with the appearance of a reptile's crest; high collar made of two rectangular yokes; long sleeves buttoned to the elbow. No label.

Estimate: 100–150 euros
Sold: 2,002 euros
Artcurial, Paris
July 6, 2012 (lot 32)
Specialist: PB Fashion

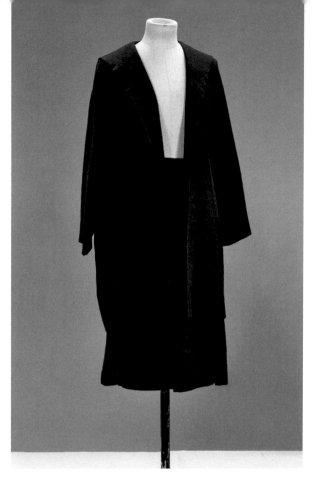

ISSEY MIYAKE

COMME DES GARÇONS

PRÊT-À-PORTER

PRÊT-À-PORTER

Taupe wool bouclé coat; wide shawl collar with two button-holes; two welted pockets; long kimono sleeves partially buttoned. Black label, gold lettering.

Black wool muslin outfit; long jacket with sailor collar; two inseam pockets; skirt gathered at the waist with two horizontal welted pockets. White label, black lettering.

Estimate: 300–350 euros
Sold: 1,500 euros
Cornette de Saint Cyr, Paris
June 30, 2012 (lot 77)
Specialists: D. Chombert and F. Sternbach

Estimate: 300–400 euros
Sold: 500 euros
Cornette de Saint Cyr, Paris
June 30, 2012 (lot 229)
Specialists: D. Chombert and F. Sternbach

COMME DES GARÇONS

PRÊT-À-PORTER

Dark blue cotton velvet unstructured asymmetric dress;
V-neckline; sloping shoulders; tailored waist; skirt
adorned with a panel on the right hip. Label "Comme des
Garçons Noir."

Estimate: 150–200 euros
Sold: 3,753 euros
Artcurial, Paris
July 6, 2012 (lot 104)
Specialist: PB Fashion

COMME DES GARÇONS

PRÊT-À-PORTER, 1988

Dress made of a short-sleeve navy blue silk T-shirt and a
muslin gathered skirt; asymmetrically cut waist. White label,
black lettering.

Estimate: 80–100 euros
Sold: 225 euros
Artcurial, Paris
July 6, 2012 (lot 67)
Specialist: PB Fashion

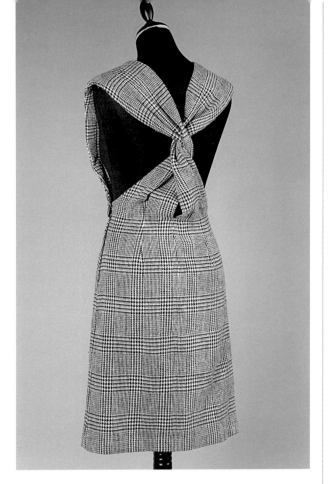

COMME DES GARÇONS

PRÊT-À-PORTER, 1989

Embossed wool pinafore dress; black and white Prince of Wales checks; round neckline; straps cross at the back. Black label, white lettering, "Tricot Comme des Garçons."

Estimate: 150–200 euros
Sold: 400 euros
Artcurial, Paris
July 6, 2012 (lot 140)
Specialist: PB Fashion

COMME DES GARÇONS

PRÊT-À-PORTER, 1988

Red poppy silk georgette and tulle gathered skirt with a reversed wool apron.

Estimate: 1,200–1,500 euros
Sold: 5,205 euros
Eve, Paris
July 12, 2011 (lot M074)
Specialist: Sylvie Daniel

AZZEDINE ALAÏA

Revered by fiercely loyal clients and admiring peers, Azzedine Alaïa was honored at the Guggenheim Museum in New York (2004) and at the Groninger Museum in the Netherlands (2011) with retrospective exhibitions that celebrated his timeless aesthetics. Alaïa is both an avid collector and fervent connoisseur of fashion history and his designs often reference the styles of the 1930s and 1950s; his allusions are always subtle but tinged with modernity.

Women are the designer's ongoing source of inspiration. Although known for his social discretion, he did reveal the following: "I work for women. I have to do it with love."

AZZEDINE AND WOMEN

Alaïa's fashion journey has always involved significant female role models. Born in Tunisia in 1940, his interest in fashion developed early. He poured through old copies of *Vogue* belonging to his mother's friend, the midwife who delivered him. His mind was filled with dreams of Parisian fashions. He learned to sew—with the help of his sister—and was soon copying haute couture designs and making dresses for his delighted neighbors.

He came to Paris in the late 1950s and worked as an assistant to the Marquise de Mazan and later to the Contesse de Blégiers. In addition to his everyday responsibilities, he made dresses for the countess, whose friends soon wanted to know more about the short man with the enormous talent. The countess recommended him to Cécile de Rothschild, Frédérique Somigli introduced him to Arletty, and Simone Zehrfuss and Louise de Vilmorin referred him to *le Tout Paris,* where a bevy of grandes dames swooned over the talented newcomer.

Alaïa spent a brief time at Christian Dior, two seasons at Guy Laroche, and a short period at Charles Jourdan, but these (masculine) names were not very significant in his life's story.

In 1965, he moved to Rue de Bellechasse. His apartment was also his atelier and the place where he entertained many elegant women, artists, and intellectuals.

After Alaïa presented his first eponymous collection in 1981, more famous women joined his "social harem": Tina Turner and Grace Jones, his muses; models Farida Khelfa and Stephanie Seymour; and Naomi Campbell, his most devoted follower, who affectionately calls him "Papa."

AZZEDINE AND A WOMAN'S BODY

The same fashion-loving midwife who shared her copies of *Vogue* with Alaïa during his childhood encouraged him to enroll at the Beaux-Arts Institute in Tunis during the 1950s, where he studied sculpture. It was not a natural medium for him, but it did shape his interpretation of a woman's body. In essence, he continued to make sculptures of women, but did so with his clothes.

The Alaïa woman represented a new kind of femininity that was both elegant and sexy: She was a real woman, whose curves were glorified by his skintight designs. As Alaïa erased the space between body and fabric, he created a brand-new sartorial aesthetic as well as a new way to appreciate a woman's body. "Alaïa likes women. His clothes caress their bodies," explains Olivier Saillard, the director of the Musée Galliera. "If a couturier is someone who reshapes bodies, then Azzedine is the only one who does that today." His impact goes beyond the surface and the fabric. His technical virtuosity in the conception and execution of the outfit (he does the design, drapes directly onto the body, cuts, and assembles himself) and his mastery of the material (especially Lycra and leather) allow him to transform the body and its anatomy. Chic sensuality and refined audacity are his signifiers.

Alaïa lives and works according to his own rules. He shows when and if he wants (and only to a limited number of people), disregards the press, and only focuses on pleasing the women he loves…who love him back.

— Azzedine Alaïa and Farida Khelfa, photograph by Jean-Paul Goude. Cutout with tape, Paris, 1985.

In 1999, Fiona Stuart, Claire Stansfield, and Steven Philip gave up their respective stalls at the Portobello market and together opened Rellik, the British destination boutique for vintage. Their shop is located at the foot of the Trellick Tower in London, itself an icon of the 1970s. For the past thirteen years, the store has attracted vintage enthusiasts from all over the world who descend into this quiet neighborhood to delight in Rellik's treasures.

A Conversation with Fiona Stuart of
RELLIK

ABOUT VINTAGE

People often ask me to define vintage. Perhaps because vintage is, by nature, always evolving, it's not easy to define. Eighteen years ago, the vintage designer market as we know it today was just beginning to see the light. Those designers whose items are so sought after today were not always popular. We never even considered brands like Hermès or Chanel that seemed so "mature." Today, all those names command very high prices.

In the past fifteen years, the word "vintage," wine vernacular to describe fine crus, shifted to the world of clothing. Certain wines age very well and the same applies to clothes.

At Rellik, we have a broad interpretation of vintage. We regularly switch from one style to another, from one period to another: One year, we'll carry a lot of Alaïa, the next year, Yves Saint Laurent. This year we have many Japanese designers.

Rellik is a small shop and we would be bored to tears if we always offered the same things. That's another great feature of vintage: You never know what you will buy next.

RELLIK'S CLIENTS

Most of our clients work in fashion. Many are designers who find inspiration in vintage clothing, so in a sense, our vintage collection will inspire tomorrow's vintage.

We also work with stylists on photo shoots, publicity campaigns, or music videos. And with individuals who want something for a special occasion or just for everyday. The best way to buy a vintage piece is to come in without anything specific in mind, to be open. That way, a vintage piece will naturally find its new owner. And a new chapter begins.

Our clients come from all over the world. Some browse, most buy. Sometimes they come directly from the airport! I am always amazed at how far people will go to buy vintage pieces.

OUR PIECES AND OUR FINDS

Any item you buy has some history. Ideally, we meet the person who owned the item, they tell us a story about it, and we can see the glint of happiness in their eyes . . . then, when we sell it, it feels so much more valuable to the buyer!

It's always rewarding to watch someone fall in love with a dress, a necklace, or any of the items we sell. Vintage pieces always seem to find new owners.

Our pieces come from all over the world. Our best pieces come from auctions and individuals. I used to go on road trips throughout the United States, traveling from city to city to look for treasures. I searched for wonderful costume jewelry from the 1960s or fur jackets by Giorgio Sant'Angelo. That was before the Internet; now, everyone is a connoisseur. As a result, today's market is saturated.

— Vintage treasures from Rellik, Fiona Stuart's fabulous shop in London.

I think the most extraordinary pieces are those from the 1920s and 1930s—all hand-sewn, they epitomize exceptional savoir faire. Almost a century later, you can still touch and appreciate the extraordinary artistic detail. Some of the most amazing pieces I have come across included an evening coat that belonged to the wife of a famous opera singer in 1910; Jerry Hall's kimono from the time of her marriage to Mick Jagger; and a hat covered in mother-of-pearl buttons that we gave to John Galliano. When we showed it to him, he told us that he had made that hat for his graduation project and that the buttons belonged to his grandmother—we had to give it to him! There is a story behind each of our pieces, you just need to dig a little, like an archeologist.

YOHJI YAMAMOTO *and* COMME DES GARÇONS

In the early 1980s, the fashion world experienced an upheaval: Two iconoclastic Japanese designers, Yohji Yamamoto and his former companion Rei Kawakubo—the founder of Comme des Garçons— presented their first Parisian prêt-à-porter collections. The two designers, who were virtually unknown in France, would change the landscape of fashion.

A NEW AESTHETIC BOTH TIMELESS AND AVANT-GARDE

Their impact on the haute couture fashion scene was seismic. "Les Japonais," as the French called them, introduced a radical and conceptually different look at a time when excess and glitz had defined the styles of the 1980s. The reviews were vicious with some journalists comparing Yohji Yamamoto's clothes to "tatters" and Rei Kawakubo's as "rags" worn by models who looked like "beggars." Still, a few praised their audacity and the poetic feel of their designs. They had definitely made an impression!

If confirmation of their status today is needed, one need look no further than the enormously successful auction organized by Artcurial on October 4, 2010: "Mode Nippone— Comme des Garçons, Yohji Yamamoto." It was a "white glove" auction, the term used when every item of the sale is sold—in this case, 478 lots that were acquired by individuals, museums, and the fashion houses themselves who wanted to complete

their archives. Based on that success, Artcurial, in collaboration with PB Fashion, planned a second auction in July 2012. This time, the sale featured a wider range of Japanese fashions, including older pieces such as traditional kimonos.

Yohji Yamamoto and Comme des Garçons have developed a parallel aesthetic, one that looks at fashion and clothes from an entirely new perspective. As architects of the 1980s avant-garde movement, they challenged the contemporary fashion scene and became part of it at the same time. They questioned the proportions of the body and introduced sensuality where it was least expected—in the space between the body and the garment. This concept was in diametric contrast to the glamorous sculpted and molded shapes of the 1980s. Rei Kawakubo pushed the limits even further, especially in the Spring/Summer 1997 and Fall/Winter 2010–2011 Comme des Garçons collections where she added "bumps" of padded fabric to the clothes, giving them the odd look of a deformed body with deplorably placed growths. While other designers reveled in the use of juxtaposed or clashing colors, *Les Japonais* focused on the basics. Yamamoto tirelessly reworked the infinite variations of black, punctuating his collections with an occasional touch of blue, red, or green. Rather than use the silhouette of the body as a starting point, he begins with the fabric, creating designs that endure and disregard current trends. The artistic bent of his creations make them appealing to collectors.

Yamamoto and Kawakubo experimented with fabric and manipulated it in new ways. They reintroduced a sense of mystery and modesty at a time when the body had been so overexposed. Their work is infused with references to the past and allusions to the history of fashion: Yohji Yamamoto's Spring/Summer 1997 collection was a homage to the haute couture of Dior and Chanel. In his Spring/Summer and Fall/Winter collections of 1995, he reinterpreted the kimono, the traditional Japanese garment, and in the Spring/Summer 2008 collection he revisited both eighteenth-century crinolines and work overalls. The Spring/Summer 2012 Comme des Garçons collection recalls the eighteenth century with cage crinolines reduced to their basic structure as well as the styles of the 1960s with architectural shapes reminiscent of Balenciaga.

In their ongoing quest, they deconstruct to better reconstruct; they "debone" each piece to reveal its structure, thus reducing the garment to its essence.

DEVOTED FANS

Having revealed their vision of the world through their designs, Yamamoto and Kawakubo have developed a loyal group of admirers, a circle of insiders who are attracted to fashion that flirts with the abstract. Devoted celebrities who wear their creations would be hard-pressed to combine them with more mainstream designs. The followers of Japanese designers are almost considered a sect whose members recognize each other easily by their instantly identifiable silhouettes.

- *Opposite, left*: Photograph by Nick Knight on the cover of the catalog for the Fall/Winter 1986–1987 Yohji Yamamoto collection.
- *Opposite, right*: Look 43 on the catwalk at the Comme des Garçons show, Fall/Winter 2010–2011.
- *Above, left*: Look 3 on the catwalk at the Yohji Yamamoto Femme show, Spring/Summer 1997.
- *Above, right*: Look 34 on the catwalk at the Yohji Yamamoto Femme show, Spring/Summer 1995.

The LABEL

In the same way an artist signs his work, the modern couturier needed to sign his. The signature took the form of a small piece of cloth sewn into the garment that bore the name of the fashion house. The label could now identify the piece and its provenance.

THE LABEL AS A MEANS OF IDENTIFICATION AND VALUE

The function of a label is obvious: It authenticates a garment, indicates its provenance, and determines its value. In fact, it does even more—it increases a garment's value by adding an element of prestige.

The label of a fashion house can change over time: The name itself might change, and the lettering and colors can be altered. Yves Saint Laurent is a perfect example, especially the "Rive Gauche" division. At one point it was called "Saint Laurent Rive Gauche," then simply "Rive Gauche." As the line evolved, the labels changed. The name—and the label—would change once again in 2012 when Hedi Slimane, the newly appointed creative director, sent shockwaves through the fashion world: He felt that "Yves" had had his moment and it was time to rebrand the company as "Saint Laurent Paris."

Such decisions have temporal consequences: Any garment labeled "Saint Laurent" will be easily identified as post 2012. This applies to other houses as well: A label, by its design, can place a garment in a time frame that explains its creative context. As certain periods in a couture house's history are more significant than others, the time-based reference can be a barometer of the garment's value.

WHEN THERE ARE NO LABELS

A label, however, is not always a toolproof indicator of value. A garment that is missing its label can be the work of a renowned designer. This is often true for older garments, especially those dating back to the first half of the twentieth century. Some labels have not withstood the passage of time and some have simply fallen off or disappeared. They might have been attached to a slip or lining that have worn out. The owner might also have removed the label intentionally, never thinking that her dress would outlive her or that she could decrease its future value by removing a small piece of material sewn into the lining.

Fortunately, there are other ways to determine a garment's provenance. Older pieces rarely have labels but specialists can identify a garment by its construction, its finish, and its details. The iconic Chanel jacket is a perfect example; besides the label, many other details make it easily recognizable: the buttons, the print of the lining, the distinctive panels, and the chain in the hem that ensures that the jacket falls perfectly. The authentication process is a little more difficult for creations by Madeleine Vionnet but a knowledgeable eye will easily recognize the approach, cut, and special technique she used to assemble the different panels of her dresses. An anonymous piece can still be as valuable as one with a label. Buyers usually recognize that even without the small strip of identifying evidence, a garment can still come from a prestigious fashion house.

THE PARADOX OF THE LABEL

Since the presence of a label can increase the value of an item, label switching has become an unfortunate consequence. Placing a fraudulent label in an anonymous but old and potentially interesting piece can substantially raise its value. Anonymous pieces that have been on the market for some time have been known to suddenly turn up with a label. Fortunately, a small number of experts keep a watchful eye on the market.

Today, the paradox of the label has taken an amusing turn at the Maison Martin Margiela. For reasons of aesthetic discretion, the Belgian designer decided that his clothes should have no label at all. Instead, he affixed either a white or a numbered piece of cloth on the inside of his garments that was secured by four pickstitches visible on the outside and easily removable. But his clients decided otherwise, proudly showing off the four visible white stitches that have become a status symbol recognizable only by those in the know.

1990s

The Advent of Minimalism

Minimalism reigns supreme, as designers explore variations on the "me" theme.

Rather than sit on their laurels, designers from the late eighties looked back over the decade to reconsider their own journey, while creating cutting-edge designs for the nineties. Yves Saint Laurent and Jean-Charles de Castelbajac continued to draw inspiration from the world of art and Azzedine Alaïa, Thierry Mugler, and Jean Paul Gaultier toyed with history.

Simplification was the order of the day, a return to basics. Issey Miyake, Rei Kawakubo, and Yohji Yamamoto kept their momentum from the eighties going strong, while newcomers quickly picked up on the iconoclastic trend: Helmut Lang adopted minimalism, Martin Margiela approached simplicity with humor, and Belgian designers proposed a frugal and radical aesthetic.

But sartorial austerity was not to everyone's taste: Moschino, Versace, and Lacroix embraced the baroque while others favored animal prints.

The end of the millennium signaled the arrival of the British bad boys: Alexander McQueen and John Galliano became the creative forces at Givenchy and Dior, the premier French couture houses. Galliano's exit following the 2011 scandal only made his creations soar in value while McQueen's suicide in 2010 turned his tortured creations into collectible works of art.

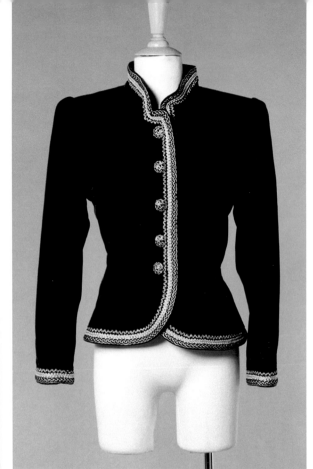

YVES SAINT LAURENT

PRÊT-À-PORTER

Short quilted cotton jacket in a multicolored stylized floral print with a red background, trimmed with red braiding; round neckline; single-breasted closure. Label "Yves Saint Laurent Rive Gauche."

Estimate: 50–80 euros
Sold: 111 euros
Deburaux & Associés, Paris
March 27, 2012 (lot 91)
Specialist: PB Fashion

YVES SAINT LAURENT

PRÊT-À-PORTER

Fitted black velvet jacket with gold braided trim; stand-up collar; single-breasted closure with gold metal buttons, repeated at the cuffs; small peplum. Label "Yves Saint Laurent Rive Gauche."

Estimate: 60–80 euros
Sold: 347 euros
Artcurial, Paris
February 7, 2011 (lot 470)
Specialist: PB Fashion

YVES SAINT LAURENT

PRÊT-À-PORTER, Fall/Winter 1990–1991

Wool muslin ensemble in a multicolored floral print on a navy background; quilted bolero jacket embellished with wool braiding; long-sleeve blouse; wraparound skirt with multicolored fringe. Label "Yves Saint Laurent Rive Gauche."

BIBLIOGRAPHY: Similar styles appear on p. 285 in *Designers History, 10 Years: YSL 1985–1995*, Yashiaki Yanada, Gap, Japan, 1996.

Estimate: 90–100 euros
Sold: 867 euros
Artcurial, Paris
February 7, 2011 (lot 324)
Specialist: PB Fashion

YVES SAINT LAURENT

PRÊT-À-PORTER, Fall/Winter 1992–1993

Double-breasted jacket in multicolored wool plaid; notched collar; wood buttons repeated at the cuffs; one breast pocket and two patch pockets. Label "Yves Saint Laurent Rive Gauche."

BIBLIOGRAPHY: The identical style appears on p. 154 in *Designers History, 10 Years: YSL 1985–1995*, Yashiaki Yanada, Gap, Japan, 1996.

Estimate: 50–80 euros
Sold: 87 euros
Artcurial, Paris
February 7, 2011 (lot 157)
Specialist: PB Fashion

YVES SAINT LAURENT

N ° 071125
COUTURE

Black bouclé wool coat; size 7/8; notched collar; double-breasted closure; vertical pockets; turnback cuffs. White label, black lettering.

Estimate: 500–600 euros
Sold: 625 euros
Gros & Delettrez, Paris
February 6–7, 2012 (lot 134)
Specialists: D. Chombert and F. Sternbach

YVES SAINT LAURENT

PRÊT-À-PORTER

Blue wool jacket edged with dark purple and black wool trim; adorned with two tassels on the front; small stand-up collar; single-breasted closure with wood buttons, repeated at the cuff; two diagonal pockets.

Estimate: 150–250 dollars
Sold: 146 dollars
Leslie Hindman Auctioneers, Chicago
April 17, 2012 (lot 150)
Specialist: Abigail Rutherford

JEAN-CHARLES DE CASTELBAJAC

PRÊT-À-PORTER

Bubblegum pink mohair and wool coat; size 9/10; trimmed with blue and brown braiding; convertible hood with snaps; two patch pockets; half belt at the back. Ivory label, black lettering.

Estimate: 100–150 euros
Sold: 225 euros
Artcurial, Paris
October 3, 2011 (lot 367)
Specialist: PB Fashion

JEAN-CHARLES DE CASTELBAJAC

PRÊT-À-PORTER, Fall/Winter 1993–1994

Raspberry and purple wool coat with a removable leather hood; fringed closure; inseam pockets; self belt.

Estimate: 300–500 dollars
Sold: 519 dollars
Leslie Hindman Auctioneers, Chicago
December 16, 2010 (lot 315)
Specialist: Abigail Rutherford

CHANEL

YVES SAINT LAURENT

PRÊT-À-PORTER, Fall/Winter 1990–1991
by Karl Lagerfeld

PRÊT-À-PORTER, Spring/Summer 1991

Strapless black silk crepe mini dress with a bow at the front; small buttons down the back. Label "Chanel Boutique."

Black satin cotton bouffant dress with elasticized asymmetric neckline and right sleeve; two vertical pockets. Label "Yves Saint Laurent Rive Gauche."

BIBLIOGRAPHY: The identical design appears on p. 253 in *Designers History, 10 Years: YSL 1985–1995*, Yashiaki Yanada, Gap, Japan, 1996.

Estimate: 80–120 euros
Sold: 250 euros
Artcurial, Paris
June 11, 2012 (lot 415)
Specialist: PB Fashion

Estimate: 150–200 euros
Sold: 688 euros
Artcurial, Paris
April 18, 2012 (lot 236)
Specialist: PB Fashion

THIERRY MUGLER

PRÊT-À-PORTER,
Spring/Summer 1992

Faux two-piece ensemble; black piqué cotton halter top; back peplum becomes a belt with a buckle at the front; gingham patterned cotton voile skirt. Blue label, silver lettering.

Estimate: 200–250 euros
Sold: 625 euros
Cornette de Saint Cyr, Paris
June 30, 2012 (lot 349)
Specialists: D. Chombert and F. Sternbach

YVES SAINT LAURENT

N° 075324
COUTURE

Navy blue silk one-shoulder cocktail dress; draped panel with a bow at the waist; straight skirt. White label, black lettering.

Estimate: 500–600 euros
Sold: 2,500 euros
Cornette de Saint Cyr, Paris
July 2, 2010 (lot 122)
Specialists: D. Chombert and F. Sternbach

VALENTINO

PRÊT-À-PORTER

Black silk and cotton dress with a white gazar double-scalloped collar; single row of buttons down the entire front of the dress; two flap pockets. Label "Valentino Boutique."

Estimate: 80–120 euros
Sold: 186 euros
Artcurial, Paris
June 27, 2011 (lot 11)
Specialist: PB Fashion

JEAN-CHARLES DE CASTELBAJAC

CLAUDE MONTANA

PRÊT-À-PORTER, Fall/Winter 1999–2000
Collection "État d'urgence"

Silver down puffer coat with a hood; zipper closure; two pockets with zippers.

BIBLIOGRAPHY: A similar style in a different color is featured on p. 31 in *JC de Castelbajac, Mémoire de la mode*, Florence Müller, Assouline, 2000.

PRÊT-À-PORTER

Copper taffeta ensemble; tapered jacket with a stand-up collar; front zipper closure; zippers at the bottom of the narrow sleeves and on the two vertical pockets; drawstring belt at the back with a buckle in the front; straight short skirt.

Estimate: 200–300 euros
Sold: 225 euros
Artcurial, Paris
October 3, 2011 (lot 366)
Specialist: PB Fashion

Estimate: 120–150 euros
Sold: 99 euros
Artcurial, Paris
February 7, 2011 (lot 382)
Specialist: PB Fashion

GIANNI VERSACE

GIANNI VERSACE

COUTURE

COUTURE, Spring/Summer 1997

Pale green and yellow wool crepe mini dress; square neckline; deep armholes edged with yellow padded trim and cut away at the back.

Cocktail dress of silver tone chain mail; low-cut round neckline with thin straps; open back; bias-cut drop-waist skirt of green chain mail with insert on one side. Black label, white and gold lettering.

BIBLIOGRAPHY: A similar design is featured on pp. 126–127 in the catalog of the Metropolitan Museum of Art exhibition, *Gianni Versace*, Richard Martin, Harry N. Abrams, 1997.

Estimate: 500–700 dollars
Sold: 1,098 dollars
Leslie Hindman Auctioneers, Chicago
September 20, 2011 (lot 217)
Specialist: Abigail Rutherford

Estimate: 3,000–4,000 euros
Sold: 3,375 euros
Cornette de Saint Cyr, Paris
July 4, 2011 (lot 308)
Specialists: D. Chombert and F. Sternbach

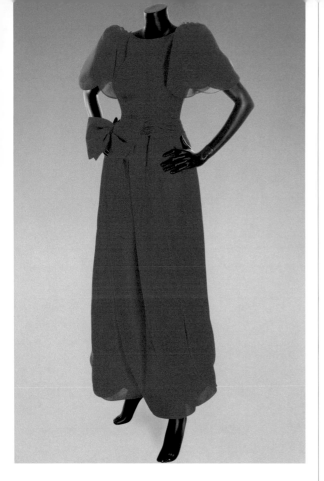

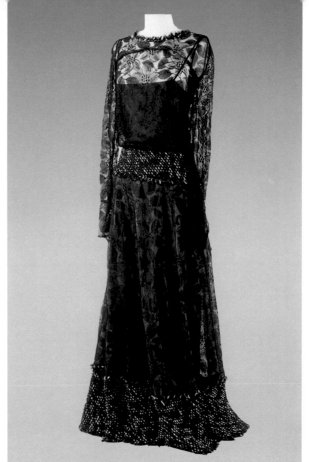

VALENTINO

CHANEL

COUTURE

N° 03427
COUTURE
by Karl Lagerfeld

Red organza evening gown; short sleeves; long skirt with layered petal-shaped panels; draped belt with a bow. Label "Valentino Couture."

Evening gown of see-through black guipure over a navy chiffon bustier; round neckline; white and navy tweed band at the hips and hem. No label.

Estimate: 800–1,500 pounds
Sold: 750 pounds
Christie's, London
December 1, 2001 (lot 59)
Specialist: Patricia Frost

Estimate: 1,200–1,300 euros
Sold: 2,125 euros
Gros & Delettrez, Paris
November 7, 2011 (lot 289)
Specialists: D. Chombert and F. Sternbach

THIERRY MUGLER

PRÊT-À-PORTER,
Spring/Summer 1992

Bias-cut black crepe evening gown; black velvet architectural bodice with molded bra; empire waist with small gathers; fluid skirt.

FILMOGRAPHY: A similar dress is worn by Demi Moore in *Indecent Proposal*, directed by Adrian Lyne (1992).

Estimate: 1,000–2,000 dollars
Sold: 3,416 dollars
Leslie Hindman Auctioneers, Chicago
December 16, 2010 (lot 349)
Specialist: Abigail Rutherford

THIERRY MUGLER

PRÊT-À-PORTER,
Fall/Winter 1998–1999

Midnight blue crepe sheath dress; asymmetric one-shoulder neckline with black velvet detail; bias-cut skirt.

Estimate: 600–800 dollars
Sold: 744 dollars
Leslie Hindman Auctioneers, Chicago
April 17, 2012 (lot 124)
Specialist: Abigail Rutherford

THIERRY MUGLER

PRÊT-À-PORTER,
Fall/Winter 1998–1999

Strapless evening gown; corset-shaped black velvet bustier with molded bra and cutouts; tapered and asymmetric silk crepe skirt gathered at the waist; seam detail at the waistline; draped back. Blue label, silver lettering.

Estimate: 200–300 euros
Sold: 7,500 euros
Cornette de Saint Cyr, Paris
April 4, 2012 (lot 462)
Specialists: D. Chombert and F. Sternbach

THIERRY MUGLER

THIERRY MUGLER

PRÊT-À-PORTER, 1990

PRÊT-À-PORTER

Sand-colored cotton serge dress; asymmetric notched collar; snap closure all the way down the front of the slightly tapered skirt; cap sleeves with cuffs; two patches at the bustline that form mini-pockets; belt with a buckle. Label "Thierry Mugler Activ."

Gray denim suit; short and fitted jacket with turndown collar; zipper closure; two pockets with zippers; straight skirt. Label "Thierry Mugler Activ."

Estimate: 40–60 euros
Sold: 125 euros
Artcurial, Paris
October 3, 2011 (lot 40)
Specialist: PB Fashion

Estimate: 40–60 euros
Sold: 50 euros
Artcurial, Paris
October 3, 2011 (lot 146)
Specialist: PB Fashion

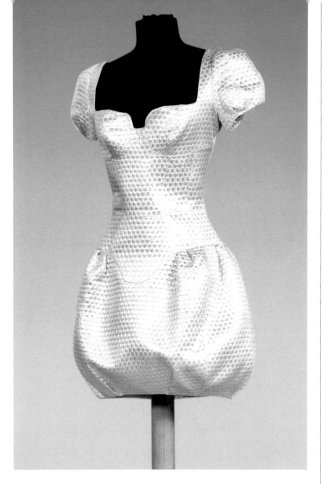

THIERRY MUGLER

PRÊT-À-PORTER, Fall/Winter 1994–1995

Silver brocade cocktail dress in a mosaic pattern; square neckline; long-waisted push-up bustier; bubble skirt. Blue label, silver lettering.

Estimate: 250–300 euros
Sold: 250 euros
Cornette de Saint Cyr, Paris
June 30, 2012 (lot 321)
Specialists: D. Chombert and F. Sternbach

YVES SAINT LAURENT

COUTURE

Sand-colored raw silk dress; Peter Pan collar with faux wood button closure on the left shoulder; short sleeves with cuffs; wraparound skirt; two pockets. Worn with a decorative caramel leather belt. White label, black lettering.

Estimate: 120–150 euros
Sold: 150 euros
Artcurial, Paris
June 11, 2012 (lot 296)
Specialist: PB Fashion

THIERRY MUGLER

PRÊT-À-PORTER, Spring/Summer 1998

Form-fitting black satin cocktail dress; asymmetric one-shoulder neckline with velvet detail.

Estimate: 500–700 dollars
Sold: 1,220 dollars
Leslie Hindman Auctioneers, Chicago
April 21, 2010 (lot 203)
Specialist: Abigail Rutherford

THIERRY MUGLER

PRÊT-À-PORTER, Spring/Summer 1995

Form-fitting black crepe sculptural dress embellished with raffia fringe; sweetheart neckline with tassel detail; built-in bra; cap sleeves with cuffs; two patch pockets.

Estimate: 300–500 dollars
Sold: 1,220 dollars
Leslie Hindman Auctioneers, Chicago
April 21, 2010 (lot 205)
Specialist: Abigail Rutherford

THIERRY MUGLER

PRÊT-À-PORTER, Fall/Winter 1998–1999

Black wool crepe suit; form-fitting jacket with rhinestone detail; V-neckline with faux-fur trim, repeated at the cuffs; single-breasted closure with snaps; straight skirt. Blue label, silver lettering.

Estimate: 150–200 euros
Sold: 150 euros
Cornette de Saint Cyr, Paris
April 4, 2012 (lot 409)
Specialists: D. Chombert and F. Sternbach

THIERRY MUGLER

PRÊT-À-PORTER, Fall/Winter 1996–1997
Collection "Amazones"

Black wool crepe jacket with quilted faux-leather embellishments; round neckline; single-breasted closure with snaps; two breast pockets; asymmetric peplum; longer at the back. Blue label, silver lettering.

Estimate: 120–150 euros
Sold: 173 euros
Artcurial, Paris
February 7, 2011 (lot 116)
Specialist: PB Fashion

THIERRY MUGLER

THIERRY MUGLER

PRÊT-À-PORTER, Fall/Winter 1994–1995

PRÊT-À-PORTER, Fall/Winter 1990–1991

Form-fitting burgundy wool gabardine suit; V-neckline jacket fitted at the waist and adorned with a black velvet star, repeated at the bottom of the long raglan sleeves and the skirt; snap closure; fuller cut over the hips; straight skirt. Blue label, silver lettering.

Black crepe wool suit with velvet detail; jacket with a peplum; round neckline with an opening; snap closure; straight skirt. Blue label, silver lettering.

Estimate: 100–150 euros
Sold: 375 euros
Cornette de Saint Cyr, Paris
April 4, 2012 (lot 419)
Specialists: D. Chombert and F. Sternbach

Estimate: 150–200 euros
Sold: 350 euros
Cornette de Saint Cyr, Paris
April 4, 2012 (lot 543)
Specialists: D. Chombert and F. Sternbach

THIERRY MUGLER

THIERRY MUGLER

PRÊT-À-PORTER, Fall/Winter 1991–1992

PRÊT-À-PORTER, Spring/Summer 1995

Cornflower blue polyester crepe suit; jacket with a peplum embellished with metallic cubes on the shoulders and cuffs; small shawl collar; snap closure; pencil skirt. Worn with a belt.

Form-fitting black crepe suit; fitted jacket with nylon tulle cinching the waist with stays; notched collar with a small bow; two flap pockets; straight skirt. Blue label, silver lettering.

Estimate: 40–60 euros
Sold: 50 euros
Artcurial, Paris
October 3, 2011 (lot 321)
Specialist: PB Fashion

Estimate: 180–200 euros
Sold: 475 euros
Artcurial, Paris
October 3, 2011 (lot 465)
Specialist: PB Fashion

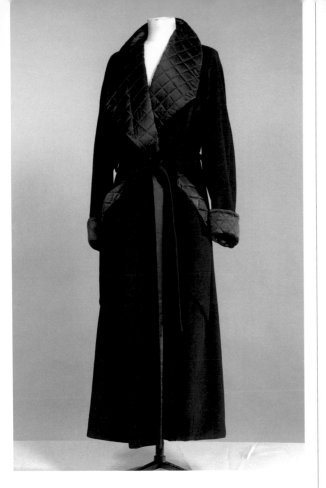

THIERRY MUGLER

THIERRY MUGLER

PRÊT-À-PORTER, Fall/Winter 1993–1994

PRÊT-À-PORTER

Black wool robe; shawl collar; cuffs and pocket flaps of quilted black satin; belt. Blue label, silver lettering.

Black wool redingote-style coat embellished with velvet; notched collar; single-breasted closure; corset-like detail at the hips; skirt with godets. Blue label, black lettering.

Estimate: 150–200 euros
Sold: 625 euros
Cornette de Saint Cyr, Paris
April 4, 2012 (lot 526)
Specialists: D. Chombert and F. Sternbach

Estimate: 400–600 euros
Sold: 1,125 euros
Cornette de Saint Cyr, Paris
June 30, 2012 (lot 210)
Specialists: D. Chombert and F. Sternbach

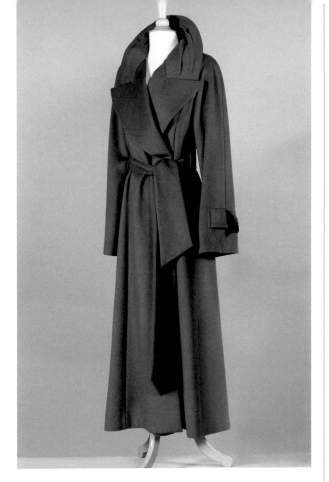 

CLAUDE MONTANA

CHLOÉ

PRÊT-À-PORTER

PRÊT-À-PORTER, Fall/Winter 1995–1996
by Karl Lagerfeld

Taupe wool oversized coat; partially draped and wide notched collar; edge-to-edge facings without buttons; belt; tabs on the cuffs.

Light blue mohair evening coat with a train, embellished with multicolored florets, rhinestones, clear sequins, and wool crocheted motifs; double turndown collar with ties; slit; scalloped hemline.

Estimate: 600–700 euros
Sold: 875 euros
Cornette de Saint Cyr, Paris
July 2, 2010 (lot 210)
Specialists: D. Chombert and F. Sternbach

Estimate: 1,200–1,400 euros
Sold: 1,500 euros
Cornette de Saint Cyr, Paris
April 4, 2012 (lot 350)
Specialists: D. Chombert and F. Sternbach

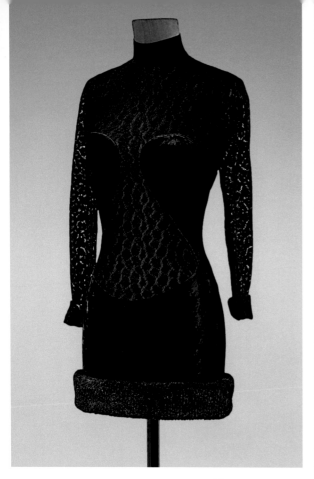

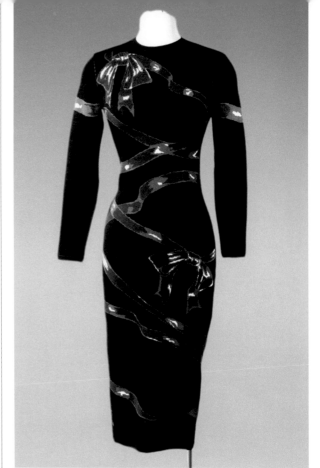

AZZEDINE ALAÏA

AZZEDINE ALAÏA

PRÊT-À-PORTER, Fall/Winter 1991–1992

PRÊT-À-PORTER

Black lace and panne velvet short dress with a black-on-black pattern; short stand-up collar with ribbed edge; faux-fur trim at the hem.

Form-fitting jacquard stretch knit dress with a design of bronze, gray, and white bows on a black background; round neckline; zipper at the back and bottom of the skirt.

BIBLIOGRAPHY: Similar styles are featured on p. 58 of *Alaïa*, François Baudot, Assouline, 1996.

Estimate: 150–200 euros
Sold: 2,231 euros

Artcurial, Paris
June 27, 2011 (lot 92)

Specialist: PB Fashion

Estimate: 120–150 euros
Sold: 1,053 euros

Artcurial, Paris
June 27, 2011 (lot 198)

Specialist: PB Fashion

AZZEDINE ALAÏA

AZZEDINE ALAÏA

PRÊT-À-PORTER, Spring/Summer 1991

PRÊT-À-PORTER, Spring/Summer 1991

Jacquard stretch cotton blend dress; jewel neckline; short sleeves. The black and white checked pattern is inspired by the logo of Tati, a popular chain of French discount stores.

BIBLIOGRAPHY: The same style in an identical fabric is featured on pp. 174–175 in *Alaïa*, Steidl, 1998.

Jacquard stretch cotton blend dress; scoop neckline; buttons at the front; short sleeves. The pink and white checked pattern fabric is inspired by the logo of Tati, a popular chain of French discount stores.

BIBLIOGRAPHY: The same style in an identical fabric is featured on pp. 174–175 in *Alaïa*, Steidl, 1998.

Estimate: 300–500 dollars
Sold: 366 dollars
Leslie Hindman Auctioneers, Chicago
April 11–12, 2011 (lot 214)
Specialist: Abigail Rutherford

Estimate: 80–120 euros
Sold: 248 euros
Artcurial, Paris
June 27, 2011 (lot 398)
Specialist: PB Fashion

AZZEDINE ALAÏA

AZZEDINE ALAÏA

COUTURE

COUTURE

Entirely pleated black crepe mini dress; plunging neckline and bare back; two leather belts, one at the waist, one under the bustline; short skirt with many slits.

BIBLIOGRAPHY: The identical style in a different color is featured on p. 18 in the exhibition catalog *Alaïa: Azzedine Alaïa in the 21st Century*, Groninger Museum, the Netherlands, December 11, 2011–May 6, 2012.

Entirely pleated white crepe jersey dress; halter neckline over viscose bra in faux fur; open back; skirt made of four floating panels.

Estimate: 180–220 euros
Sold: 4,337 euros
Artcurial, Paris
June 27, 2011 (lot 263)
Specialist: PB Fashion

Estimate: 200–300 euros
Sold: 6,816 euros
Artcurial, Paris
June 27, 2011 (lot 348)
Specialist: PB Fashion

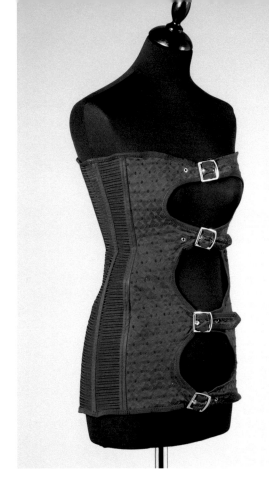

JEAN PAUL GAULTIER

JEAN PAUL GAULTIER

PRÊT-À-PORTER, Spring/Summer 1992
Collection "Concours d'élégance"

Navy jersey girdle bustier that closes at the front with four buckles; side panels of boned netting; lacing up the back. Label "Jean Paul Gaultier Femme."

PRÊT-À-PORTER

Tunic with straps composed of a black satin bra with molded cups and topstitching, attached to the lower portion of a burgundy wool jacket with buttons in the front and two flap pockets. Label "Jean Paul Gaultier Femme."

Estimate: 150–200 euros
Sold: 438 euros
Artcurial, Paris
April 18, 2012 (lot 366)
Specialist: PB Fashion

Estimate: 100–150 euros
Sold: 563 euros
Artcurial, Paris
April 18, 2012 (lot 444)
Specialist: PB Fashion

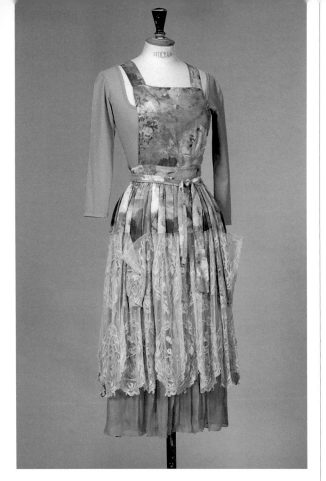

JEAN PAUL GAULTIER

JEAN PAUL GAULTIER

PRÊT-À-PORTER

Flesh-toned polyester jersey dress; round neckline; single-breasted closure; three-quarter sleeves; beige chiffon skirt worn under a floral-print chiffon pinafore adorned with ivory lace; two pockets and a belt that ties in the front. Black label, green lettering, "Jean Paul Gaultier Femme."

PRÊT-À-PORTER

Strapless dress; black poplin panel wraps around the bust over chocolate brown netting; a second panel is wrapped around the hips over a black polyester straight skirt. White label, green lettering, "Jean Paul Gaultier Femme."

Estimate: 250–300 euros
Sold: 325 euros
Cornette de Saint Cyr, Paris
June 30, 2012 (lot 117)
Specialists: D. Chombert and F. Sternbach

Estimate: 1,000–1,200 euros
Sold: 1,625 euros
Cornette de Saint Cyr, Paris
June 30, 2012 (lot 116)
Specialists: D. Chombert and F. Sternbach

JEAN PAUL GAULTIER

JEAN PAUL GAULTIER

PRÊT-À-PORTER, Fall/Winter 1992–1993
Collection "L'Europe de l'avenir"

Moss green fitted wool jacket with black vinyl appliqués and white topstitching; notched collar; single-breasted closure with snaps; two flap pockets and one breast pocket; peplum. Black label, green lettering, "Jean Paul Gaultier Femme."

PRÊT-À-PORTER, Fall/Winter 1998–1999
Collection "Élégance parisienne"

Red leather Perfecto-inspired coat; size 9/10; notched collar; asymmetric zipped closure, repeated on the pockets and at the cuffs. Worn with a belt with a buckle. Label "Jean Paul Gaultier Femme."

Estimate: 150–200 euros
Sold: 225 euros
Artcurial, Paris
October 3, 2011 (lot 177)
Specialist: PB Fashion

Estimate: 300–400 euros
Sold: 563 euros
Artcurial, Paris
October 3, 2011 (lot 265)
Specialist: PB Fashion

MOSCHINO

PRÊT-À-PORTER, Spring/Summer 1991

Roy Lichtenstein comic book–print silk suit; double-breasted closure; notch collar; covered buttons; two flap pockets; straight skirt; sleeveless blouse with round neckline and a little bow. Label "Cheap and Chic by Moschino."

Estimate: 120–150 euros
Sold: 350 euros
Artcurial, Paris
April 18, 2012 (lot 238)
Specialist: PB Fashion

JEAN-CHARLES DE CASTELBAJAC

PRÊT-À-PORTER, Spring/Summer 1998

Clear PVC raincoat with multicolored design; four flap pockets, two on the inside; stand-up collar; snap closure.

Estimate: 120–150 euros
Sold: 150 euros
Artcurial, Paris
April 18, 2012 (lot 365)
Specialist: PB Fashion

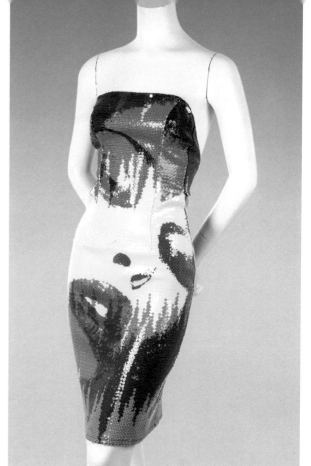

GIANNI VERSACE

GIANNI VERSACE

PRÊT-À-PORTER, 1991

PRÊT-À-PORTER

Warhol-print suit featuring portraits of Marilyn Monroe and James Dean; jacket trimmed with electric blue topstitched braiding; single cuffs; round neckline; single-breasted closure with rhinestone buttons; short, straight skirt.

Sequin-covered strapless cocktail dress in a pop art design. Label "Versus Versace."

Estimate: 800–1,200 dollars
Sold: 1,220 dollars
Leslie Hindman Auctioneers, Chicago
April 21, 2010 (lot 234)
Specialist: Abigail Rutherford

Estimate: 300–500 dollars
Sold: 1,342 dollars
Leslie Hindman Auctioneers, Chicago
April 21, 2012 (lot 224)
Specialist: Abigail Rutherford

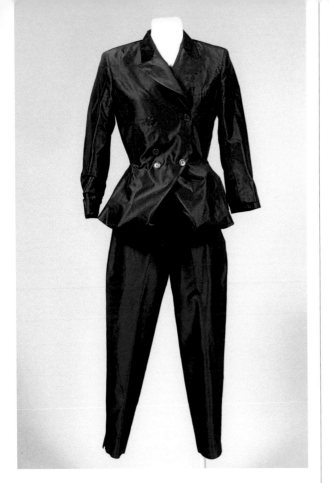

JEAN PAUL GAULTIER

JEAN PAUL GAULTIER

PRÊT-À-PORTER

Taffeta suit; purple jacket with bouffant peplum at the front; turndown collar; double-breasted closure; breast pocket; layered cuffs; bottle-green tapered pants. Label "Jean Paul Gaultier Classique."

PRÊT-À-PORTER, Fall/Winter 1997–1998
Collection "La culture noire et sa force"

Straight dress of printed panne velvet and printed crepe with repeated photographic portraits; small stand-up collar. Black label, green lettering, "Jean Paul Gaultier Femme."

Estimate: 120–150 euros
Sold: 370 euros
Artcurial, Paris
October 4, 2010 (lot 44)
Specialist: PB Fashion

Estimate: 60–80 euros
Sold: 100 euros
Artcurial, Paris
October 3, 2011 (lot 293)
Specialist: PB Fashion

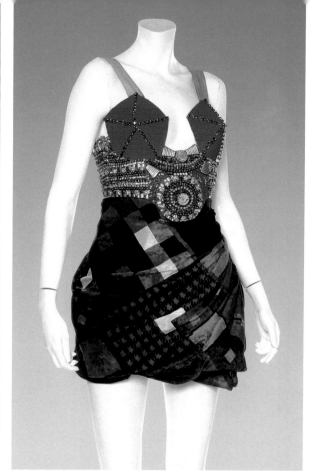

ISSEY MIYAKE

GIANNI VERSACE

PRÊT-À-PORTER

COUTURE

Oversized kimono-coat in multicolored woven wool blend; wide asymmetric turndown collar; two buttons; two diagonal pockets with piping; turnback cuffs. White label, black lettering.

Mini dress with orange hexagonal bra cups covered in red sequins and a small corset entirely embroidered with beads, sequins, and small gold metal ornaments; draped skirt of multicolored printed velvet. Label "Gianni Versace Couture."

ICONOGRAPHY: Iman wore this dress on the catwalk.

Estimate: 300–500 euros
Sold: 1,500 euros
Cornette de Saint Cyr, Paris
July 2, 2010 (lot 189)
Specialists: D. Chombert and F. Sternbach

Estimate: 2,000–3,000 pounds
Sold: 6,875 pounds
Christie's, London
December 2, 2010 (lot 195)
Specialist: Patricia Frost

JEAN-CHARLES DE CASTELBAJAC

PRÊT-À-PORTER, Spring/Summer 1997

Black gazar bolero with an image of the *Mona Lisa* on the back; stand-up collar; hidden snap closure.

Estimate: 100–150 euros
Sold: 375 euros
Artcurial, Paris
April 18, 2012 (lot 262)
Specialist: PB Fashion

MOSCHINO

PRÊT-À-PORTER

Black cotton serge mini skirt covered with playing cards. Label "Moschino Jeans."

Estimate: 70–90 euros
Sold: 688 euros
Artcurial, Paris
April 18, 2012 (lot 243)
Specialist: PB Fashion

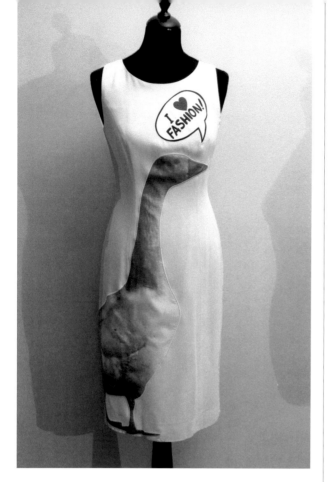

MOSCHINO

PRÊT-À-PORTER

Ivory silk crepe dress with appliqués of a goose and a speech bubble exclaiming, "I love Fashion!"

BIBLIOGRAPHY: The identical style appears in a different color on p. 38 in *Moschino*, Luca Stoppini and Mariuccia Casadio, Skira, 2001.

Estimate: 100–150 euros
Sold: 389 euros
Bailly-Pommery & Voutier, Paris
April 23, 2012 (lot 81)
Specialist: PB Fashion

JEAN-CHARLES DE CASTELBAJAC

PRÊT-À-PORTER, Spring/Summer 1999
Model "Premier Secours"

Strapless dress of woven raffia; bustline adorned with a V-shaped revers with a fringe; clear PVC inserts at the waist, repeated at the hemline.

Estimate: 80–120 euros
Sold: 137 euros
Bailly-Pommery & Voutier, Paris
April 23, 2012 (lot 142)
Specialist: PB Fashion

AZZEDINE ALAÏA

YVES SAINT LAURENT

PRÊT-À-PORTER, Fall/Winter 1991–1992

PRÊT-À-PORTER

Leopard-patterned wool and viscose bodysuit with visible seams and push-up bra.

BIBLIOGRAPHY: The identical style is featured on p. 56 in *Alaïa*, François Baudot, Assouline, 1996; the model Nadège wore the identical style, which is featured on pp. 166–167 in *Alaïa*, Steidl, 1998; the identical style also appears on p. 13 in the exhibition catalog *Alaïa: Azzedine Alaïa in the 21st Century*, Groninger Museum, the Netherlands, December 11, 2011–May 6, 2012.

Green and navy leopard-print two-piece outfit; wool knit sweater with round neckline and ribbed cuffs and hem; straight skirt in ottoman cotton. Label "Saint Laurent Rive Gauche."

Estimate: 80–120 euros
Sold: 682 euros
Artcurial, Paris
June 27, 2011 (lot 346)
Specialist: PB Fashion

Estimate: 50–60 euros
Sold: 100 euros
Artcurial, Paris
October 3, 2011 (lot 92)
Specialist: PB Fashion

THIERRY MUGLER

AZZEDINE ALAÏA

PRÊT-À-PORTER, Spring/Summer 1996

PRÊT-À-PORTER

Giraffe-print loose-fit silk tunic; boat neckline; three-quarter sleeves; ties at the front. Blue label, silver lettering.

Viscose and wool jacquard two-piece set in a caramel, pale yellow, brown, and soft green print; fitted sweater; round neckline; ribbing at the cuffs and hem of the sweater; straight skirt.

Estimate: 80–120 euros
Sold: 75 euros
Artcurial, Paris
October 3, 2011 (lot 380)
Specialist: PB Fashion

Estimate: 100–120 euros
Sold: 397 euros
Artcurial, Paris
June 27, 2011 (lot 90)
Specialist: PB Fashion

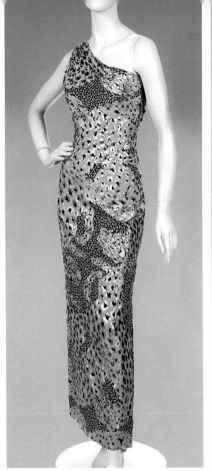

YVES SAINT LAURENT

PRÊT-À-PORTER, 1993

Gold leopard-print one-shoulder evening gown. Label "Yves Saint Laurent Rive Gauche."

ICONOGRAPHY: The identical design was photographed by Helmut Newton for a publicity campaign.

Estimate: 800–1200 dollars
Sold: 2,074 dollars
Leslie Hindman Auctioneers, Chicago
December 6, 2011 (lot 130)
Specialist: Abigail Rutherford

THIERRY MUGLER

**PRÊT-À-PORTER,
Spring/Summer 1996**

Form-fitting leopard-print silk dress; deep notch collar; snap closure all the way to the bottom of the straight skirt; breast pockets and pockets at the hips; belt. Blue label, silver lettering.

Estimate: 500–600 dollars
Sold: 525 euros
Cornette de Saint Cyr, Paris
December 12, 2011 (lot 350)
Specialists: D. Chombert and
F. Sternbach

AZZEDINE ALAÏA

**PRÊT-À-PORTER,
Fall/Winter 1991–1992**

Leopard-print wool and viscose sheath; cowl collar with a revers; zippers at the bottom of the skirt.

BIBLIOGRAPHY: The identical style is featured on p. 57 in *Alaïa*, François Baudot, Assouline, 1996; a similar style is featured on pp. 166–167 in *Alaïa*, Steidl, 1998; the identical style is featured on p. 12 in the exhibition catalog *Alaïa: Azzedine Alaïa in the 21st Century*, Groninger Museum, the Netherlands, December 11, 2011–May 6, 2012.

Estimate: 200–300 euros
Sold: 2,231 euros
Artcurial, Paris
June 27, 2011 (lot 264)
Specialist: PB Fashion

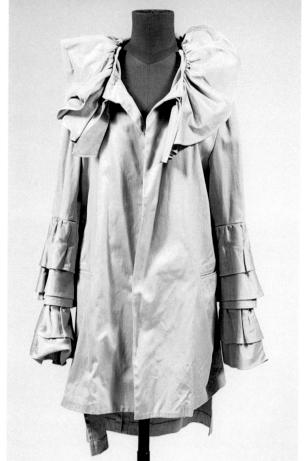

COMME DES GARÇONS

PRÊT-À-PORTER

Long greenish-brown cotton blend skirt with large darts and a gathered hem; the bronze jersey lining has a side slit and is longer than the skirt. Worn with a silk, cotton, and linen blend cardigan. Black labels, gold lettering.

Estimate: 70–90 euros
Sold: 112 euros
Artcurial, Paris
October 4, 2010 (lot 3)
Specialist: PB Fashion

YOHJI YAMAMOTO

PRÊT-À-PORTER, Spring/Summer 1999

Cappuccino cotton gabardine coat; size 7/8; round neckline with a large jabot ruffle, repeated at the cuffs; two piped pockets; zipper at the back with a tab; asymmetric length.

BIBLIOGRAPHY: The identical style appears on p. 300 in *Histoire idéale de la mode contemporaine, les plus beaux défilés de 1971 à nos jours*, Olivier Saillard, éditions Textuel, 2009.

Estimate: 180–220 euros
Sold: 434 euros
Artcurial, Paris
October 4, 2010 (lot 42)
Specialist: PB Fashion

ISSEY MIYAKE

ISSEY MIYAKE

PRÊT-À-PORTER

PRÊT-À-PORTER

Crumpled gazar faux two-piece dress with a licorice black plant motif trimmed in silver; boat neckline; dropped armholes enhanced with two flounces. White label, black lettering.

Copper silk and polyester outfit with permanent pleats; kimono poncho; turndown collar with small slit; long, unstructured skirt. White label, black lettering.

Estimate: 300–400 euros
Sold: 500 euros
Cornette de Saint Cyr, Paris
July 2, 2010 (lot 144)
Specialists: D. Chombert and F. Sternbach

Estimate: 300–400 euros
Sold: 750 euros
Cornette de Saint Cyr, Paris
July 2, 2010 (lot 113)
Specialists: D. Chombert and F. Sternbach

JOHN GALLIANO

ISSEY MIYAKE

PRÊT-À-PORTER

PRÊT-À-PORTER

Wool drape coat with multicolored ethnic patterns of American Indian inspiration; fringe trim; notched lapel partially garnished with zebra-stripe cowhide; flap pockets; asymmetric length. Burgundy label, sky blue lettering.

Unstructured chocolate and dark burgundy polyester outfit with permanent pleats; jacket with draped turndown collar; asymmetric side panels; full skirt.

Estimate: 800–900 euros
Sold: 1,750 euros
Cornette de Saint Cyr, Paris
June 30, 2012 (lot 70)
Specialists: D. Chombert and F. Sternbach

Estimate: 300–500 dollars
Sold: 671 dollars
Leslie Hindman Auctioneers, Chicago
April 17, 2012 (lot 227)
Specialist: Abigail Rutherford

COMME DES GARÇONS

PRÊT-À-PORTER

Navy blue pinstripe wool outfit adorned with Lurex; unstructured jacket with asymmetric length, fastened with a large safety pin; pea jacket inspiration; slit in the back lets the lining show through; armhole cutouts with raw edges; double mid-length skirt with a wraparound look, also fastened with a large safety pin and embellished with a polyester insert printed with stylized multicolored starfish. Black label, gold lettering.

Estimate: 200–300 euros
Sold: 595 euros
Artcurial, Paris
October 4, 2010 (lot 50)
Specialist: PB Fashion

COMME DES GARÇONS

PRÊT-À-PORTER

Gray wool blend dress with white pinstripes embellished with camouflage print muslin inserts; double-breasted jacket with notched lapels; two flap pockets on the peplum, gathered in the back; skirt pleated from the hips. White label, black lettering.

Estimate: 200–300 euros
Sold: 248 euros
Artcurial, Paris
October 4, 2010 (lot 239)
Specialist: PB Fashion

COMME DES GARÇONS

PRÊT-À-PORTER

Patchwork skirt made from various pieces of cotton, wool and viscose; the fabric is shirred in places and the patterns range from plaid to floral and striped; covered elastic waistband. White label, black and blue lettering.

Estimate: 60–80 euros
Sold: 300 euros
Artcurial, Paris
July 6, 2012 (lot 421)
Specialist: PB Fashion

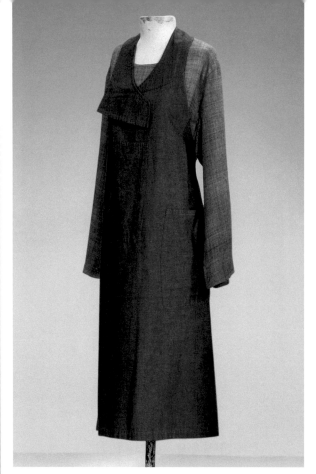

JOHN GALLIANO

YOHJI YAMAMOTO

PRÊT-À-PORTER, Fall/Winter 1997–1998
Collection "Suzy Sphinx"

Gray wool tapered jacket with very thin pinstripes; turndown collar; single-breasted closure with covered buttons with loop fasteners; waist embellished with smocked circular pattern securing small gatherings. Burgundy label, blue lettering.

PRÊT-À-PORTER

Gray wool muslin and silk sack dress; round neckline; buttons on the cuffs. Worn with a charcoal gray cotton apron; cuffed bib; two large asymmetric patch pockets. Gray label, black lettering.

Estimate: 100–150 euros
Sold: 125 euros
Artcurial, Paris
July 6, 2012 (lot 330)
Specialist: PB Fashion

Estimate: 120–150 euros
Sold: 563 euros
Cornette de Saint Cyr, Paris
June 30, 2012 (lot 247)
Specialists: D. Chombert and F. Sternbach

COMME DES GARÇONS

PRÊT-À-PORTER

Cotton-candy pink jacket; small turndown polyester collar; side panels decorated with flowers, petals, ruches, and fringe in cascading pieces of fabric made from diverse materials of the same color; long sleeves with barrel cuffs; slit in the back. Black label, gold lettering.

Estimate: 150–200 euros
Sold: 372 euros
Artcurial, Paris
October 4, 2010 (lot 271)
Specialist: PB Fashion

COMME DES GARÇONS

PRÊT-À-PORTER, 1994

Slightly unstructured white cotton A-line dress adorned with horizontal ruches from the bust; round neckline. White label, black lettering.

Estimate: 250–350 euros
Sold: 1,001 euros
Artcurial, Paris
July 6, 2012 (lot 150 bis)
Specialist: PB Fashion

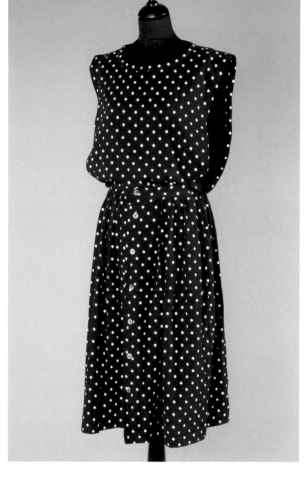

HANAE MORI

N º 1277
COUTURE, 1993

Two-tone black and white duchesse satin cocktail dress; wide asymmetric shawl collar partially draped over the left shoulder; tight-fitting skirt adorned on the front with a floating panel fastened with small hooks. White label, black lettering.

Estimate: 200–300 euros
Sold: 248 euros
Artcurial, Paris
October 4, 2010 (lot 455)
Specialist: PB Fashion

COMME DES GARÇONS

PRÊT-À-PORTER

Navy blue wool crepe dress with white polka dots; bodice with round neckline and floating panel over the front; gathered buttoned skirt. Label "Tricot Comme des Garçons."

Estimate: 100–150 euros
Sold: 751 euros
Artcurial, Paris
July 6, 2012 (lot 250)
Specialist: PB Fashion

YOHJI YAMAMOTO

HERVÉ LÉGER

Black crepe dress; boat neckline; shoulder straps and cross strap in the back; belt; flowing skirt with cut panels at the bottom; asymmetric hemline.

Black jersey short fitted sheath; round neckline; straps crossing over the front; gathered openwork bust.

Estimate: 600–800 euros
Sold: 805 euros
Eve, Paris
May 6, 2011 (lot M056)
Specialist: Sylvie Daniel

Estimate: 400–600 dollars
Sold: 682 dollars
Leslie Hindman Auctioneers, Chicago
April 17, 2012 (lot 128)
Specialist: Abigail Rutherford

ROMEO GIGLI

YOHJI YAMAMOTO

PRÊT-À-PORTER

Draped green velvet egg-shaped coat; wide lapels extending around the neck.

PRÊT-À-PORTER

Black wool coat with turndown collar over crossed side panels; single-breasted look; high waist adorned with a belt secured with loops; hips set off with a scalloped cut.

Estimate: 300–500 dollars
Sold: 183 dollars
Leslie Hindman Auctioneers, Chicago
April 11–12, 2011 (lot 210)
Specialist: Abigail Rutherford

Estimate: 500–700 dollars
Sold: 610 dollars
Leslie Hindman Auctioneers, Chicago
December 16, 2010 (lot 352)
Specialist: Abigail Rutherford

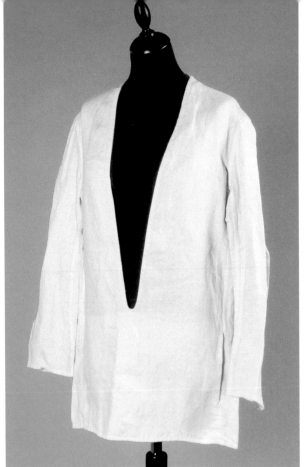

HERMÈS

HERMÈS

PRÊT-À-PORTER, Fall/Winter 1999–2000
Model "Turbo" *by Martin Margiela*

PRÊT-À-PORTER, Fall/Winter 1998–1999
by Martin Margiela

Black lambskin cloak with horizontal cuts; turndown collar
and lapels; vertical pockets.

Ivory linen tunic; V-neckline to the waist; two inseam
pockets.

BIBLIOGRAPHY: The identical model is reproduced in a
different material on p. 285 in *Histoire idéale de la mode
contemporaine, les plus beaux défilés de 1971 à nos jours*, Olivier
Saillard, éditions Textuel, 2009.

Estimate: 1,200–1,400 euros
Sold: 1,500 euros
Gros & Delettrez, Paris
June 4, 2012 (lot 158)
Specialists: D. Chombert and F. Sternbach

Estimate: 40–60 euros
Sold: 313 euros
Artcurial, Paris
July 6, 2012 (lot 181)
Specialist: PB Fashion

COMME DES GARÇONS

PRÊT-À-PORTER

Navy blue single-breasted frock-inspired coat; long sleeves of embossed wool with charcoal gray and plum herringbone weave; half belt at the back; two inseam pockets. Black label, golden yellow lettering.

Estimate: 200–300 euros
Sold: 1,001 euros
Artcurial, Paris
July 6, 2012 (lot 287)
Specialist: PB Fashion

VIVIENNE WESTWOOD

PRÊT-À-PORTER

Eighteenth-century-inspired black grain de poudre jacket with very thin pinstripes and a tiny white and red speckled motif; V-neckline lapel and single-breasted closure with logo buttons; two pockets; cuffs. White label, gold lettering, logo.

Estimate: 400–450 euros
Sold: 500 euros
Cornette de Saint Cyr, Paris
July 2, 2010 (lot 152)
Specialists: D. Chombert and F. Sternbach

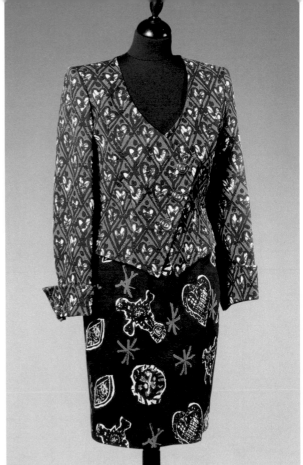

VIVIENNE WESTWOOD

PRÊT-À-PORTER, Spring/Summer 1999
Collection "La Belle Hélène"

Black and red vichy silk taffeta blouse embellished with lace; fitted with a built-in corset with boning; wide neckline set off with large lapels; asymmetrical snap closure; three-quarter sleeves. White label, gold lettering.

Estimate: 60–80 euros
Sold: 150 euros
Artcurial, Paris
April 18, 2012 (lot 476)
Specialist: PB Fashion

CHRISTIAN LACROIX

PRÊT-À-PORTER

Quilted cotton print suit; tailored short jacket with black and white stylized heart pattern on a vermilion background; V-neckline; gold metal asymmetric buttons, repeated on the cuffs; straight skirt.

Estimate: 40–60 euros
Sold: 100 euros
Artcurial, Paris
April 18, 2012 (lot 267)
Specialist: PB Fashion

VIVIENNE WESTWOOD

PRÊT-À-PORTER

Red, black, and ivory Scottish plaid dress; neckline creates the look of an uplifted bust; bouffant asymmetric peplum over a straight skirt. Black label, gold lettering, logo, "Vivienne Westwood Anglomania."

Estimate: 400–500 euros
Sold: 688 euros
Cornette de Saint Cyr, Paris
July 2, 2010 (lot 42)
Specialists: D. Chombert and F. Sternbach

CHRISTIAN LACROIX

PRÊT-À-PORTER

Red, green, and yellow Scottish plaid silk taffeta cocktail dress; halter top adorned with a bow at the back; apron skirt with darts and a two-layered black guipure bustle. Fuchsia label, black lettering.

Estimate: 300–400 euros
Sold: 625 euros
Cornette de Saint Cyr, Paris
June 30, 2012 (lot 197)
Specialists: D. Chombert and F. Sternbach

CHRISTIAN DIOR

CHRISTIAN DIOR

COUTURE
by John Galliano

Cocktail dress with georgette crepe top; asymmetric draped panel falling on the wool crepe gored skirt; boat neckline set off with caparisons on the shoulders. White label, black lettering.

PRÊT-À-PORTER
by John Galliano

Black brocade floral-pattern silk evening coat inspired by the 1920s; collar-scarf adorned with tinted fox fur with tassels, partially trimmed with gold metallic mesh; kimono sleeves. Label "Christian Dior Boutique."

Estimate: 900–1,000 euros
Sold: 11,250 euros
Cornette de Saint Cyr, Paris
December 12, 2011 (lot 322)
Specialists: D. Chombert and F. Sternbach

Estimate: 500–600 dollars
Sold: 780 dollars
Charles A. Whitaker Auction Company, Philadelphia
October 28–29, 2011 (lot 816)
Specialist: Charles A. Whitaker

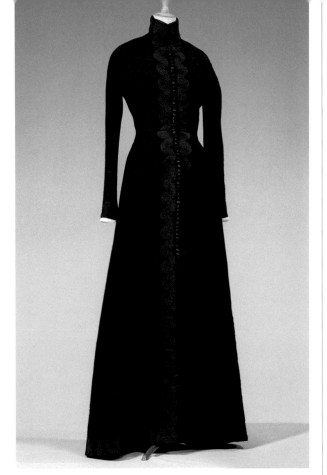

CHRISTIAN DIOR

ALEXANDER McQUEEN

COUTURE, Fall/Winter 1998–1999
by John Galliano (Embroidery: Vermont)

Black wool crepe evening coat; soutache trim with tracings and arabesques inspired by fifteenth-century Spanish clothing; high collar; snaps and hook-and-eye fasteners under satin buttons; long sleeves with cuffs adorned with white ruffs. White label, black lettering.

Estimate: 2,500–3,500 euros
Sold: 16,250 euros
Cornette de Saint Cyr, Paris
December 12, 2011 (lot 321)
Specialists: D. Chombert and F. Sternbach

PRÊT-À-PORTER, Fall/Winter 1998–1999
Model "Joan"

Black cashmere tailored jacket; high neck; single-breasted closure with straightened shoulders and back; side panels with buttons from the bust; buttons also run from neck to hem.

BIBLIOGRAPHY: The identical model is reproduced on p. 47 in the exhibition catalog *Alexander McQueen: Savage Beauty*, Andrew Bolton, the Metropolitan Museum of Art, New York, May 4–July 31, 2011.

Estimate: 6,000–8,000 dollars
Sold: 15,600 dollars
Augusta Auctions, New York
March 21, 2012 (lot 305)
Specialist: Karen E. Augusta

— Lady Belle boots by Noritaka Tatehana, probably from
the Fall/Winter 2010–2011 collection. Part of "The
Daphne Guinness Collection" auction held at Christie's
on June 27, 2012 (sold: 8,125 pounds).

The DAPHNE GUINNESS COLLECTION
Auction at Christie's

New world records were set at Christie's when Britain's high-profile heiress auctioned off her own clothes to benefit the Isabella Blow Foundation in 2012.

The Daphne Guinness auction was remarkable for many reasons. For one, all the proceeds would go to the organization Guinness founded in honor of her friend, the late Isabella Blow, British stylist and muse of milliner extraordinaire, Philip Treacy. Guinness had acquired her friend's collection in its entirety. The foundation's mission was to preserve, maintain, and exhibit Isabella's collection as well as support young British artists and bring attention to issues of depression and mental health.

The auction was also remarkable for its content. A personal collection always has a special emotional dimension because every piece reflects a facet of its owner's personality. Each lot of the Guinness collection was revealing in its own way. Together, they formed a coherent picture of Daphne Guinness, a woman well versed in both art and fashion who, over the years, had acquired several spectacular pieces, ranging from the most traditional Parisian haute couture to the wildest designs imagined by British creators. Most were one-of-a-kind pieces and all shared a sense of modernity infused with avant-garde: Totem shoes such as the sculpture-like (and precariously shaky) boots made especially for Guinness by Noritaka Tatehana sold for 8,125 pounds; one of many dramatic dresses, a metallic mini dress by Alexander McQueen, accompanied by a photograph published in *Harper's Bazaar* of Guinness wearing the dress, sold for 79,250 pounds; the empire-line dress from "The Girl Who Lives in the Tree" collection, also accompanied by a photograph, sold for 85,250 pounds. The amounts paid for both dresses set new world records for Alexander McQueen's designs. Another record was achieved when a photograph of Daphne Guinness, taken by Mario Testino for British *Vogue*, sold for 133,250 pounds—the highest amount ever paid for a photograph by the Peruvian photographer and the top sale of the auction. The 102 lots featured many other outstanding pieces from Prada, Christian Lacroix, Gareth Pugh, and Cristóbal Balenciaga.

The combined star power of the late Isabella Blow and Daphne Guinness turned the auction into a media event. Both women were considered British fashion icons for their very English sense of style and sartorial audacity, and for their ability to discover and champion new talent. Other boldface names involved in the auction included the late Alexander McQueen—a Guinness favorite—whose many listed pieces defied all estimates. Lady Gaga, a *fashionista* in her own right and a close friend of the late McQueen, was a surprise guest and bidder at the auction.

"I'm overwhelmed by how many bidders took part this evening and I'm particularly moved by Lady Gaga's support for the foundation. I like her very much, and it's lovely to see the nascent beginnings of something that may help other people," declared Daphne Guinness after the event. The sale achieved 476,000 pounds, more than four times the amount that had been anticipated—compelling motivation for Christie's to hold more celebrity auctions like those for Elizabeth Taylor (see pages 228–229), Anna Piaggi, Erin O'Connor, and Lady Diana.

VINTAGE
ENTHUSIASTS

ICONS OF VINTAGE FASHION
Spotlight

One expects bidders at a vintage fashion auction to be a microcosm of professionals: curators hoping to enrich the fashion collections of museums, entrepreneurs who buy with the intention of reselling, and several fashion houses looking to complete their own archives.

But, among the auction-circuit regulars are a small group of savvy enthusiasts who are also there to buy—possibly for resale—but who are mainly interested in acquiring pieces for themselves.

Among them is Michèle Richoux, a regular at Drouot since the mid-1990s. One day, as she wandered through the maze of auction rooms at Drouot, Richoux bypassed her usual haunts devoted to art, antiques, and crystal and visited the adjacent rooms dedicated to fashion. There, she realized that "fashion is an art unto itself" and that its presence alongside paintings and other collector's objects was indeed justified. More pragmatically, she appreciated the fact that these purchases could be worn on a daily basis and that she could acquire clothes "that maintain their elegance despite the years" and whose quality, materials, and finish were "so far superior than anything one can buy today." Buying at auction would make it possible for her to own designer pieces that she might not otherwise be able to afford.

While she does not consider herself a collector, she recognizes that she has become somewhat of a conservator: "I wear things for a long time, a very long time, and I hold onto things; I have a really hard time parting with anything I buy." She may not be a collector or a professional, but she is an educated customer. Michèle Richoux has taken full advantage of auctions to broaden her knowledge of fashion. She is well versed on the styles of the 1930s, a period she particularly admires, noting that she has come across pieces from the past that have clearly continued to influence contemporary designers. She singles out "the exceptional" Schiaparelli who, sadly, remains beyond her reach.

Michèle Richoux's friend Christine Gérald has attended auctions for over forty years. While she adores jewelry from the 1950s, Gérald buys far less than she used to because it has become so much harder to find good buys today. Still, with "the benefit of age" her eye is more discerning. When she was younger, it never would have occurred to her to buy second-hand clothes because, in her view, anything that was not current was out of style. Now, she thinks of vintage pieces as synonymous with a bygone style that will return or has never really left, "because fashion is an endless renewal." Three years ago, she bought a perfect and timeless black coat by Jean Patou from the 1930s that she never tires of wearing. If a piece is in good condition, the years mean nothing. Like her friend Michèle, Christine recognizes the finesse and craftsmanship of the cut and fabric of vintage designs. She buys clothes to wear them, not save them, and is willing to let go of pieces that are "no longer age appropriate." She recently sold her entire collection of Alaïa creations, nearly fifty pieces she acquired during the 1980s when she was friendly with the couturier's sister. Her collection included peplum jackets, mini skirts, and complete ensembles, all of which had been carefully conserved. She has no regrets, as the collection "is now in good hands," but does concede that it is still hard for her to part with certain pieces to which she was very attached. But, as she does not have the room to keep everything, she forces herself to sell and feels that she has shifted to the other side of the mirror, having become more a seller than a buyer.

— The Hôtel Drouot, located at 9 Rue Drouot in the ninth arrondissement, is the premier auction house in Paris.

CELEBRITIES
and VINTAGE

Because of the media frenzy surrounding movie stars and socialites, every public appearance is photographed, filmed, and endlessly analyzed. Deciding what to wear has become an all-important choice as celebrities rely on red-carpet moments to increase their visibility. While some celebrities have an inner sense of style and manage on their own to make the best-dressed lists that have become a ubiquitous feature of magazines, others turn to personal stylists, professionals who help them achieve a look that is both contemporary and personal.

WHY VINTAGE?

Celebrities have access to (almost) all the couture collections, fresh off the catwalk or even before they appear on the runways. Why then, with such exceptional access to the *now* and future, would they choose instead to turn to the past?

Many factors explain the growing appeal of vintage for film stars, models, and other celebrities.

First, wearing vintage suggests a certain understanding of fashion and fashion history, and the ability to select a design that is relevant because of its style, fabric, or detailing.

Second, wearing vintage requires a certain attitude. You can't simply wear a vintage piece; you must appropriate it. You might be wearing a garment from another time, but you are wearing it today.

Third, wearing vintage allows you to eschew the frivolous aspect of choosing an outfit. A vintage dress has a story and a past.

Finally, wearing vintage defines your originality and ensures that your look will be unique. It is a declaration of sartorial independence at a time when choices are often constrained by contracts between celebrities and the brands they represent.

Conscious that every style they wear will be endlessly analyzed, celebrities take all the above factors into consideration when they choose a vintage creation.

A FEW HIGHLIGHTS

Celebrities have made vintage glamorous. No longer the domain of specialized collectors or a few eccentrics who like to dwell in the past, vintage is and can be worn at the most important events.

In 1997, the *New York Times* published an article* about the increasing popularity of vintage clothing and credited Barbra Streisand for pioneering the movement.

The phenomenon started off slowly, but 2001 marked a turning point when Renée Zellweger attended the Oscars in a yellow strapless gown designed by Jean Dessès in 1950. Julia Roberts, who won an Oscar that year, wore a Valentino haute couture dress from 1992 that was immediately described as "vintage" by the press. The appeal of vintage caught on, and soon many Hollywood celebrities were seen wearing vintage couture. In 2003, Jennifer Aniston wore a Halston dress from 1970; Drew Barrymore chose a dress by Janine that she bought for just a few dollars; and Reese Witherspoon attended the 2006 Academy Awards in a spectacular beaded gown by Christian Dior.

Some credit the rise of vintage's popularity to the supermodels of the 1990s—Naomi Campbell and Kate Moss were among the first to wear vintage couture. Kate Moss and her vintage gown made the headlines at the *Golden Age of Couture* exhibition at the Victoria and Albert Museum in 2007. Moss was wearing a Christian Dior gown from the 1950s that tore during the evening. Undeterred, Moss rolled it up, turning the gown into a mini dress that would eventually be sold at auction to raise money for charity.

*Mitchell Owens, "Couture Shock: Vintage Clothes as Collectibles," *New York Times*, January 5, 1997.

— Kate Moss in vintage Christian Dior, at the Victoria and Albert Museum gala celebrating *The Golden Age of Couture*, September 22, 2007–January 6, 2008.

Accessories

The Handbag

The ultimate accessory, the handbag is exceptionally positioned to represent and advertise a luxury brand name.

Slung over a shoulder, held in the crook of the arm, or clutched in one's hand, a handbag is instantly visible and easy to identify. It is a status symbol and, unlike certain clothing, a handbag remains in style for many seasons, even generations. A luxury handbag is an investment enjoyed on a daily basis, one that can be passed down to the next generation as it ages well and becomes more valuable with time. One does not have to be a specialist to recognize a handbag by Chanel, Hermès, or Louis Vuitton. Accessories are of paramount importance for those institutions as they generate the bulk of their business. These luxury brands are perennial favorites at auctions, turning up again and again as customers never tire of them. Handbags don't need to fit. They look great on every woman.

At auctions, handbags offer immediate gratification—no more waiting lists or production delays and discontinued styles are once again available. There is a huge market for this accessory, which shows off one's identity and personality. Even the bags have emblematic names. Shoulder bags, satchels, purses, and minaudières have names befitting their individuality: Vuitton has chosen "Speedy" and "Keepall," Chanel honors the creation date of its iconic bag by naming it the "2.55," while Hermès prefers the mythic symbolism of "Kelly" and "Birkin."

CHANEL

White quilted lambskin 2.55 bag with gold hardware.

Estimate: 1,200–1,300 euros
Sold: 1,750 euros
Gros & Delettrez, Paris, February 6, 2012 (lot 272)
Specialists: D. Chombert and F. Sternbach

White quilted leather flap bag, embellished with a floral motif and chrome hardware.

Estimate: 150–200 euros
Sold: 854 euros
Chayette & Cheval, Paris, February 5, 2012 (lot 433)
Specialist: PB Fashion

Metallic gold leather evening flap bag with gold hardware.

Estimate: 300–500 euros
Sold: 1,376 euros
Artcurial, Paris, June 11, 2012 (lot 436)
Specialist: PB Fashion

CHANEL

Black quilted lambskin Classique bag with gold hardware.

Estimate: 500–700 euros
Sold: 1,254 euros
Millon & Associés, Brussels, October 7, 2012 (lot 185)
Specialist: PB Fashion

Black quilted caviar leather 2.55 bag with gold hardware.

Estimate: 1,000–1,200 euros
Sold: 2,000 euros
Cornette de Saint Cyr, Paris, February 13, 2012 (lot 234)
Specialists: D. Chombert and F. Sternbach

Black quilted patent leather Jumbo bag with chrome hardware.

Estimate: 1,500–1,700 euros
Sold: 1,875 euros
Cornette de Saint Cyr, Paris, February 13, 2012 (lot 164)
Specialists: D. Chombert and F. Sternbach

CHANEL

Black quilted lambskin Jumbo bag with gold hardware.

Estimate: 2,000–2,200 euros
Sold: 2,625 euros
Gros & Delettrez, Paris, February 6, 2012 (lot 268)
Specialists: D. Chombert and F. Sternbach

Brown quilted lambskin flap bag with gold hardware.

Estimate: 500–700 euros
Sold: 2,383 euros
Millon & Associés, Brussels, October 7, 2012 (lot 303)
Specialist: PB Fashion

Black quilted lambskin bag with gold hardware.

Estimate: 700–800 euros
Sold: 875 euros
Gros & Delettrez, Paris, February 6, 2012 (lot 168)
Specialists: D. Chombert and F. Sternbach

CHANEL

Olive green quilted caviar leather briefcase with gold logo turn-lock clasp.

Estimate: 500–700 dollars
Sold: 1,708 dollars
Leslie Hindman Auctioneers, Chicago, April 17, 2012 (lot 398)
Specialist: Abigail Rutherford

Black quilted patent leather briefcase with gold turn-lock clasp.

Estimate: 1,200–1,400 euros
Sold: 1,750 euros
Gros & Delettrez, Paris, February 6, 2012 (lot 347)
Specialists: D. Chombert and F. Sternbach

Black quilted lambskin bag with gold hardware.

Estimate: 600–800 dollars
Sold: 1,342 dollars
Leslie Hindman Auctioneers, Chicago, April 17, 2012 (lot 406)
Specialist: Abigail Rutherford

CHANEL

Brown eel-skin bag with gold hardware and double chain-link strap.

Estimate: 600–800 euros
Sold: 1,125 euros
Cornette de Saint Cyr, Paris, February 13, 2012 (lot 94)
Specialists: D. Chombert and F. Sternbach

Paris-Shanghai Collection

Black silk and green sequins 2.55 bag with gold hardware.

Estimate: 3,000–3,200 euros
Sold: 4,500 euros
Cornette de Saint Cyr, Paris, February 14, 2012 (lot 503)
Specialists: D. Chombert and F. Sternbach

Silver metallic leather "ice cube" bag with matte gray hardware.

Estimate: 1,300–1,500 euros
Sold: 1,875 euros
Cornette de Saint Cyr, Paris, February 13, 2012 (lot 361)
Specialists: D. Chombert and F. Sternbach

ICONS OF VINTAGE FASHION
Accessories

CHANEL

Woven toile bag in blue, caramel, and ivory with metal chrome hardware.

Estimate: 600–700 euros
Sold: 875 euros
Cornette de Saint Cyr, Paris, February 13, 2012 (lot 137)
Specialists: D. Chombert and F. Sternbach

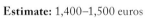

Gray and pink tweed and Lurex bag with metal chrome hardware.

Estimate: 1,400–1,500 euros
Sold: 2,225 euros
Cornette de Saint Cyr, Paris, February 14, 2012 (lot 510)
Specialists: D. Chombert and F. Sternbach

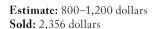

Printed silk hard-sided bag featuring a stylized design of Coco Chanel.

Estimate: 800–1,200 dollars
Sold: 2,356 dollars
Leslie Hindman Auctioneers, Chicago, April 17, 2012 (lot 405)
Specialist: Abigail Rutherford

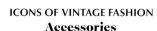

CHANEL

1960s

Navy quilted jersey 2.55 bag with gold hardware.

Estimate: 800–900 euros
Sold: 1,875 euros
Cornette de Saint Cyr, Paris, April 4, 2012 (lot 404)
Specialists: D. Chombert and F. Sternbach

Brown quilted lambskin 2.55 bag with gold hardware.

Estimate: 400–600 euros
Sold: 626 euros
Artcurial, Paris, March 19, 2012 (lot 139)
Specialist: PB Fashion

Black quilted lambskin flap bag with gold hardware.

Estimate: 500–600 euros
Sold: 1,752 euros
Artcurial, Paris, April 18, 2012 (lot 41)
Specialist: PB Fashion

CHANEL

Fall/Winter 1994–1995

Gold metal and black leather bottle holder with a shoulder strap.

Estimate: 180–200 euros
Sold: 640 euros
Bailly-Pommery & Voutier, Paris, April 23, 2012 (lot 447)
Specialist: PB Fashion

Small apple green quilted crepe bag with gold hardware and a cable chain shoulder strap interlaced with black cord.

Estimate: 150–250 euros
Sold: 815 euros
Millon & Associés, Brussels, October 7, 2012 (lot 236)
Specialist: PB Fashion

Black quilted patent leather Jumbo XXL bag with matte silver metal hardware.

Estimate: 2,100–2,300 euros
Sold: 3,375 euros
Cornette de Saint Cyr, Paris, February 13, 2012 (lot 312)
Specialists: D. Chombert and F. Sternbach

CHANEL

Red quilted lambskin bag with gold hardware.

Estimate: 300–500 dollars
Sold: 1,037 dollars
Leslie Hindman Auctioneers, Chicago, April 17, 2012 (lot 403)
Specialist: Abigail Rutherford

Taupe quilted caviar leather Mademoiselle bag with silver metal hardware.

Estimate: 800–1,000 euros
Sold: 1,944 euros
Millon & Associés, Brussels, October 7, 2012 (lot 391)
Specialist: PB Fashion

Red quilted lambskin bag with gold hardware and tassel.

Estimate: 600–800 dollars
Sold: 976 dollars
Leslie Hindman Auctioneers, Chicago, April 17, 2012 (lot 397)
Specialist: Abigail Rutherford

ICONS OF VINTAGE FASHION
Accessories

CHANEL

Dusty pink quilted iridescent patent leather Timeless Baguette bag with silver gray hardware.

Estimate: 300–400 euros
Sold: 1,191 euros
Millon & Associés, Brussels, October 7, 2012 (lot 337)
Specialist: PB Fashion

Coffee-colored shiny lizard flap bag with gray trim, gold metal hardware, and tassel.

Estimate: 200–300 euros
Sold: 626 euros
Artcurial, Paris, July 6, 2012 (lot 315)
Specialist: PB Fashion

Brick-colored, tubular-patterned, quilted lambskin bag with metal chrome hardware.

Estimate: 400–600 euros
Sold: 475 euros
Artcurial, Paris, March 19, 2012 (lot 247)
Specialist: PB Fashion

CHANEL

Mini black quilted lambskin Timeless bag with gold hardware.

Estimate: 300–400 euros
Sold: 1,881 euros
Millon & Associés, Brussels, October 7, 2012 (lot 380)
Specialist: PB Fashion

Navy trapeze-shape quilted lambskin bag with gold hardware.

Estimate: 600–800 euros
Sold: 1,376 euros
Artcurial, Paris, April 18, 2012 (lot 458)
Specialist: PB Fashion

Black quilted patent leather tote bag with double gold chain-link shoulder straps.

Estimate: 600–800 dollars
Sold: 1,464 dollars
Leslie Hindman Auctioneers, Chicago, April 17, 2012 (lot 401)
Specialist: Abigail Rutherford

CHANEL

Small gray leather bag with black logo, gold hardware, and tassel.

Estimate: 180–220 euros
Sold: 313 euros
Artcurial, Paris, March 19, 2012 (lot 436)
Specialist: PB Fashion

2003

Black and white tote bag with camellia design.

Estimate: 300–400 euros
Sold: 815 euros
Millon & Associés, Brussels, October 7, 2012 (lot 88)
Specialist: PB Fashion

Black quilted lambskin Speedy bag.

Estimate: 800–900 euros
Sold: 1,250 euros
Cornette de Saint Cyr, Paris, February 14, 2012 (lot 624)
Specialists: D. Chombert and F. Sternbach

HERMÈS

1986

"H" red Togo leather Kelly bag with gold metal hardware; 40 cm.

Estimate: 2,500–3,500 pounds
Sold: 2,500 pounds
Christie's, London, May 30, 2012 (lot 310)
Specialist: Patricia Frost

Navy box leather Kelly bag with gold metal hardware; 33 cm.

Estimate: 1,100–1,200 euros
Sold: 1,750 euros
Gros & Delettrez, Paris, June 4, 2012 (lot 302)
Specialists: D. Chombert and F. Sternbach

1998

Black *Varanus niloticus* lizard Kelly bag with gold metal hardware; 25 cm.

Estimate: 10,000–12,000 pounds
Sold: 10,625 pounds
Christie's, London, May 30, 2012 (lot 334)
Specialist: Patricia Frost

HERMÈS

1998

Tan and black bicolor box leather Kelly bag with gold metal hardware; 32 cm.

Estimate: 2,000–4,000 pounds
Sold: 4,375 pounds
Christie's, London, May 30, 2012 (lot 329)
Specialist: Patricia Frost

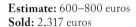

Natural leather and beige "H" toile Kelly bag with gold metal hardware; 32 cm.

Estimate: 600–800 euros
Sold: 2,317 euros
Artcurial, Paris, May 9, 2012 (lot 45)
Specialist: Cyril Pigot

1996

Eggshell lizard Kelly bag with gold metal hardware; 28 cm.

Estimate: 12,000–14,000 euros
Sold: 14,157 euros
Artcurial, Paris, July 25, 2012 (lot 16)
Specialist: Cyril Pigot

HERMÈS

Black ostrich Kelly bag with gold metal hardware; 35 cm.

Estimate: 7,000–7,500 euros
Sold: 9,000 euros
Gros & Delettrez, Paris, February 6, 2012 (lot 358)
Specialists: D. Chombert and F. Sternbach

1997

Chocolate brown Togo leather Birkin bag with gold metal hardware; 35 cm.

Estimate: 3,500–4,500 pounds
Sold: 5,000 pounds
Christie's, London, May 30 2012 (lot 303)
Specialist: Patricia Frost

2001

Cognac ostrich Birkin bag with gold metal hardware; 35 cm.

Estimate: 10,000–12,000 euros
Sold: 22,523 euros
Artcurial, Paris, July 25, 2012 (lot 21)
Specialist: Cyril Pigot

HERMÈS

2005

Matte chocolate brown *niloticus* crocodile Birkin bag with gold metal hardware; 30 cm.

Estimate: 30,000–35,000 euros
Sold: 38,611 euros
Artcurial, Paris, July 25, 2012 (lot 27)
Specialist: Cyril Pigot

Matte caramel *porosus* crocodile Birkin bag with silver palladium hardware; 35 cm.

Estimate: 28,000–33,000 euros
Sold: 44,500 euros
Gros & Delettrez, Paris, June 5, 2012 (lot 620)
Specialists: D. Chombert and F. Sternbach

Dark gray *porosus* crocodile Birkin bag with silver palladium hardware; 35 cm.

Estimate: 28,000–33,000 euros
Sold: 45,000 euros
Gros & Delettrez, Paris, June 5, 2012 (lot 529)
Specialists: D. Chombert and F. Sternbach

HERMÈS

2011

Electric blue *niloticus* crocodile Birkin bag with silver palladium hardware; 25 cm.

Estimate: 30,000–35,000 euros
Sold: 38,611 euros
Artcurial, Paris, July 25, 2012 (lot 28)
Specialist: Cyril Pigot

Matte havana *porosus* crocodile Birkin bag with silver palladium hardware; 35 cm.

Estimate: 30,000–35,000 euros
Sold: 38,611 euros
Artcurial, Paris, July 25, 2012 (lot 27)
Specialist: Cyril Pigot

2009

Black *porosus* crocodile Birkin bag with silver palladium hardware; 35 cm.

Estimate: 24,000–26,000 euros
Sold: 46,046 euros
Artcurial, Paris, July 25, 2012 (lot 39)
Specialist: Cyril Pigot

HERMÈS

2008

Anise green swift calfskin Birkin bag with gold metal hardware; 30 cm.

Estimate: 7,000–8,000 pounds
Sold: 10,000 pounds
Christie's, London, May 30, 2012 (lot 348)
Specialist: Patricia Frost

2000

Gold Courchevel leather and beige "H" toile Birkin bag with gold metal hardware; 35 cm.

Estimate: 4,000–5,000 euros
Sold: 10,296 euros
Artcurial, Paris, May 9, 2012 (lot 348)
Specialist: Cyril Pigot

2001

Chocolate brown Togo leather Birkin bag with gold metal hardware; 35 cm.

Estimate: 4,500–5,500 pounds
Sold: 8,125 pounds
Christie's, London, May 30, 2012 (lot 368)
Specialist: Patricia Frost

HERMÈS

2010

Rose and amethyst bicolor Epsom calfskin Birkin bag with palladium silver hardware; 35 cm.

Estimate: 5,000–7,000 pounds
Sold: 15,000 pounds
Christie's, London, May 30, 2012 (lot 358)
Specialist: Patricia Frost

White Togo calfskin Birkin bag with silver palladium hardware; 35 cm.

Estimate: 3,200–3,600 euros
Sold: 5,500 euros
Cornette de Saint Cyr, Paris, April 4, 2012 (lot 470)
Specialists: D. Chombert and F. Sternbach

2009

Red, saffron, and brown tricolor goatskin Birkin bag with gold metal hardware; 25 cm.

Estimate: 4,000–5,000 pounds
Sold: 15,625 pounds
Christie's, London, May 30, 2012 (lot 366)
Specialist: Patricia Frost

HERMÈS

Beige "H" toile and natural Chamonix calfskin Saint Aubin bag.

Estimate: 600–800 euros
Sold: 1,158 euros
Artcurial, Paris, May 9, 2012 (lot 536)
Specialist: Cyril Pigot

1950s

Beige "H" toile and bottle green box leather Farming bag with gold metal hardware.

Estimate: 300–400 euros
Sold: 890 euros
Millon & Associés, Brussels, October 7, 2012 (lot 433)
Specialist: PB Fashion

1970s

Beige "H" toile and natural vache leather Ulysse bag.

Estimate: 800–1000 euros
Sold: 1,066 euros
Millon & Associés, Brussels, October 7, 2012 (lot 431)
Specialist: PB Fashion

HERMÈS

Navy calfskin and beige "H" toile Evelyne bag with gold metal hardware.

Estimate: 800–1,200 dollars
Sold: 580 dollars
Leslie Hindman Auctioneers, Chicago, April 17, 2012 (lot 296)
Specialist: Abigail Rutherford

2003

Barénia calfskin and beige "H" toile Haut à Courroies bag with gold metal hardware.

Estimate: 3,500–4,500 pounds
Sold: 3,750 pounds
Christie's, London, May 30, 2012 (lot 339)
Specialist: Patricia Frost

2009

Beige "H" toile and gold Togo calfskin Birkin bag with silver palladium hardware; 30 cm.

Estimate: 6,000–8,000 pounds
Sold: 10,625 pounds
Christie's, London, May 30, 2012 (lot 346)
Specialist: Patricia Frost

HERMÈS

2009

Varanus niloticus lizard Birkin bag with silver palladium hardware; 25 cm.

Estimate: 10,000–12,000 pounds
Sold: 27,500 pounds
Christie's, London, May 30, 2012 (lot 363)
Specialist: Patricia Frost

Natural Courchevel leather Haut à Courroies bag with gold metal hardware; 32 cm.

Estimate: 4,000–5,000 euros
Sold: 5,268 euros
Artcurial, Paris, May 9, 2012 (lot 589)
Specialist: Cyril Pigot

1997

Black Courchevel leather Haut à Courroies bag with gold metal hardware.

Estimate: 2,500–3,000 pounds
Sold: 5,625 pounds
Christie's, London, May 30, 2012 (lot 338)
Specialist: Patricia Frost

HERMÈS

Navy box leather Mangeoire bag with gold metal hardware.

Estimate: 250–300 euros
Sold: 313 euros
Artcurial, Paris, March 19, 2012 (lot 289)
Specialist: PB Fashion

Rust "H" toile and white calfskin Heeboo bag.

Estimate: 300–500 euros
Sold: 869 euros
Artcurial, Paris, May 9, 2012 (lot 56)
Specialist: Cyril Pigot

1985

Cognac ostrich Market bag with gold metal hardware.

Estimate: 4,000–5,000 euros
Sold: 4,505 euros
Artcurial, Paris, July 25, 2012 (lot 64)
Specialist: Cyril Pigot

HERMÈS

"H" red leather Manille bag with chrome metal hardware.

Estimate: 250–350 euros
Sold: 313 euros
Artcurial, Paris, March 19, 2012 (lot 48)
Specialist: PB Fashion

Gold Courchevel leather Trim bag with gold metal hardware.

Estimate: 300–500 euros
Sold: 375 euros
Artcurial, Paris, June 11, 2012 (lot 176)
Specialist: PB Fashion

Natural calfskin Trim bag with gold metal hardware.

Estimate: 1,000–2,000 dollars
Sold: 1,984 dollars
Leslie Hindman Auctioneers, Chicago, April 17, 2012 (lot 294)
Specialist: Abigail Rutherford

HERMÈS

Cognac crocodile Piano bag with gold metal hardware.

Estimate: 1,500–2,000 pounds
Sold: 1,750 pounds
Christie's, London, May 30, 2012 (lot 350)
Specialist: Patricia Frost

Chocolate brown *porosus* crocodile Piano bag with gold metal hardware.

Estimate: 1,500–2,000 euros
Sold: 1,931 euros
Artcurial, Paris, May 9, 2012 (lot 577)
Specialist: Cyril Pigot

Cognac caviar calfskin Piano bag with gold metal hardware.

Estimate: 120–150 euros
Sold: 188 euros
Millon & Associés, Brussels, October 7, 2012 (lot 382)
Specialist: PB Fashion

HERMÈS

1950s

Black box leather Ring bag with gold metal hardware.

Estimate: 600–1,000 pounds
Sold: 1,000 pounds
Christie's, London, May 30, 2012 (lot 352)
Specialist: Patricia Frost

1960s

Black *porosus* crocodile Poulie bag with gold metal hardware.

Estimate: 600–800 euros
Sold: 1,001 euros
Artcurial, Paris, June 11, 2012 (lot 421)
Specialist: PB Fashion

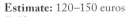

Natural vache leather Drag bag with gold metal hardware.

Estimate: 120–150 euros
Sold: 314 euros
Millon & Associés, Brussels, October 7, 2012 (lot 338)
Specialist: PB Fashion

HERMÈS

Beige "H" toile and chocolate brown box leather Constance bag with gold metal hardware.

Estimate: 1,000–1,500 pounds
Sold: 3,750 pounds
Christie's, London, May 30, 2012 (lot 311)
Specialist: Patricia Frost

"H" red box leather Constance bag with gold metal hardware.

Estimate: 1,500–2,000 euros
Sold: 2,766 euros
Artcurial, Paris, May 9, 2012 (lot 355)
Specialist: Cyril Pigot

2001

Black box leather Constance bag with gold metal hardware.

Estimate: 1,500–2,000 pounds
Sold: 5,250 pounds
Christie's, London, May 30, 2012 (lot 317)
Specialist: Patricia Frost

HERMÈS

1998

Black alligator Constance bag with gold metal hardware.

Estimate: 3,000–5,000 euros
Sold: 10,296 euros
Artcurial, Paris, July 25, 2012 (lot 36)
Specialist: Cyril Pigot

White ostrich Constance bag with gold metal hardware.

Estimate: 1,400–1,600 euros
Sold: 1,750 euros
Gros & Delettrez, Paris, June 4, 2012 (lot 301)
Specialists: D. Chombert and F. Sternbach

Navy box leather Balle de Golf bag with gold metal hardware.

Estimate: 250–300 euros
Sold: 965 euros
Artcurial, Paris, May 9, 2012 (lot 242)
Specialist: Cyril Pigot

HERMÈS

2004

Black Togo calfskin Birkin shoulder bag with silver palladium hardware.

Estimate: 3,500–4,500 pounds
Sold: 5,000 pounds
Christie's, London, May 30, 2012 (lot 336)
Specialist: Patricia Frost

Honey crocodile 404 bag with gold metal hardware.

Estimate: 200–300 euros
Sold: 726 euros
Artcurial, Paris, June 11, 2012 (lot 307)
Specialist: PB Fashion

Black box leather and *officier* toile Kelly Lakis bag with silver palladium hardware.

Estimate: 4,500–6,500 euros
Sold: 5,368 euros
Chayette & Cheval, Paris, November 24, 2012 (lot 258)
Specialist: PB Fashion

HERMÈS

"H" red box leather Jige clutch with white contrast stitching.

Estimate: 600–800 euros
Sold: 1,287 euros
Artcurial, Paris, May 9, 2012 (lot 154)
Specialist: Cyril Pigot

1930s

Black crocodile Pan evening clutch with silver metal closure.

Estimate: 800–1,000 euros
Sold: 3,604 euros
Artcurial, Paris, May 9, 2012 (lot 381)
Specialist: Cyril Pigot

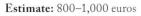

Pumpkin *porosus* crocodile Goya clutch with gold metal closure.

Estimate: 8,000–9,000 euros
Sold: 12,875 euros
Cornette de Saint Cyr, Paris, April 4, 2012 (lot 531)
Specialists: D. Chombert and F. Sternbach

HERMÈS

Cherry *porosus* crocodile Mini Plume bag with gold metal hardware.

Estimate: 4,200–4,500 euros
Sold: 5,000 euros
Gros & Delettrez, Paris, June 5, 2012 (lot 526)
Specialists: D. Chombert and F. Sternbach

2005

Cyclamen goatskin Plume bag with silver palladium hardware; 28 cm.

Estimate: 3,000–4,000 euros
Sold: 3,218 euros
Artcurial, Paris, July 25, 2012 (lot 8)
Specialist: Cyril Pigot

Raspberry *alligator mississippiensis* Plume Elan bag with silver palladium hardware.

Estimate: 4,000–6,000 pounds
Sold: 5,250 pounds
Christie's, London, May 30, 2012 (lot 354)
Specialist: Patricia Frost

HERMÈS

Brown Courchevel leather Bolide bag; 37 cm.

Estimate: 800–1,000 euros
Sold: 1,544 euros
Artcurial, Paris, May 9, 2012 (lot 267)
Specialist: Cyril Pigot

2004

Olive green ostrich Bolide bag with gold metal
hardware; 25 cm.

Estimate: 4,000–5,000 euros
Sold: 5,792 euros
Artcurial, Paris, July 25, 2012 (lot 18)
Specialist: Cyril Pigot

Elephant-skin Duffel bag with gold metal hardware.

Estimate: 900–1,000 euros
Sold: 1,063 euros
Gros & Delettrez, Paris, June 5, 2012 (lot 528)
Specialists: D. Chombert and F. Sternbach

LOUIS VUITTON

LV Monogram canvas and natural cowhide leather Alma bag.

Estimate: 180–220 euros
Sold: 250 euros
Gros & Delettrez, Paris, May 14, 2012 (lot 161)
Specialists: D. Chombert and F. Sternbach

N° 01915

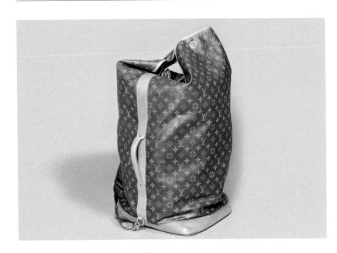

LV Monogram canvas and natural cowhide leather Marin bag.

Estimate: 400–500 euros
Sold: 1,189 euros
Artcurial, Paris, April 18, 2012 (lot 114)
Specialist: PB Fashion

LV Monogram canvas and natural cowhide leather Speedy bag; 40 cm.

Estimate: 200–300 euros
Sold: 375 euros
Artcurial, Paris, March 19, 2012 (lot 40)
Specialist: PB Fashion

LOUIS VUITTON

LV Monogram canvas and natural cowhide leather Plat bag.

Estimate: 200–300 euros
Sold: 438 euros
Artcurial, Paris, March 19, 2012 (lot 238)
Specialist: PB Fashion

LV Monogram canvas and natural cowhide leather Lockit bag.

Estimate: 300–500 dollars
Sold: 992 dollars
Leslie Hindman Auctioneers, Chicago, April 17, 2012 (lot 388)
Specialist: Abigail Rutherford

LV Monogram canvas and natural cowhide leather Steamer bag.

Estimate: 400–600 euros
Sold: 815 euros
Millon & Associés, Brussels, October 7, 2012 (lot 19)
Specialist: PB Fashion

LOUIS VUITTON

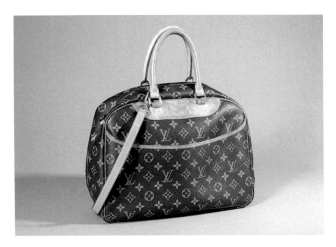

LV Monogram and natural cowhide leather Deauville bag.

Estimate: 400–600 euros
Sold: 525 euros
Artcurial, Paris, June 11, 2012 (lot 95)
Specialist: PB Fashion

LV Monogram and natural cowhide leather Chantilly bag with initials *C.S.*

Estimate: 150–200 euros
Sold: 275 euros
Gros & Delettrez, Paris, May 14, 2012 (lot 94)
Specialists: D. Chombert and F. Sternbach

LV Monogram and natural cowhide leather tote.

Estimate: 150–250 dollars
Sold: 589 dollars
Leslie Hindman Auctioneers, Chicago, April 17, 2012 (lot 378)
Specialist: Abigail Rutherford

LOUIS VUITTON

Brown ostrich Loch Ness bag.

Estimate: 800–1,000 euros
Sold: 2,502 euros
Artcurial, Paris, March 19, 2012 (lot 249)
Specialist: PB Fashion

Damier canvas and chocolate patent leather Neverfull bag.

Estimate: 350–400 euros
Sold: 563 euros
Gros & Delettrez, Paris, May 14, 2012 (lot 95)
Specialists: D. Chombert and F. Sternbach

Damier canvas and chocolate patent leather Saleya bag.

Estimate: 300–400 euros
Sold: 500 euros
Artcurial, Paris, March 19, 2012 (lot 245)
Specialist: PB Fashion

LOUIS VUITTON

N º 2058
1996 by Azzedine Alaïa

LV Monogram canvas and leopard-print pony Alma bag with accessories created to celebrate the hundredth anniversary of the LV Monogram, 1896–1996.

BIBLIOGRAPHY: The identical style appears on p. 12 in the catalog illustrating the collaboration between Louis Vuitton and seven designers: Manolo Blahnik, Romeo Gigli, Helmut Lang, Isaac Mizrahi, Sybilla, Vivienne Westwood, and Azzedine Alaïa.

Estimate: 2,200–2,800 euros
Sold: 4,625 euros
Groz & Delettrez, Paris, May 14, 2012 (lot 101)
Specialists: D. Chombert and F. Sternbach

Spring/Summer 2002
Collection "Contes de fées musette"

Black silk LV Monogram shoulder bag/clutch with patchwork appliqués.

Estimate: 120–150 euros
Sold: 220 euros
Chayette & Cheval, Paris, February 5, 2012 (lot 426)
Specialist: PB Fashion

N º 0690
1996 by Isaac Mizrahi

Clear vinyl and natural cowhide leather maxi tote created to celebrate the hundredth anniversary of the LV Monogram, 1896–1996.

BIBLIOGRAPHY: The identical style appears on p. 12 in the catalog illustrating the collaboration between Louis Vuitton and seven designers: Manolo Blahnik, Romeo Gigli, Helmut Lang, Isaac Mizrahi, Sybilla, Vivienne Westwood, and Azzedine Alaïa.

Estimate: 400–600 euros
Sold: 500 euros
Artcurial, Paris, March 19, 2012 (lot 233)
Specialist: PB Fashion

LOUIS VUITTON

Yellow Epi leather Saint-Jacques bag.

Estimate: 300–400 euros
Sold: 350 euros
Gros & Delettrez, Paris, May 14, 2012 (lot 249)
Specialists: D. Chombert and F. Sternbach

Cognac Epi leather Noé bag.

Estimate: 250–280 euros
Sold: 350 euros
Gros & Delettrez, Paris, May 14, 2012 (lot 249)
Specialists: D. Chombert and F. Sternbach

Blue, red, and green tricolor Epi leather Noé bag.

Estimate: 380–430 euros
Sold: 688 euros
Gros & Delettrez, Paris, May 14, 2012 (lot 219)
Specialists: D. Chombert and F. Sternbach

LOUIS VUITTON

Silver LV Monogram *miroir* leather Alma bag; 45 cm.

Estimate: 600–800 euros
Sold: 1,001 euros
Artcurial, Paris, July 6, 2012 (lot 362)
Specialist: PB Fashion

by Takashi Murakami

Multicolored LV Monogram canvas and natural cowhide leather Alma bag.

Estimate: 650–750 euros
Sold: 750 euros
Gros & Delettrez, Paris, May 14, 2012 (lot 208)
Specialists: D. Chombert and F. Sternbach

Silver LV Monogram *miroir* leather Speedy bag; 37 cm.

Estimate: 1,500–1,700 euros
Sold: 2,125 euros
Gros & Delettrez, Paris, May 14, 2012 (lot 92)
Specialists: D. Chombert and F. Sternbach

LOUIS VUITTON

Gold LV Monogram *miroir* leather Papillon bag.

Estimate: 800–900 euros
Sold: 1,000 euros
Gros & Delettrez, Paris, February 6, 2012 (lot 128)
Specialists: D. Chombert and F. Sternbach

by Takashi Murakami

LV Monogram canvas and natural cowhide leather Speedy bag; 25 cm.

Estimate: 900–1,000 euros
Sold: 2,125 euros
Gros & Delettrez, Paris, May 14, 2012 (lot 85)
Specialists: D. Chombert and F. Sternbach

Gold LV Monogram *miroir* leather Speedy bag; 34 cm.

Estimate: 1,100–1,300 euros
Sold: 1,250 euros
Gros & Delettrez, Paris, May 14, 2012 (lot 40)
Specialists: D. Chombert and F. Sternbach

LOUIS VUITTON

by Stephen Sprouse

Graffiti Monogram canvas and natural cowhide leather Speedy bag; 30 cm.

Estimate: 1,000–1,100 euros
Sold: 2,125 euros
Gros & Delettrez, Paris, May 14, 2012 (lot 174)
Specialists: D. Chombert and F. Sternbach

by Stephen Sprouse

Graffiti Monogram canvas and natural cowhide leather Speedy bag; 40 cm.

Estimate: 1,000–1,200 euros
Sold: 1,688 euros
Gros & Delettrez, Paris, May 14, 2012 (lot 169)
Specialists: D. Chombert and F. Sternbach

by Stephen Sprouse

Graffiti Monogram canvas and natural cowhide leather Speedy bag; 30 cm.

Estimate: 900–1,100 euros
Sold: 1,125 euros
Cornette de Saint Cyr, Paris, April 4, 2012 (lot 466)
Specialists: D. Chombert and F. Sternbach

LOUIS VUITTON

by Richard Prince

Watercolor Monogram canvas and natural cowhide leather Speedy bag; 30 cm.

Estimate: 1,100–1,300 euros
Sold: 1,875 euros
Gros & Delettrez, Paris, May 14, 2012 (lot 218)
Specialists: D. Chombert and F. Sternbach

by Stephen Sprouse

White and beige patent leather Alma bag.

Estimate: 600–800 euros
Sold: 1,001 euros
Artcurial, Paris, April 18, 2012 (lot 387)
Specialist: PB Fashion

by Stephen Sprouse

Black and white patent leather Alma Long bag.

Estimate: 600–700 euros
Sold: 1,250 euros
Cornette de Saint Cyr, Paris, April 4, 2012 (lot 405)
Specialists: D. Chombert and F. Sternbach

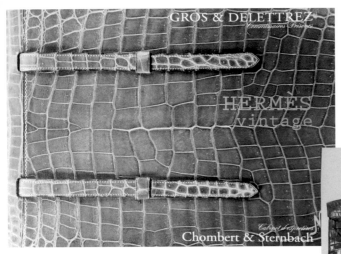

HERMÈS AUCTIONS

F our times each year, for over twenty years, auctions devoted exclusively to Hermès items have attracted countless enthusiasts who worship the products of the famed Rue du Faubourg Saint Honoré saddlemaker.

Begun on a small scale in 1993 by fashion experts Dominique Chombert and Françoise Sternbach, the successful auctions soon grew in both size and frequency and launched the popular trend of thematic sales. That first auction, featuring fifty Hermès pieces, was held in one of Drouot's smallest rooms and the bidding was so heated that shoving and fainting ensued.

After this resounding and unexpected success, the apparent void was quickly filled: The number of lots, size of the auction rooms, number of bidders, and volume of sales grew exponentially. Gros & Delettrez has held two auctions per year. For the past twelve years, Artcurial and the specialist Cyril Pigot also organized biannual Hermès vintage sales. The sales

are planned well in advance and eagerly awaited, and these four dates attract buyers from all over the world.

What items are featured at these auctions? There are handbags of course, many handbags: ostrich Kelly bags, crocodile Birkin bags, Constance, Plume, Picotin, Evelyne, and other limited editions or special-order styles. The Hermès auctions are filled not only with the splendid trophy bags but also with jewelry, watches, small leather goods, ties, scarves, prêt-à-porter, gloves, shoes, accessories, desk items, linens, and even beach towels—so many choices that you might think you are in a Hermès store. And the prices would only confirm that: Some items sell for nearly the same amount as they would at retail—or more. This is especially true for handbags, specifically the timeless and iconic Kelly and Birkin bags, the flagship items of the house of Hermès. It might seem incongruous to pay more for a secondhand bag than for a brand-new one, but the age of the bag is not a negative factor: There are no outdated styles and the bags are all manufactured in the same way. In fact, the prices have soared! A blazing red crocodile Kelly bag sold for over 53,000 euros at the May 11, 2011, auction at Artcurial and a gray Birkin bag sold for 36,000 euros at the Gros & Delettrez sale on June 5, 2012. There is a reason for this seemingly irrational phenomenon: A purchase at auction is immediately gratifying, whereas buying a brand-new bag often involves a waiting period of several months. Stock for Birkin and Kelly bags is usually very low or non-existent, as most items are fabricated on demand. Moreover, thematic sales attract customers who are specifically interested in acquiring Hermès items; they know what they want and know they will find it at these auctions. Competition is heated and prices are high for the most desirable pieces, sometimes surpassing the actual retail price. It is still possible, however, to find a good deal: At the Hermès vintage sale organized by Gros & Delettrez at Drouot on June 4–5, 2012, a Hermès scarf in "Le Perroquet" pattern sold for 70 euros, a secondhand Kelly handbag sold for 500 euros, a cashmere robe for 120 euros, and a men's cardigan for 40 euros. At the Artcurial auction on May 9, 2012, a pair of gloves sold for 77 euros, earrings for 105 euros, ballet flats for 129 euros, and a leather notepaper holder for 142 euros.

The phenomenon of these unique Hermès auctions illustrates the enormous appeal of legendary French workmanship and the ongoing success and savoir faire of the legendary house of Hermès.

— Sales catalogs for Hermès vintage auctions organized by Gros & Delettrez.

LOUIS VUITTON
and MARC JACOBS

The Louis Vuitton and Marc Jacobs *exhibition held at the Musée des Arts Décoratifs (March 9–September 16, 2012) suggested a hypothetical meeting between Louis Vuitton, creator and founder of the famed luggage company, and designer Marc Jacobs, the company's artistic director since 1997.*

LOUIS VUITTON, AT THE TIME OF ITS FOUNDING

Born in 1821 in the Jura region of France, Louis Vuitton established his eponymous company in 1854, near the Rue de la Paix. He started his own small revolution within the larger context of industrialization. Positioned at a moment of great social transition, the young, ambitious luggage manufacturer would see his business grow and thrive.

The bourgeoisie were prospering and people traveled with increasing frequency, going farther away and for longer periods of time. Louis Vuitton would simplify the process for his worldly and adventurous first-class customers—Empress Eugénie among them—by providing the means to take along everything they might need for their journeys. His ingeniously designed cases with intricate compartments allowed his clients to transport, in perfect condition, day and evening dresses (even those made of gossamer fabric or involving many crinolines), elaborate hats, and precious shoes. The luggage was covered in thick gray Trianon canvas that was impervious to water and personalized with the customer's initials.

Concerned that his designs might be imitated, Louis Vuitton devised a way to protect them: The gray canvas soon gave way to different color stripes, then to a check pattern that included, for the first time, the name of its creator, and later to the LV Monogram that was conceived by his son Georges in 1896. Was it clever foresight or the ultimate irony? Today, the two famous initials have become the favorite target of counterfeit merchandise dealers and it is often difficult to tell the original from the copy. Still highly sought after by buyers and collectors, authentic Vuitton pieces are well represented at auctions, with entire auctions devoted to the brand: Old steamer trunks, limited-edition items, and the great classic pieces have timeless appeal.

MARC JACOBS REINTERPRETS THE LEGACY

When he was named creative director of Vuitton in 1997, Marc Jacobs, as Louis Vuitton did before him, would start his own revolution, this time within the context of globalization. At that point, the company did not have a prêt-à-porter line and the appointment of a young American to head a company so anchored in Parisian tradition raised many eyebrows. Jacobs, on the other hand, was thrilled to be living in the city of his dreams and was ready for the challenge. He transformed Vuitton into a *maison de couture*. He held spectacular runway shows and presented collections that defined the look of a season. The most memorable shows featured nurses in Monogram

caps (Spring/Summer 2008), neo-vintage corolla skirts (Fall/Winter 2010–2011) and a *Night Porter*-inspired fetish fantasy theme (Fall/Winter 2011–2012).

Jacobs brought a new dimension to Vuitton's already iconic leather goods. His daring collaborations with artists such as Takashi Murakami, Stephen Sprouse, and Yayoi Kusama taunted but never eclipsed the mythic Monogram. Jacobs was a master at balancing the past and the present. He respected and retained the legacy of the hundred-year-old firm while still introducing a brand-new style each season—styles that were often provocative and occasionally garish. Not one to play it safe, Marc Jacobs, like his predecessor, moved to the beat of his generation, but in his own, radical way.

Exhibited on different floors of the museum, the exhibit's mythical encounter between two men and their respective centuries was left to the imagination. Their stories, however, share many similarities as both men had the intuitive ability to embrace the spirit of their time.

- *Opposite: Cabine double* trunk in Monogram toile. Part of the "Chanel—Louis Vuitton" auction organized by Artcurial on July 9, 2012, with PB Fashion (sold: 9,384 euros).
- *Above:* Speedy handbag in Monogram toile; 25 cm; limited edition; part of the Cherry Blossom collection by Takashi Murakami. Part of the "Chanel—Louis Vuitton" auction organized by Artcurial on July 9, 2012 (sold: 630 euros).

Index

AUSTRALIA

[Buy/Sell]

Grandma Takes a Trip
263 Crown Street
Surry Hills, Sydney, NSW 2010
www.grandmatakesatrip.com

Harlequin Market
Shop 8, 20–26 Cross Street
Double Bay, Sydney, NSW 2028
www.harlequinmarket.com

Martin Fella
556 Queensberry Street
North Melbourne, VIC 3051
www.facebook.com/martin.fella.
vintage

Shag
259 Collins Street
Melbourne, VIC 3181
www.shagshop.com.au

BELGIUM

[View]

**ModeMuseum Provincie
Antwerpen - MoMu**
Nationalestraat 28
2000 Anvers
www.momu.be

**Musée du Costume
et de la Dentelle**
Rue de la Violette, 12
1000 Bruxelles
www.museeducostume
etdeladentelle.be

[Buy/Sell]

RA
Bvba Kloosterstraat 13
2000 Antwerp
www.ra13.be

Katheley's
www.katheleys.com

Addresses

CHILE

[View]

Museo de la Moda
Vitacura 4562, Santiago
www.museodelamoda.cl

FRANCE

[Auction Houses]

Aguttes
www.aguttes.com

Artcurial
www.artcurial.com

Artfact
www.artfact.com

**AuctionArt - Rémy Le Fur &
Associés**
www.auctionart.auction.fr

Bailly-Pommery & Voutier
www.bpv.fr

Beaussant-Lefèvre
www.beaussant-lefevre.com

Camard & Associés
www.camardetassocies.com

Chayette & Cheval
www.chayette-cheval.com

Cornette de Saint Cyr
www.cornettedesaintcyr.fr

Coutau-Begarie
www.coutaubegarie.com

Deburaux & Associés
www.deburaux-associes.fr

Drouot
www.drouot.com

Drouot Live
www.drouotlive.com

Eve
www.auctioneve.com

Guizzetti & Collet
www.guizzetticollet.com

Gros & Delettrez
www.gros-delettrez.com

Lafon Castandet
www.lafon-castandet.com

Millon & Associés
www.millon-associes.com

Piasa
www.piasa.fr

Tajan
www.tajan.com

Thierry de Maigret
www.thierrydemaigret.com

[View]

Musée de la Mode
17, rue de la Souque
81000 Albi
www.musee-mode.com

Musée de la Chemiserie
Rue Charles-Brillaud
36200 Argenton-sur-Creuse

Musée du Costume
6, rue Belgrand
89200 Avallon

Musée du Chapeau
16, route de Saint-Galmier
42140 Chazelles-sur-Lyon
www.museeduchapeau.com

Musée Christian Dior
Villa Les Rhumbs
1, rue d'Estouteville
50400 Granville
www.musee-dior-granville.com

Musée du Gant
79, rue Nicolas-Chorier
38000 Grenoble

**Musée des Tissus et des Arts
décoratifs**
34, rue de la Charité
69002 Lyon
www.musee-des-tissus.com

**Les Docks, cité de la Mode et
du Design**
34, quai d'Austerlitz
75013 Paris
www.paris-docks-en-seine.fr

**Fondation Pierre Bergé–
Yves Saint Laurent**
5, avenue Marceau
75116 Paris
www.fondation-pb-ysl.net

**Musée de la Mode et du
Costume Palais Galliera**
10, avenue Pierre-le-de-Serbie
75116 Paris

**Musée de la Mode et du
Textile–Musée des Arts
décoratifs**
107, rue de Rivoli
75001 Paris
www.lesartsdecoratifs.fr

Musée Pierre Cardin
33, boulevard Victor-Hugo
93400 Saint-Ouen
www.pierrecardin.com

[Buy/Sell]

**Les Collections Vintage
Boutique**
1, rue Trarieux
92600 Asnières-sur-Seine

L'Antiquaire et la Mode
8, rue Hélène-Vagliano
06400 Cannes

Marché du Vintage of Lyon
www.marchemodevintage.com

Anouschka
By appointment:
6, passage du Coq
75009 Paris

Chez Chiffons
47, rue de Lancry
75010 Paris
www.chezchiffons.fr

Des-Voyages
By appointment:
82, rue Saint-Louis-en-l'Ile
75004 Paris
www.des-voyages.fr

Didier Ludot
24, Galerie Montpensier
75001 Paris
www.didierludot.fr

Falbalas
Marché Dauphine
140, rue des Rosiers
93400 Saint-Ouen
www.falbalas.puces.free.fr

Gabrielle Geppert
31-34, Galerie Montpensier
Jardins du Palais-Royal
75001 Paris
www.gabriellegeppert.com

La Tienda Loca
By appointment:
1, rue de Maubeuge
75009 Paris
www.latiendaloca.com

Les Collections Vintage
www.lescollectionsvintage.com

**Les Trois Marches de
Catherine B.**
1-3 rue Guisarde, 75006 Paris
www.catherine-b.com

Mademoiselle Steinitz
19, rue de la Grange-Batelière
75009 Paris
www.sarahsteinitz.com

Quidam de Revel
By appointment :
55, rue des Petites-Écuries
75010 Paris

RA
14, rue de la Corderie
75003 Paris
www.ra13.be

Ragtime
Françoise Auguet
23, rue de l'Échaudé
75006 Paris

Renaissance
14, rue de Beaune
75007 Paris
www.renaissance75007.com

Thanx God I'm a V.I.P
12, rue de Lancry
75010 Paris
www.thanxgod.com

Patricia Attwood
Marché Serpette
96-112, rue des Rosiers
93400 Saint-Ouen
www.that-little-pink-shop.fr

Histoire(s) de Mode
Les Puces du canal
Allée C - 1, rue du Canal
69100 Villeurbanne

Dressing Factory
www.dressing-factory.com

ITALY

[View]

Museo Gucci
Palazzo della Mercanzia
Piazza della Signoria, 10
50100 Florence
www.gucci.com

Museo Salvatore Ferragamo
Via Tornabuoni, 2
50123 Florence
www.ferragamo.com

Palazzo Fortuny
Sestiere San Marco 3958
30124 Venise
www.fortuny.visitmuve.it

[Buy/Sell]

Vintage Delirium
Via Sacchi, 3
20121 Milan
www.vintagedeliriumfj.com

Cavalli e Nastri
Via Brera, 2
20121 Milano *et*
Via Gian Giacomo Mora, 3
20123 Milano
www.cavallienastri.com

Memory Lane
Via Galeazzo Alessi, 8
20123 Milano
www.memorylanevintagemilano.com

Tara Vintage
www.taravintage.com

JAPAN

[View]

The Kyoto Costume Institute
103, Shichi-jo Goshonouchi
Minamimachi, Shimogyo-ku
600-8864 KYOTO
www.kci.or.jp

SPAIN

[View]

Cristóbal Balenciaga Museoa
Almadar Parkea 6
20808 Getaria- Gipuzkoa
www.cristobalbalenciagamuseoa.com

[Buy/Sell]

Lotta Vintage
Calle de Hernán Cortés, 9
28004 Madrid
www.lottavintage.com

Paris Vintage
Calle Rossello 237
Entresuelo, 1ro
08008 Barcelone
www.parisvintage.net

SWITZERLAND

[View]

Musée suisse de la Mode
1400 Yverdon-les- Bains
www.museemode.ch

[Buy/Sell]

Julia's Dressing
Rue Jean-Violette, 18
1205 Genève
www.juliasdressing.com

UNITED KINGDOM

[Auction Houses]

Christie's
www.christies.com

Kerry Taylor
www.kerrytaylorauctions.com

[View]

Fashion Museum
Assembly Rooms, Bennett Street -
BA1 2QH Bath
www.museumofcostume.co.uk

Victoria and Albert Museum
Cromwell Road
SW7 2RL London
www.vam.ac.uk

[Buy/Sell]

Blackout II
51 Endell Street, Covent Garden
WC2H 9AJ London
www.blackout2.com

Rellik
8, Golborne Road
W10 5NW London
www.relliklondon.co.uk

Sheila Cook
26 Addison Place, Holland Park,
W11 4RJ London
www.sheilacook.co.uk

Vintage Fashion Fair
www.vintagefashionfairlondon.co.uk

UNITED STATES

[Auction Houses]

Augusta Auction
www.augusta-auction.com

Charles A. Whitaker Auction Company
www.whitakerauction.com

Leslie Hindman Auctioneers
www.lesliehindman.com

[View]

Museum of Fine Arts, Boston
Avenue of the Arts
465 Huntington Avenue
Boston, MA 02115
www.mfa.org

The Costume Institute, The Metropolitan Museum of Art
1000 Fifth Avenue
New York, NY 10028
www.metmuseum.org

Fashion Institute of Technology
227 West 27th Street
New York, NY 10001
www.fitnyc.edu

[Buy/Sell]

C Madeleine's
13702 Biscayne Blvd
North Miami Beach, FL 33181
www.cmadeleines.com

Decades
8214½ Melrose Avenue
Los Angeles, CA 90046
www.decadesinc.com

Lily & Cie
9044 Burton Way
Beverly-Hills, CA 90211
www.lilyetcie.com

Manhattan Vintage Clothing Show
127 North Lake Ave.
Albany, NY 12206
www.manhattanvintage.com

Marlene Wetherell
40 West 25th Street
New York, NY 10010
www.marlenewetherell.com

New York Vintage
117 West 25th Street
New York, NY 10001
www.newyorkvintage.com

Rare Vintage
24 West 57th Street
New York, NY 10019
www.rarevintage.com

Resurrection
217 Mott Street
New York, NY 10012
www.resurrectionvintage.com

What Goes Around Comes Around
351 West Broadway
New York, NY 10013
www.whatgoesaroundnyc.com

Credits

**THE AUTHORS
WISH TO THANK:**

Nicolas Aksil, Azzedine Alaïa, Montassar Alaya, Pierre-Dominique Antonini, Aziz Arslan,
Soizic Audouard, Karen Augusta, Babar, Odile Babin, Eva Barat, Lili Barbery, Carole Barlot,
Marianne Beck, Sue Bell, Véronique Belloir, Sihem Bengarrach, Sandrine Benichou,
Olivia Berghauer, Mélissa Besnard, Morgane Bichot, Jeanne Biehn Sall, Nadine Bisson,
Brooke Blair, Bruno Blanckaert, Gilles and Nadège Blanckaert, Marie-Claire Blanckaert,
Marie-Pacifique Blanckaert, Robinson Blanckaert, Edgar Blanckaert Vincent, Marc Blondeau,
Carl Bocksch-Juul, Isabelle Boisgirard, Isabelle Boudot de La Motte, Vivianne Bourillet de Béchon,
Marie Boury, Victoire Boyer Chammard, Raymonde Branger, Coralie Cadène, Henric Caldas,
Agnès and Sylvie Carton, Marie Castro, Anne-Charlotte Cauchard-Morin, Armelle Chalm Kergall,
Olivier Châtenet, Dominique Chombert, Margot Christmann, Olivier Colinet, Thierry Collet,
Laurent Cotta, Charles Cuvillier, Chantal Dagommer, Charlotte Daniel, Cathy Dechezelle,
Sylviane de Decker, Lucas Delattre, Isabelle Delesalle, Chantal Delinot, Léocadie De Vos,
Christian Doldi, Nathalie Dufour, Claire Duplessis, Olivier Duplessis, Acacia Echazarreta,
Hedi El Chikh, Mara Estes, Moji Farhat, Hubert Felbacq, Marie-Laure Feltz,
Erwan and Françoise de Fligué, Jean-Denis Franoux, Christine Freeland, Patricia Frost,
Maryse Gaspard, Évelyne Gaud, Coralie Gauthier, Pascal Gautrand, Sylvie Gautrelet,
Marie-Christine Gérald, Cécile Goddet-Dirles, Pamela Golbin, Jean-Paul Goude, France Grand,
Sophie Grossiord, Liliane Grunewald, Julia Guillon, Pierre-Pascal Guizzetti, Laure Harivel,
Nathalie Hatala, Réjane Henri, Mathieu and Albertine Hernu, Anne Hernu, Anastasia Hirt,
Christophe Honoré, Alix Huguenin, Françoise Huguier, François Hurteau-Flamand,
Barbara Jeauffroy-Mairet, Julie Jouitteau, Denise Kohn, Sylvie Krumula, Lilith Laborey,
Joséphine de La Celle, Christine Lamoureux, Katell Le Bourhis, Rémy Le Fur, Caroline Legrand,
Germaine and Gérard Legroux, Martine Leherpeur, Constance Le Nay, Bérengère Lepeu,
Catherine Leroy, Sébastien Lévy, Cécile Liard, Catherine Longuet, Didier Ludot, Florent Magnin,
Sabine Maïda, Ségolène de Malherbe, Gaël Mamine, Caroline Mangin, Sandrine Mantelet,
Aya Marmion-Soucadaux, Charles Marmion, Bleue-Marine Massard, Damien Messager,
Jessica Meza, Alexandre Millon, Romain Monteaux-Sarmiento, Hadrien de Montferrand,
Jean de Moüy, Jean-Paul Najar, Alain Nave, Laurence Neveu, Géraldine Noël, Minako Norimatsu,
Robert Normand, Marie Ollier, Mariko Omura, Olivier Pacteau, Pamela Parmal, Fabio Perrone,
Jean Piccioli, Leonie Pitts, Aurore Pommery, Marilyn Porlan, Enrique Portocarrero, Romain Poujol,
Éric Pujalet, Éric Reinard, Georges Richard, Michèle Richoux, Jean-Philippe Rincheval,
Nicole and Michel Rincheval, Lucie-Eléonore Riveron, Bob Ross, Camille Rouze, Françoise Sackrider,
Chloé Saillard, Kuki de Salvertes, Susana Santos, Denise Sarrault, Antoine Saulnier,
Antigone Schilling, Caroline Schwartz-Mailhe, Philippe Sébert, Irène Silvagni, Cameron Silver,
Géraldine Sommier, Brigitte Stepputtis, Françoise Sternbach, Marc Stoltz, Pénélope Strintz,
Fiona Stuart, Antoine Taillandier, Joëlle Tardieu, Élisabeth Telliez, Marie-Christine Thévenet,
Safia Thomass Bendali, Loredana de Tommaso, Alicia de Toro, Catherine and François Trèves,
Sabine Trèves, Igor Uria Zubizarreta, Bernard Utudjian, Nathalie Valax,
Charlotte and Aymar Van Gaver, Bruno Vaysette, Blanche Viart, Pauline Vidal, Annabelle Vinbert,
Philippe Vincent, Irina Volkonskii, François Wedrychowski, Naïda and Thierry Winsall, Kirsten Winter,
Charles Whitaker, Jorge Yarur.

FRENCH EDITION

Documentation
Victory Boyer Chammard
Graphic Design and Layout
Annalisa Pagetti, Aplusdesign Paris
Proofreading
Armelle Heron
Photogravure
APS Chromostyle

ABRAMS EDITION

Editor
Laura Dozier
Designer
Shawn Dahl, dahlimama inc
Cover design
John Gall
Production Manager
Erin Vandeveer

Library of Congress Control Number: 2013935984

ISBN: 978-1-4197-1042-1

Printed and bound in China
10 9 8 7 6 5 4 3 2 1

Abrams books are available at special discounts when purchased
in quantity for premiums and promotions as well as fundraising or
educational use. Special editions can also be created to specification.
For details, contact specialsales@abramsbooks.com or the address below.

THE ART OF BOOKS SINCE 1949

115 West 18th Street
New York, NY 10011
www.abramsbooks.com